"The moment I met Bob Kauflin I liked him (a lot!). The more I have gotten to know him, the more I have respected and appreciated him. The more I have listened to and read him on the subject of the corporate worship of our gracious God, the more I have been edified, instructed, humbled, and helped. Whether you are a choir director or minister of music in a congregation with a more traditional form of public worship or a worship team leader in a church with a more contemporary style or a pastor trying to think hard (and biblically) about congregational worship or a Christian wanting to make sure you understand the privilege of 'giving to the Lord the glory due his name in the company of the saints' in a way that helpfully prepares you to do just that, this book will be a blessing to you (as it already has been to me). The things that Bob addresses here transcend style and situation and point us to enduring and universal Christian priorities. I love the wisdom—the Christ-exalting, gospel-derived wisdom—displayed in the challenge Bob asks us to consider, the important things he calls us to, the tasks he reminds us of, the tensions that he bids us hold, and the right relationships he exhorts us to embrace. Very wise. Very timely. Profoundly biblical, theological, devotional, pastoral, and practical. Thanks, Bob. I am your debtor once again."

—LIGON DUNCAN, Senior Minister, First Presbyterian Church,
    Jackson, Mississippi; President, Alliance of Confessing Evangelicals;
    Adjunct Professor, Reformed Theological Seminary

"Humility. Self-deprecating humor. Practical wisdom. And not just for music leaders. What a refreshing read! I've gained from Bob Kauflin, and if you read this, you will too. Clearly structured, well illustrated, engagingly written, biblically saturated, theologically careful, this book gives us a rich treatise on how we can follow Christ ourselves and call others to do the same. This book helps musicians, pastors, elders, and other Christians understand better what we're called to do when we're together."

—MARK DEVER, Pastor of Capitol Hill Baptist Church;
    head of 9Marks Ministries

"God is seeking those who worship him in spirit and in truth. Bob Kauflin is a man whose passion for true worship is both infectious and instructive. In *Worship Matters* he offers profound and powerful observations about the task of leading God's people in worship—observations missing from much of the conversation about worship today. Bob Kauflin is driven by a passion for God's glory, and his reflections on music and worship are grounded in biblical truth and keen theological insight. In a day of such confusion about worship, I welcome this important book."

—R. ALBERT MOHLER JR., President, The Southern Baptist Theological
    Seminary, Louisville, Kentucky

"For some years Sovereign Grace Ministries has blessed the church with music that greatly enhances worship. I have been moved especially by their music CDs, which combine solid biblical doctrine, music skillfully played and sung, and a great passion for Christ. One rarely finds these qualities combined with such balance. That is a gift of God's grace, but also (by God's grace) the result of careful thinking. Now we have access to that thinking, in Bob Kauflin's wonderful *Worship Matters: Leading Others to Encounter the Greatness of God*. This book is thoroughly biblical, comprehensive, balanced, clear, and engaging. Worship leaders must read it, and it will be a great help to anyone interested in finding out what biblical worship is about and how to worship from the heart."

> —JOHN FRAME, Professor of Systematic Theology and Philosophy,
> Reformed Theological Seminary

"In every conversation or correspondence I've had with Bob Kauflin, one thing always shines through—a burning desire to 'get it right' when it comes to the worship of God. Bob loves God, values theology, and cares about people. This mix is found throughout this wonderful and helpful book. *Worship Matters* will inspire you as a worshiper and spur you on as a leader of worship."

> —MATT REDMAN, lead worshiper and song-writer, Brighton, UK

"Here is a rare book: a practical treatment of corporate worship that nevertheless reflects deep theological commitments. One may disagree here and there with some of the judgments, but it is demonstrably unfair to imagine that Bob Kauflin has not thought about these matters deeply—and he has done so in a context where he is teaching a new generation to take corporate worship seriously in a fashion that is simultaneously biblically faithful and addressing today's culture."

> —D. A. CARSON, Research Professor of New Testament,
> Trinity Evangelical Divinity School

"Bob Kauflin has written an amazingly rich and wise book on worship. It is biblical, Christ-honoring, relevant, practical, enjoyable, and everything else I could have asked for. It's full of tested insights, coming out of the author's disciplined contemplation and long experience as a leader among worship leaders. I know and respect Bob and have thoroughly enjoyed following his lead in worshiping our Lord. Bob lives what he writes; so his emphasis on character, integrity, and humility has credibility. I enthusiastically recommend this book to all who wish to cultivate in our churches deeper and more Christ-centered worship."

> —RANDY ALCORN, author of *Heaven* and *The Treasure Principle:
> Unlocking the Secrets of Joyful Giving*

"Rich and glorious theology, discerning and judicious insight, faithful and seasoned experience, practical and humble wisdom—these are some of the marked qualities of Bob Kauflin's treasure trove, *Worship Matters*. With deep concern both for the rightful glory of God and for the edification of God's people through responsible and heart-felt worship, Kauflin provides an array of insights and instruction covering many practical issues, all of which are wrapped in an overarching theology of the triune God, the gospel of grace, and the centrality of the cross. What a needed contribution to our understanding of the nature and practice of worship. May the vision of God and the

model of worship conveyed by Kauflin spread widely and enrich many churches, for the glory of God's great name."
　　—Bruce Ware, Professor of Christian Theology, Southern Baptist
　　　Theological Seminary

"Bob Kauflin is my favorite worship leader, but for reasons that may be surprising to some. Sure, he is an exceptional pianist, songwriter, pastor, and leader, but it's his humility and heart to serve that sets him apart. I know of no man more qualified to write this book than Bob. And I know of no more important, useful work for those who would lead God's people in worship than *Worship Matters*."
　　—C. J. Mahaney, Sovereign Grace Ministries

"I've known Bob Kauflin for many years, and he is truly a remarkable man. First, he's tall—really tall. Second, he manages to combine a widely-read, biblically grounded, deep-thinking spiritual maturity with enthusiasm, passion, and a depth of commitment that puts me to shame. That's a pretty powerful combination in one man. When he told me he was writing a book on worship, I was excited. And I have not been disappointed. Bob's approach is humble, yet authoritative; comprehensive, yet inspirational. And if you take his gentle but clear teaching onboard, it will help make you fully equipped in mind, heart, and spirit to lead others in worship. I wholeheartedly recommend it."
　　—Stuart Townend, Christian song-writer

"It rings true! This is how I continually reacted to *Worship Matters* as I made my way through it. It rings true because Bob Kauflin rings true. I know him; I have worked and fellowshiped with him; we e-mail each other somewhat regularly. He has always been ointment to my battered and redeemed life, and his personal example continues to humble me. But this book above all rings true because Bob rings true to his God, his Word, his Son, his Spirit, and God's relentless desire for the nations through the completed work of his only Son. Thus, page after page Bob brings his work under the scrutiny of the Word; he summons the worship and music of the people of God to its commandments, instructions, and promises, and he does so with clarity and order. So what he says in his book and how he lives his personal and vocational life are entirely consonant. *Worship Matters* should matter deeply to those for whom it is primarily written: young, eager, Christ-centered musician-leaders—people who, at least for the present, are called worship leaders and on whose shoulders a heavy burden has been thrust. The author's wisdom shows continually. His ability to simplify the complex without cheapening it; his rich artistic eclecticism; his love for great music; his insistence on theological and doctrinal literacy; his respect for church history and its various worship and musical dialects; his passion for sensible speech, rich prayer, soul-deepening books; and his obvious freedom from the very practices to which he gives his attention—in this case, contemporary worship leading—these together make this a necessary book. Were the young to read it honestly and be deeply changed by it, were the old to see in it something beyond the 'contemporary,' were all of us to understand that new, old, and everything in between have no life in themselves and must be continually rescued both from self-conscious novelty and self-preserving stodginess, that would bring much needed reform to the unnecessarily confused worlds of worship and music making."

    —HAROLD M. BEST, author of *Music Through the Eyes of Faith* and
        Unceasing Worship: Biblical Perspectives on Worship and the Arts

"Bob Kauflin's new book *Worship Matters* is an outstanding book both for those who lead worship and also for every Christian who wants to worship God more fully. The book is biblical, practical, interesting, wise, and thorough in its treatment of the topic. Though it treats many practical details, it rightly puts primary emphasis on the worship leader's character and relationship to God, and on the Bible's own teaching about worship. The next time I teach on worship, I plan to make this the required text."

    —WAYNE GRUDEM, Research Professor of Bible and Theology,
        Phoenix Seminary

"Bob Kauflin combines musical expertise with theological and pastoral insight. With clarity and passion, he gives biblical and practical guidance to those responsible for leading congregational worship, and in the process builds creative bridges between evangelical and charismatic traditions."

    —DAVID PETERSON, author of *Engaging with God*

"No one has taught me more about worship than Bob Kauflin. If he were just a veteran musician and worship leader, he'd deserve a hearing. If he were only a skilled teacher with a zeal for biblical theology, you would be wise to pay attention. If he were simply a skilled pastor with a heart to see Christians grow in their knowledge of and love for God, you could learn from him. But he's not just one—he's all three. Bob is a pastor, a teacher, and a skilled musician. And this book captures his heart, his zealous pursuit of God, and his many years of real-life experience leading worship. That's why his book deserves the careful study of pastors and worship leaders alike."

    —JOSHUA HARRIS, Senior Pastor, Covenant Life Church,
        Gaithersburg, Maryland

WORSHIP
MATTERS

Leading Others to *Encounter the Greatness of God*

Bob Kauflin

foreword by Paul Baloche

CROSSWAY BOOKS
WHEATON, ILLINOIS

Library of Congress Cataloging-in-Publication Data
Kauflin, Bob.
   Worship matters : leading others to encounter the greatness of God /
Bob Kauflin.
      p. cm.
   Includes bibliographical references and index.
   ISBN-13: 978-1-58134-824-8 (tpb)
   1. Worship—Biblical teaching. I. Title.
BS680.W78K38   2008
264—dc22   2007041082

VP		18	17	15	14	13	12	11	10	09	08
15	14	13	12	11	10	9	8	7	6	5	4	3	2

To my grandsons,

ETHAN, TYLER, JACK, AND GAVIN.

*May you be among those who
lead your generation to encounter
the greatness of God in Jesus Christ
through the power of the Holy Spirit.*

PSALM 71:18

CONTENTS

FOREWORD

The first worship conference that I ever attended was just outside of Philadelphia in 1984. Bob Kauflin was one of the speakers. It was an eye-opening experience that inspired in me the dream of being involved in music that had the potential to help people truly worship God.

Bob's passion for the Lord lit up in his face as he led us in song and taught from the Scriptures. Being raised in a denomination where drums and prayers never mixed, this was a totally new experience for me. The music Bob was talking about was powerful in the way that it could impact others both immediately and eternally. My high-school years were spent playing in various garage bands, highlighted by occasional gigs around Philadelphia bars or clubs along the Jersey Shore. Besides the occasional "folk mass," I had never heard others singing to God with guitars in their hands. That day was the beginning of my journey to encourage others in their walk in the Lord. I wanted to do what Bob Kauflin did. I wanted to encourage others as I had been encouraged. As the years have passed I've crossed paths with Bob at various events, and I always walk away wanting to be a better husband, a better father, and a better lover of God. Those are the qualities in Bob that inspire me more than anything.

In *Worship Matters*, Bob leads us skillfully through the Scriptures and through his experiences to better understand the why and how of biblical worship, regardless of the style or form. From the spiritual aspects of cultivating a devotional life, to the practicalities of putting together a song list, he unfolds the essentials required to effectively fulfill the call of God on our lives. Thankfully, Bob is brutally honest about his own struggles with music, ministry, ego, identity, and failure. If you have been involved in any kind of music ministry, you can't help but see yourself in the mirror of his personal anecdotes. I have wrestled with many of the same issues over the years and found great insight and hope from Bob's conversational confessions in this book.

Bob Kauflin is an important voice in this season of worship-style wars, pointing us to the point of it all—pointing us to the Savior. This is an essential book for anyone considering a role of any kind in worship ministry. As

Jesus shared in the Sermon on the Mount, we can build our lives (or ministries) on the rock or on the sand. The truths in this book are rock-solid and vital to any foundation for lasting ministry. It is the most complete and most readable discussion on the art and the heart of worship that I have ever read. As a worship pastor for the past eighteen years, I felt personally challenged to reexamine and rethink some of the ways that I approach and conduct worship ministry in my own life.

So for those who are just beginning their journey and for those who have been on this road awhile, get ready to be inspired to love your God even more by "putting away childish things" and "pressing on to take hold of that for which Christ Jesus took hold of you."

Paul Baloche

part one

THE LEADER

chapter 1

THE IMPORTANT THINGS

It was my dream job. I'd just become Director of Worship Development for Sovereign Grace Ministries. After pastoring for twelve years, I was now studying worship and training worship leaders full-time.

I was leading worship at a conference and should have been exhilarated. After praying with the worship team I headed up the stairs to start the meeting. The room was overflowing, the atmosphere electric. Every heart was ready to praise God.

Well, almost. From the outside I'm sure no one could tell what *I* was thinking. That was a good thing.

As I made my way to the stage, I suddenly found myself battling doubts.

What difference will this make tonight? Will it have any eternal value? People will sing, raise their hands, get excited . . . and go home. And I'll do this over and over and over again. For the rest of my life.

Suddenly it all seemed empty. Dry. Pointless.

Ever been there? Have you found yourself wondering where your joy went or if what you do really matters?

A friend of mine confided that one of his greatest struggles in leading worship is fighting the feeling that he has to "get up and do it again" for the two-hundredth time. He has to resist going through the motions and simply "mailing it in."

I don't think he's alone.

IS THIS WHAT I SIGNED UP FOR?

Don't get me wrong. I think leading God's people in worship is one of the most fulfilling, enjoyable, exciting, sobering, life-changing jobs on the planet. We're helping people connect with the purpose for which they were created—to glorify the living God. We're pointing their hearts toward the Sovereign One who is greater than their trials and kinder than they could ever imagine. We get to display the matchless Savior who died in our place, conquering sin, death, and hell in the process.

We watch in amazement as the Spirit of God transforms lives and gives people a fresh encounter with God's faithfulness, love, and power.

At times like these we think, *I can't believe I get to do this.* (And if you're on a church staff, you might add, "I can't believe I get *paid* to do this.")

But then come the times we'd be happy to pay someone *else* to do this.

• Your lead vocalist is sick, your bass player's out of town, and your keyboardist slept in. And no one called to find a sub.

• A small but influential group in the church just informed the pastor they don't like the songs you've been teaching.

• After two years in your new church, you still don't have a drummer who can keep steady time.

• Your best singer just told you she's not coming to this week's rehearsal unless she gets to sing the solo.

• For the fifth week in a row, your pastor e-mailed to say the music went too long and you talked too much.

Moments like these make you think that leading worship would be a joy if it didn't involve working with others.

But just as often we struggle with our own hearts:

• No one seems to appreciate or even notice that on top of a full-time job you put in at least ten hours each week for the worship team.

• The last time you taught a new song was eight months ago, and CDs are piled on your desk that you still haven't listened to.

• You put off confronting a guitarist whose critical and proud attitude is affecting the whole team.

• You can't remember the last time you prayed more than five minutes, and you feel like a hypocrite as you lead on Sundays.

• You never have enough hours to plan, prepare, study, practice, or work with the music team. Which makes you wonder what in the world you're doing with your time.

And yet . . .

Despite these and other difficulties, you believe the joys of leading worship far outweigh the challenges. You wouldn't think of giving it up.

You just want to do it better. More effectively. More skillfully. More faithfully.

I'm guessing that's why you picked up this book. I hope so because that's why I wrote it.

But I have to confess something.

I didn't write this book simply to help you be a better worship leader. There's more at stake here.

After thirty years of leading worship, I've realized that worship isn't just an opportunity to use my musical gifts. It's more than a heightened emotional experience or a way to make a living. It's way more than what we do on Sunday morning.

Worship is about what we love. What we live for.

It's about who we are before God.

This book is filled with practical ideas for leading worship. But we don't start there. These initial chapters are about the way we think and live. I want to challenge, encourage, and inspire you to live your life for the glory and praise of Jesus Christ. Holding nothing back. Giving no ground. It's the only kind of life that makes sense for someone who leads worship.

But first, a little background.

HOW I GOT HERE

My first experience of music in a church context came as a Catholic, when I played the organ for Masses, weddings, and funerals. There wasn't much "leadership" involved. I just played what I was told. When I could, I'd sneak in "sacred" versions of Beatles tunes, college fight songs, or nursery rhymes to make it interesting.

In the early seventies, I majored in piano at Temple University in Philadelphia. I became a Christian during my first year and started visiting a Baptist church on campus. When my friends and I noticed we were the only people in the church under sixty, we tried starting our own church in the dorms. That lasted two meetings.

Then someone invited us to a charismatic church in Center City Philadelphia. We heard the meetings were pretty lively, especially when they broke into line dancing around the pews. I helped with the worship team there and eventually was asked to lead, to use the term generously.

Between my junior and senior years at Temple, I came across a small, humble group of Christians in rural Pennsylvania who claimed Scripture as their only doctrine. The women wore head coverings, the men had beards, and they sang without instruments.

My worship world was diversifying.

After getting married and graduating from college in 1976, my wife, Julie, and I spent eight years with the Christian music group GLAD. We traveled across the U.S. learning what worship meant to Baptists, Assemblies of God, Catholics, Methodists, Lutherans, Episcopalians, Presbyterians, and a host of nondenominational churches.

Some churches followed centuries-old liturgies. Others were "Spirit-filled" and looked for God to show up in prophetic words, tongues, or some other spontaneous event.

In too many churches we detected a disconnect between the God they worshiped on Sundays and the one they seemed to follow during the week.

I continued to lead worship in my local church when we weren't traveling. But in 1984 I said good-bye to life on the road. I thought I might be called to be a pastor.

The following year I joined the staff of a church related to Sovereign Grace Ministries, led by C. J. Mahaney. I led the worship team there for six years, then helped plant what's now Crossway Community Church in Charlotte, North Carolina. I experienced firsthand the challenges and joys of overseeing a worship team in a new church.

In 1997 C. J. invited me to Covenant Life Church, a congregation of 3,000-plus members near Washington, D.C., to serve in my present role. As you might guess, leading worship in a large congregation is different from a church plant. More people to organize, more songs to learn, more meetings to work around, more equipment to deal with, and more potential problems.

But the important things haven't changed.

This book is about the important things.

WHAT REALLY MATTERS?

Maybe you're just getting started as a worship leader or think God wants you to be one. Perhaps you've been in music ministry for decades and are feeling a little weary. You might be part of a music team or a worship planning committee. Maybe you're a pastor and want to understand more clearly what worship is supposed to look like in your church. Or it could be you're the kind of person who wants to get your hands on anything that feeds your love for God.

Whatever your situation, I want to help you avoid going through what

I described at the beginning of this chapter—when I stepped up to lead worship, and it all seemed empty, dry, and pointless. It isn't.

But the Lord graciously reminded me, "That's exactly what it would be like without me—pointless."

Worship matters. It matters to God because he is the one ultimately worthy of all worship. It matters to us because worshiping God is the reason for which we were created. And it matters to every worship leader, because we have no greater privilege than leading others to encounter the greatness of God. That's why it's so important to think carefully about what we do and why we do it.

Discovering what matters in worship is a journey I've been on for thirty years, and one I'll be on for the rest of my life. I'm glad you've joined me.

And if you don't feel adequate for the task . . . you're in the perfect place for God to use you.

chapter 2

MY HEART: WHAT DO I LOVE?

What's the greatest challenge you face as a worship leader? You might think it's deciding which songs to sing, getting along with your pastor, receiving feedback from church members, or leading a team of unorganized, independent musicians.

Nope. Your greatest challenge is what you yourself bring to the platform each and every Sunday.

Your heart.

For years we've read about or experienced firsthand the "worship wars"—conflicts over music styles, song selections, and drums. But far too little has been said about the worship wars going on inside us. And they're much more significant.

Each of us has a battle raging within us over what we love most—God or something else.

Whenever we love and serve anything in place of God, we're engaging in idolatry. We love our idols because we think they'll provide the joy that comes from God alone. We think having them will truly satisfy us. We think they're worthy of our worship.

Of course, we're wrong.

Throughout Scripture, idolatry is the greatest snare the people of God encounter. God condemns idolatry repeatedly in his Word. He hates it when we pursue, serve, or are emotionally drawn to other gods, which are not really gods at all. Idols enslave us and put us to shame (Isaiah 45:16; Psalm

106:36). The apostle John warned his readers and us, "Little children, keep yourselves from idols" (1 John 5:21). Idols are powerless to help us and end up making us into their own image (Psalm 115:8). Like David, we should hate idols and those who pay regard to them (Psalm 31:6). Too often, though, we ourselves are the idolaters.

When some of us hear the word *idolatry*, we picture primitive tribesmen bowing down to statues of wood, metal, or stone. Or we think of countries like India where Hindu temples dot the landscape. When I went to train pastors in India years ago, I met many men who had grown up worshiping idols as a daily ritual.

But idol worship is a daily ritual in America, too. Only it's more subtle and therefore more dangerous.

Idols are all around us. Can you spot them? They come in different forms. Material comforts. Financial security. Sensual pleasures. Musicians have their own special idols. New gear. Electronic gadgets. Hip clothes. The most powerful idols are the ones we can't even see. Things like reputation, power, and control.

As Christians we're sometimes like the people described in 2 Kings 17:33: "they feared the LORD but also served their own gods." We fear the Lord externally, doing all the right things on Sunday morning—singing, strumming a guitar, lifting our hands—yet actively serve false gods throughout the week. We profess to love the true God but actually love false idols. It's a condition that God, in his mercy, is committed to changing.

That's a lesson I learned the hard way.

IDOLS AND ME

I spent most of my early years seeking my own glory. Popularity, music, and academic excellence were my idols of choice, and I spent most of my teenage years pursuing them. When God saved me at seventeen, my sins were completely forgiven. But I had deep-rooted sin patterns that weren't going to die easily.

After becoming a pastor, I assumed my job was to serve others with my superior wisdom and discernment. My pride was exposed a few times, and patient friends tried to help me see what was going on in my heart. But I was a slow learner.

When we moved to North Carolina to help start a church, my cravings for admiration and control were constantly challenged. Some people didn't like the way we were leading the church and left. A few disgruntled parents expressed disagreement with our parent-driven youth ministry. Newcomers recommended ways the church could serve them better. A counseling situation turned ugly when a man caught in immorality claimed that I lacked compassion and had gotten angry at him.

No one knew it at the time, but God was using these situations and others to expose the long-standing sins of idolatry in my heart. I wanted everyone around me to share my high opinion of myself. My life was one extended attempt to draw attention to my gifts, my abilities, and my efforts. But it wasn't working. I wasn't getting the praise I craved, and that was affecting my soul. I increasingly struggled with feelings of anxiety, fear, and confusion. I felt like my life was about to fall apart.

One January evening in 1994 it did.

A family in the church had invited Julie and me over for dinner. In between bites, as we were engaging in small talk, I lost my grip on reality. I couldn't tell you how it happened, but in an instant I felt completely disconnected from both my past and my future. Resisting the sudden urge to jump up from the table and scream, I excused myself, went into the bathroom, and shut the door behind me.

God, what in the world is happening to me? Where are you? Who am I?

No answers came as questions raced through my mind at warp speed.

That night I began a sanctifying journey that would last nearly three years. God wanted to teach me a few things about what I loved and who I worshiped.

HOPELESS—BUT NOT ENOUGH

Over the next three months I experienced a variety of symptoms. Hollowness and tightness in my chest. Buzzing in my face. Daily thoughts of death. Itching on my arms. Panic attacks. Sleeplessness. Shortness of breath.

I woke up each morning to this thought: *Your life is completely hopeless.* And things went downhill from there.

I chose not to go to a psychologist or psychiatrist, but I'm certain they would have classified me as someone having a breakdown. I made an appointment for a complete physical with our family doctor, who said I was fine. At least that's what the tests showed.

But the tests couldn't measure what was taking place in my heart. I was battling God for his glory—and losing.

About a year after these symptoms appeared, Julie and I attended a leadership conference and shared a meal with our good friends Gary and Betsy Ricucci. I knew Gary was a wise and gracious pastor. I also knew I needed help. Desperately. Early in our conversation I confessed, "Gary, I don't know what to do. I feel hopeless all the time. Completely hopeless."

I expected Gary to say something like, "You'll be okay, Bob. God is faithful. He's working all things for your good." Instead he looked at me with compassion and stated, "I don't think you're hopeless enough."

I'm not sure what the look on my face said at that moment, but inside I was picking myself up off the floor.

Gary smiled. "If you were really hopeless, you'd stop trusting in yourself and what you can do and start trusting in what Jesus accomplished for you at the cross."

The words drifted into my head like morning fog over a field—there was a discernible shape, but I couldn't quite get my arms around it.

As I considered Gary's response in the coming weeks, the fog began to lift. I started seeing a reality that dominated my life—the reality of my sinful cravings. My problems—emotional, physical, and otherwise—stemmed from battles within my heart of which I'd been largely unaware. Yes, I wanted God to be exalted through my life, but another agenda was ruling my heart. I wanted people to approve of me, admire me, *applaud* me.

To be honest, I wanted people to *adore* me. I had an incessant passion to steal God's glory. I was a lover of myself rather than a lover of God (2 Timothy 3:2, 4). And it was killing me. The unresolved conflict in my heart spilled over into my mind and body and led to that fateful January night in 1994.

BREAKING DOWN THE BREAKDOWN

So what happened to me? Many would call it a nervous breakdown. I've learned that it was far simpler than that. And far more serious.

I was experiencing the consequences of my pride. A sin breakdown, if you will. God in his kindness was mercifully humbling me and showing me what life would be like without him.

I'd been in a relentless pursuit of glory. I relished hearing my name mentioned, reading my name in print, and being commended by others for my wisdom, my musical gifts, my parenting, and my care—even my humility. I'd grown increasingly offended when people found fault with anything I did. I bristled inwardly when someone questioned my integrity, gifting, or planning. I tried to avoid any kind of criticism and worked hard to persuade others that I was an exceptional (but humble) Christian, pastor, and worship leader.

Some people would characterize my condition as a chronic people-pleaser. A more apt description was a people-worshiper. I was striving to gain the approval of those whose approval was of no eternal significance. I'd failed to see that the only approval that matters—God's—is impossible to earn but is offered as a gift through the gospel.

And it was the gospel that set me free.

Gary had been right. I'd felt hopeless, but not hopeless enough. I knew Jesus died on the cross to save sinners from God's wrath, enduring in our place the punishment we deserved. I understood that I couldn't save myself. I just didn't think of myself as a very great sinner. Which meant I didn't need a very great Savior.

When I sought glory for myself, praise for my accomplishments, and credit for my growth, I wasn't depending on a Savior—I was searching for an audience.

God used various people and means to transform my heart. I know my wife will receive significant rewards on the last day for her support, correction, and love during that time. My friends gave me much insightful and patient counsel. Jerry Bridges's book *The Discipline of Grace* and John Owen's treatises on *Sin and Temptation* also proved to be meaningful channels of grace through which the Spirit encouraged my sin-weary soul.

Today the gospel—which I so frequently assumed but so often failed to apply—is the center and foundation of my daily life. I continue to learn about the pervasive power of sin and the greater power of Jesus Christ to redeem me from it. I love Jesus more than I ever thought I would or could.

Why have I shared all this? Because I want to make it clear from the start that worship isn't primarily about music, techniques, liturgies, songs, or methodologies. It's about our hearts. It's about what and who we love more than anything.

Here's my sobering discovery. I learned that I could lead others in worshiping God and be worshiping something else in my own heart. But by the grace of God, I was beginning to understand what worship is all about.

LOVE AND WORSHIP

In my pride I had lost sight of what really matters. I had overlooked what couldn't be clearer in Scripture. Jesus said the greatest commandment is this: "You shall *love* the Lord your God with all your *heart* and with all your soul and with all your mind" (Matthew 22:37, emphasis added). While it's simplistic to say that worship is love, it's a fact that what we love most will determine what we genuinely worship.

God wants us to love him more than our instruments and music. More than our possessions, food, and ministry. More than our wife and children.

More than our own lives.

That doesn't mean we can't love anything else. Or that we shouldn't love anything else. But we can't love anything in the right way unless we love God more. Our desires will be out of whack. We'll look to temporary pleasures like concerts, video games, and sports to fulfill eternal desires. We'll love things that aren't as worthy as God to be loved.

How do I know what I love the most? By looking at my life outside of Sunday morning. What do I enjoy the most? What do I spend the most time doing? Where does my mind drift to when I don't have anything to do? What am I passionate about? What do I spend my money on? What makes me angry when I don't get it? What do I feel depressed without? What do I fear losing the most?

Our answers to those questions will lead us straight to the God or gods we love and worship.

That's why as worship leaders our primary concern can't be song preparation, creative arrangements, or the latest cool gear. Our primary concern has to be the state of our hearts.

The great hymn-writer Isaac Watts once wrote:

> The Great God values not the service of men, if the heart be not in it: The Lord sees and judges the heart; he has no regard to outward forms of worship, if there be no inward adoration, if no devout affection be employed therein. It is therefore a matter of infinite importance, to have the whole heart engaged steadfastly for God.[1]

A matter of *infinite importance*.

Is it a matter of *infinite importance* to you?

Unquestionably it is to God. And when it becomes a matter of infinite importance to us, we're beginning to grasp the heart of leading worship.

chapter 3

MY MIND:
WHAT DO I BELIEVE?

Let's say you and I run into each other at Starbucks, and you start telling me how much you've enjoyed getting to know my son, Jordan.

I'm delighted.

You go on to describe him as a five-foot-two saxophonist who has an avid interest in cooking Italian food and playing cricket.

I give you a funny look. "You must be thinking of someone else. Jordan is a six-foot-tall drummer who loves to *eat*, not *cook*, Italian food. And though he excels in many sports, cricket isn't one of them."

But you continue extolling a short, sax-playing, pasta-cooking cricket player as you repeat several times, "He's just a great guy!"

Such praise would be meaningless because it would be based on inadequate and inaccurate information. Your "doctrine of Jordan" would be wrong. And however strong your appreciation, I think you'd like him more after discovering what he's really like.

It's like that with us and God. He calls us not only to love him but to "love the truth" about him (2 Thessalonians 2:10). We worship the One who says he *is* the truth and who tells us, "the truth will set you free" (John 14:6; John 8:32). God wants everyone "to come to the knowledge of the truth" (1 Timothy 2:4). And he reveals his wrath against those who "suppress the truth" (Romans 1:18). Jesus said he would send "the Spirit of truth," and he asked God to sanctify his disciples "in the truth," which he identified as God's Word (John 16:13; 17:17).

The better (i.e., the more accurately) we know God through his Word, the more genuine our worship will be. In fact, the moment we veer from what is true about God, we're engaging in idolatry.

Regardless of what we think or feel, there is no authentic worship of God without a right knowledge of God.

THEOLOGY AND DOCTRINE

Where do we find a right knowledge of God? In the revealed truth of Scripture. A worship leader who barely knows the Bible can't be a faithful worship leader. But how do we get our arms around everything the Bible says about God? It takes thoughtful, disciplined study.

That introduces two words many Christians are uncomfortable with— *theology* and *doctrine*. Sadly, doctrine and theology rank fairly low on the popularity scale these days. But biblical worship is impossible without them.

Theology literally means "the study of God." It includes our concept of God as a result of that study (or lack thereof). So every Christian, musical or otherwise, is already a theologian. The question is, am I a good theologian or a bad one?

We're good theologians if what we say and think about God lines up with what Scripture says and affirms.

We're bad theologians if our view of God is vague, unbiblical, distorted, or based on our own opinions.

Doctrine is a word meaning "what is taught." Doctrine is everything the Bible teaches on a particular topic, such as worship or holiness or the church or spiritual gifts. Paul told Titus that a leader in the church "must hold firm to the trustworthy word as taught, so that he may be able to give instruction in sound doctrine and also to rebuke those who contradict it" (Titus 1:9).

The study of doctrine isn't opposed to studying the Bible; it *is* studying the Bible. It's how we find out what God is like, what he wants us to believe, how he wants us to worship him.

So that means we need to be reading. We need to be studying. Because we'll be learning about God for the rest of our lives.

WE NEED HELP

I've met guys who don't read theology books because they don't want their understanding of the Bible to be influenced by anyone else. What they're saying is: "God couldn't possibly use another person to help me understand his Word more clearly." That's ridiculous. I need all the help I can get. So do you.

In a letter written from prison, Paul requested Timothy to bring him "the books" (2 Timothy 4:13). Charles Spurgeon, the nineteenth-century "prince of preachers," expressed amazement at such a request from Paul:

> He is inspired, and yet he wants books! He has seen the Lord, and yet he wants books! He has had wider experience than most men, and yet he wants books! He had been caught up in the third heaven, and had heard things unlawful for a man to utter, yet he wants books! He has written a major part of the New Testament, and yet he wants books!

Spurgeon then reminds us, "He who will not use the thoughts of other men's brains proves he has no brains of his own."[1]

But I've hung around enough worship leaders and Christian musicians over the past few decades to make this general observation: We rarely read theology books.

I know that's a broad statement, and I've met some commendable exceptions. But often when I ask worship leaders what they're reading, it's secular business best-sellers, novels, music magazines, biographies, or books about sports or history. There's always something we can learn from reading those kinds of books. But they pale in comparison to books that help us understand what God has told us about himself in his Word. Books like *Engaging with God* by David Peterson, *The Cross of Christ* by John Stott, or *Knowing God* by J. I. Packer.

When someone suggests we should be reading books that are more theologically substantive, we may tend to respond, "I'm no scholar. They're too deep." But authors of books like these can offer invaluable assistance for wrapping our minds around the Spirit-inspired teachings of Scripture. That's why we should take time not only to study Scripture, but also to learn from writers whose books challenge us and help us mine the riches of God's Word.

COMMON MISCONCEPTIONS

As I've talked to musicians and worship leaders over the years, I've encountered some common perspectives that keep us from pursuing God with our minds.

Misconception #1: Studying This Stuff Shouldn't Be So Hard

Studying doctrine and theology *is* hard. Becoming a good theologian is harder than learning a new riff, and initially not as much fun.

Getting to know God is time-consuming. We live in the age of instant everything. We want a life-changing devotional in fifteen minutes max. And why *shouldn't* God fit into the slot we've allotted him? After all, he's *God*; he knows how packed our schedule is! We open our Bibles and get bored if nothing grips us after two paragraphs. We want everything abridged, dumbed down, and in today's lingo, so we don't have to think too much or examine our lives too closely.

Those attitudes are unacceptable if we want to display the glories of God through song each Sunday. Given our small minds, our absolute dependence on revealed truth, and the immensity of God, how can we think there's an easy path to knowing the God we worship?

There are no shortcuts. Only a grace-motivated, steadfast, lifelong pursuit of the God who created and redeemed us for his glory.

Misconception #2: We Know God Better through Music than through Words

Like me, you've probably had profound encounters with God during musical worship. Just as King Saul was calmed as David played the lyre (1 Samuel 16:23), we experience an unusual peace or sense God's nearness in an unexpected way. We can start assuming that words restrict and limit the Spirit's work, while music expands the soul and opens us to new ways of powerfully experiencing God.

But being moved emotionally is different from being changed spiritually. Music affects and helps us in many ways, but it doesn't replace truth about God. Music can never by itself help us understand the meaning of God's self-existence, the nature of the Incarnation, or Christ's substitutionary atonement. Nor can an instrumental solo tell us how music functions in worshiping God. For that, we need to read our Bibles. And to know what the Bible says, we need theology. Good theology.

Good theology helps us keep music in its proper place. We learn that music isn't an end in itself but rather a means of expressing the worship already present in our hearts through the new life we've received in Jesus Christ.

Misconception #3: Theology and Doctrine Cause Problems

One worship leader told me he wasn't interested in theology because it only causes divisions. He said his theology was Jesus.

While I appreciate the simple devotion to Christ behind his comment, it raises a few questions. As we lead others in worship, how will we clarify who Jesus is? Is it a Jesus "meek and mild" who never speaks a harsh word? Or is it the holy Jesus who drove the moneychangers from the temple in righteous anger when he saw how they completely missed God's purpose for the temple? Do we worship Jesus as a champion of social justice, a divine mystic, a revolutionary religious radical, or the Savior of the world?

When we're dodgy about our theology, we're really saying we want our own Jesus. But our worship isn't based on people's personal opinions, ideas, or best guesses about Jesus. Nor should we base our understanding of him on anyone's individual experiences. He has a name, a particular history, and a specifically revealed body of teaching. *God* has theology; will we sharpen our own biblical understanding to find out what it is? Will we worship the Son of God, the Redeemer, the second person of the Trinity, the Alpha and Omega, our High Priest, sanctifier, and intercessor and seek to understand what all this means?

You might respond, "But doesn't doctrine divide the church?"

Yes and no. Sure, Christians often disagree over doctrinal issues of secondary importance. Given the degree of sin that still remains with us and the enemy's desire to separate us, that's no surprise. But divisions have also protected the church. The New Testament warned us that false prophets and teachers would infiltrate the church's ranks (Acts 20:29–30; 2 Corinthians 11:13; 2 Peter 2:1). Many of the most precious truths we live by were more clearly defined as a response to heresy. The result has been clarity and agreement on foundational truths from God's Word that the church has cherished for centuries. Truth has often been tested and confirmed in the fires of controversy and conflict.

But don't doctrine and theology make life complicated?

It depends on what you mean by *complicated*. Sometimes we expect to be able to understand God like, say, the inside of our computer. But if we could grasp God completely, he wouldn't be much of a god. We should anticipate that our minds will be stretched to their limits as we seek to take in God's revelation of himself and his universe.

Theology and doctrine make life simpler. They protect us from reading verses out of context, restricting our diet to our favorite passages, and making decisions based on impulse rather than truth. They put meat on concepts we tend to use mindlessly like *glory*, *gospel*, *salvation*, and *love*. They help us understand what we're actually doing every Sunday. What complicates life is not doctrine but *ignorance* of doctrine.

But doesn't studying doctrine just make people proud?

It shouldn't. To begin with, our knowledge of God is limited to what he has revealed to us (1 Corinthians 2:11–12). When we understand a truth, it's because God's Spirit has opened our eyes and hearts (Ephesians 1:17–19).

And the more we study God, the more we should realize that what we know will always be dwarfed by what we don't know (Romans 11:33–36).

If we're arrogant because we use big theological terms or have memorized more verses than our friends, we've lost sight of the God we claim to know. As Paul reminds us, that kind of knowledge "puffs up, but love builds up. If anyone imagines that he knows something, he does not yet know as he ought to know" (1 Corinthians 8:1–2). Good theologians are increasingly humbled and amazed by the God they study.

Instead of causing problems, doctrine and theology rightly applied will *solve* problems. They inform our minds to win our hearts, so we can love God more accurately and passionately.

MIND AND HEART TOGETHER

Mind and heart belong together. Strong, passionate *desires* for God flow from and encourage the faithful, thoughtful *study* of God—his nature, character, and works.

We're deceived when we think we can have one without the other. God intends us to have both.

If our doctrine is accurate but our hearts are cold toward God himself, our corporate worship will be true but lifeless. Or if we express fervent love for God but present vague, inaccurate, or incomplete ideas of him to those we're leading, our worship will be emotional but misleading—and possibly idolatrous. Neither option brings God glory.

My prayer for myself and every worship leader is that we'll become as familiar with the Word of Truth as we are with our instruments. Hopefully even more so. If we do, there's a strong possibility people are going to walk away from our meetings more amazed by our God than by our music.

And that will be a very good thing.

chapter 4

MY HANDS: WHAT DO I PRACTICE?

Meet Joe, the new worship leader for Crosstown Community Church. Joe is fictional, but you might recognize some of his qualities.

Joe works forty-five hours a week as a software engineer but still spends between five and ten hours preparing for Sunday morning. A lot of that time is given to reading Scripture, studying notes from the pastor's previous message, and praying for the church. Late Saturday night you'll usually find him poring over songs for the next morning.

Joe really wants to be used by God to help people grow in their love for him.

But things haven't been going too well. Last Sunday he forgot to tune his guitar. Again. After two verses it sounded so bad the pastor came up and asked the team to start over. During the third song, Joe remembered the team hadn't practiced going from the chorus to the verse. After a minor train wreck, the piano player finally got them on track.

Every week Joe fumbles through chords, misses cues, and forgets words. When others suggest he could grow in his abilities, Joe shakes his head and smiles. He's sure worship is about the *heart*, not trying to play everything perfectly. He thinks loving God and knowing him through his Word are all he needs.

The congregation wouldn't agree. They think Joe needs skill. And their worship of God is being hindered by Joe's lack of it.

Skill is the ability to do something well. It's related to qualities like expertise and competence. We can tend to undervalue it, like Joe, or idolize it, like we do in professional musicians and athletes. But rightly understood and pursued, skill can mark the difference between ineffectiveness and fruitfulness in our leading. It can contribute to, or hinder people from, engaging with God. That's why we should make it a priority.

While God can work through us in spite of our mistakes, incompetence, and lack of preparation, he commends skill and uses it for his glory. When Moses had to find men to oversee the construction of the tabernacle, he didn't pass around a sign-up list. He chose craftsmen whom God had gifted with "skill and intelligence" (Exodus 36:1). When David looked for a Levite to lead singing, he picked Kenaniah "because he was skillful at it" (1 Chronicles 15:22, NIV). Under divine inspiration, David wrote that musicians are to "play skillfully on the strings" (Psalm 33:3), and David himself, as king over the people, "guided them with his skillful hand" (Psalm 78:72). In the New Testament, Paul referred to himself as "a skilled master builder" (1 Corinthians 3:10).

Skill matters to God. It should matter to us too.

FIVE THINGS TO REMEMBER ABOUT SKILL

But simply valuing skill isn't sufficient. We need a theologically informed understanding of skill so that we can pursue it in a way that pleases God.

Here are five principles to keep in mind as we seek to become more competent in what God has called us to do.

Skill Is a Gift from God, for His Glory

None of us can claim credit for our abilities. As Paul asked the Corinthians, "What do you have that you did not receive? If then you received it, why do you boast as if you did not receive it?" (1 Corinthians 4:7).

I remember a musician in college who had trouble understanding why God should get any glory for his (the musician's) gifts. He reasoned that God wasn't the one sitting in a practice room for hours on end. This guy didn't understand grace, which provides not only our gifts but the ability and endurance to develop them. As my good friend C. J. Mahaney says, "All gifts from God are intended to direct our attention to God and create fresh affection for God."[1]

Skill Must Be Developed

We read in 1 Chronicles 25:7 that the musicians ministering at the tabernacle were those "who were *trained* in singing to the LORD, all who were *skillful*." Skill must be developed.

Wynton Marsalis, Yo-Yo Ma, Pat Metheny, and other legendary musicians have demonstrated that excellence comes not only from being gifted but from practicing harder, longer, and more comprehensively than others. The greatest musicians put in countless hours honing their talent, realizing that skill must be cultivated.

When I entered Temple University as a piano performance major, my goal was to practice enough to be able to play any piece I desired when I finished school. Over the next four years I averaged four hours a day, seven days a week. I had friends who put in even more time.

Sometimes people say to me, "I wish I could play the piano like you do." My standard reply is, "You can! It just takes a little gifting and practicing four hours a day for four years."

I shared that recently with a worship leader, and he told me it was discouraging. Who has time to practice four hours a day? No worship leader I know, that's for sure. But if you want to grow in your craft, you have to develop your skill. Even if it's only fifteen minutes a day or an hour a week, it will make a difference in the long run.

Skill Doesn't Make Worship More Acceptable before God

While God values skill, he doesn't accept our worship on the basis of it. Even if I can play the most complex chord progressions, write better songs than Matt Redman, or play a song flawlessly, I still need the atoning work of the Savior to perfect my offering of worship (1 Peter 2:5).

We worship leaders can struggle with discouragement when we miss an entrance, play a wrong chord, or forget the lyrics. We can feel elated when everything goes well. But God isn't listening to the sound of our music or the quality of our performance. He's hearing the sound of our hearts.

Years ago I heard a pastor say, "God isn't looking for something brilliant; he's looking for something broken." We'll never impress God with our musical expertise or sophistication. What impresses God is "a broken and contrite heart" (Psalm 51:17) that recognizes our weakness and puts our faith in the finished work of Christ.

Skill Should Be Evaluated by Others

Even after thirty years of leading worship, I can't always tell if what I'm doing is helpful or where I need to grow. I need the eyes and ears of those with whom I'm serving.

The feedback I receive from my team and others during rehearsals and after meetings is invaluable. *Is that arrangement working? Did I sing that chorus too many times? Was I clear? Did I play too much?* It's both humbling and helpful to hear back from people I trust who'll speak the truth. Especially my pastor.

By the way, don't give too much weight to comments from those who week after week tell you how "blessed" they were by your worship leading. Their encouragement, though sincere, won't necessarily help you grow.

Skill Is Not an End in Itself

Valuing skill too highly can yield some ugly fruit. It becomes an idol. We arrogantly think our church's worship is better than the church down the street. We over-rehearse and get impatient when others make mistakes. We minimize spiritual preparation and devote ourselves entirely to musical issues. We evaluate failure or success solely on right tempos, in-tune vocals, and well-executed plans. We take pride in our polished performance rather than being humbled by God's mercy.

After a time of corporate worship, I'm always a little disappointed when someone says, "I *loved* your keyboard playing!" I don't want them to even focus on my playing, except as it helps them see God's character and works more clearly as we sing.

God wants us to realize that the point of our practice isn't to receive the praise of others. It's to bring him glory.

WHAT SKILL HELPS US DO

A divine perspective on skill will both motivate us to develop skill and protect us from exalting it. That's because God wants us to be skillful for specific reasons. Here are just a few.

Skill Helps Us Focus on God

I've been asked numerous times, "How can you concentrate on worshiping God while you're leading others?"

Becoming more skillful is part of the answer. The more comfortable I am with practical aspects of leading, the more I can think about the One to whom I'm singing. I focus on developing skill so I'll be able to focus more on God. We want to get to the place where musical, administrative, and leadership issues become second nature as a result of rehearsal, repetition, and careful planning.

And remember, the goal of practice isn't doing something until you get it right. It's doing it until you can't get it wrong.

Can we worship God even if we aren't thoroughly familiar with the practical skills required for leading? Sure. God can use whatever we can manage. But my lack of skill can tempt people to be distracted, confused, and potentially irritated. I might be worshiping God, but I'm not doing all I can to help everyone else join me.

Skill Helps Us Serve the Church

Joe, our friend at the beginning of this chapter, really wants to bring glory to God with his gifts. What he doesn't understand is that his lack of skill is an obstacle. God gives us gifts so that we can "serve one another" (1 Peter 4:10).

How do we serve one another?

By leading clearly so people aren't wondering what words to sing next or what the melody is. By using fresh arrangements that aren't distracting.

And by possessing a calm and joyful countenance that expresses the hope in the God we're singing about. "Those who look to him are radiant" (Psalm 34:5). If I'm trying to remember the lyrics to verse 2, how to play a B7sus, or how the bridge melody goes, I'll have a hard time looking to the One I'm worshiping, and my face will be anything but radiant.

But if I don't have to think much about the mechanics of leading, I'll be free to look to the One I'm worshiping, and my face will show it. And that will serve the people I'm leading.

Skill Multiplies Serving Opportunities

A few years ago, we were looking for a music and worship intern at my church. The individual we were considering had a master's degree in organ performance. In some churches that would be a requirement, but in our situation it didn't carry much weight. In fact, it was a strike against him. We don't have an organ and don't plan to purchase one.

But this man had also spent a significant amount of time developing his improvisation skills on the piano and had experience in songwriting, choir-leading, and arranging. Because he broadened his skill set, he was able to serve in more areas and was a perfect fit for us.

SKILLS TO DEVELOP

Our varied skills should function like the frame around a classic painting. If the frame is too bold or extravagant, we'll hardly notice the picture it displays. On the other hand, if the frame is cheap, shabby, or marred, we'll wonder why such a masterpiece is surrounded by junk. The right frame complements the picture in all the right ways, directing our eyes to the brilliance of the artist, not to the frame.

John Piper calls the right balance "undistracting excellence."[2] It's a proficiency that doesn't draw attention to itself but rather points away from itself.

We can pursue undistracting excellence in a number of areas. The first and most important is our knowledge of God and his Word, which we looked at in the last chapter. But the nature of worship leading requires us to give attention to other areas as well.

Leadership

Perhaps the most neglected skill among worship leaders is leadership. We think, "I'm not a pastor, so I don't really have the responsibility for leading." But we do. And by God's grace we can be better leaders than we currently are. We can define our goals more clearly and pursue them more faithfully.

Do you have a plan and a purpose on Sunday morning, or do you walk in unprepared and unconcerned? Skilled leaders have a clear vision of what we've gathered to do. They enable us to see things we wouldn't see on our own. That may involve explaining why we're singing a certain song or making connections between a song and the sermon. It could also mean letting a song speak for itself.

Good leaders draw our attention to what's most important. They make choices that help us focus. That means I take responsibility for what people are getting out of a song and don't assume everyone is equally engaged or aware of what they should be thinking about. I try to minimize distractions and clear up confusion.

Skilled leadership always involves saying yes to some things and no to others. In my experience, saying no is more difficult. It often requires forgoing something good to choose something better. I might have to cut a song or what I'd planned to say because we've run over. I may have to say no to someone's joining the team. Maybe I'll have to explain why we can't sing a song someone really likes because the lyrics are weak or unclear. And of course, in saying yes to one soloist, I'm automatically saying no to everyone else.

Being a leader inevitably involves disappointing people. Someone will eventually misunderstand or criticize our decisions. But our goal is pleasing God, not trying to make everyone happy. Our goal is to serve the church with our gift of leadership.

Musicianship

Being skilled musically involves different components. One is *technique*, which simply means mastering the mechanics or building blocks of a style. It's having the actual ability to play or sing whatever is required in a situation. Developing technique is probably the most difficult and unexciting aspect of musicianship, which is why we tend to spend so little time on it. Depending on the instrument, it can include practicing scales, riffs, chord progressions, strum patterns, different beats, or vocal exercises.

A second aspect of musicianship is *theory*—understanding how music works. Because music is made up of repeatable patterns and sounds, we can figure out what the interval of a fourth sounds like, what the minor 6 chord is in the key of D, and how to modulate from F to G. Musicians who don't understand music theory are lost if they have a memory slip during a song. Theory is like a road map that helps us get our bearings and return to the right path. If you don't know the basics of chord structure, notation, and intervals, consider checking out the many theory courses on the Internet[3] or taking classes at a local college. The benefits will far surpass the time and money you invest.

You can excel at technique and theory but still make music that's cold, boring, or inappropriate. That's why a third requirement in skilled musicianship is *taste*. Taste is knowing what fits. It comes primarily through listening to music purposefully and picking apart exactly what musicians are doing or not doing. Taste involves dynamics, phrasing, rhythmic patterns, voicings, and instrumentation. Probably the most challenging part of good musical taste is knowing what to leave out. Great musicianship is less about what you play and more about what you don't play. I've been telling worship teams for years that "less is more," but when I listen to a recording of my own playing, I still probably play twice as much as I need to. If I'm not the only member of the band, I shouldn't play like I am. More notes rarely equals greater effectiveness.

Sometimes we try to grow in multiple areas of skill at once and become discouraged. Don't go down that path. Focus on one or two areas at a time. If you're a pianist wanting to learn to read music better, try sight-reading a hymn or two every day. If you want to grow in technique as a guitarist, practice chords from a chord book or riffs you've picked up from listening to CDs. If you want to grow in playing by ear, find a CD you like and start copying what you hear.

Diverse musical skills give us more tools to choose from. My background as a trained classical pianist enables me to choose songs out of songbooks without having heard them, to write out lead sheets and vocal parts, and to accompany soloists. Playing by ear helps me play chord charts, use creative musical transitions, and respond to a spontaneous direction during a meeting. Both skills have been valuable in my role as a worship leader.

If you want to grow in a particular area, private lessons are often the best option. Many community colleges offer music training and courses that are well worth the price. Training videos are another route, and they're getting better every year.[4] Bookstores also offer a wide variety of helpful music books.

How much should you practice? It depends on what else you do and what your goals are. At the very least you should be able to play the songs you need to play without any interruptions. But that's a minimum. A higher standard is to continually add to your skills so you can serve whatever needs arise.

Communication

You might think your primary means of communicating to others is music. Maybe you get tongue-tied when you try quoting a Bible verse, or you lose your train of thought trying to explain what a song means. So you end up defaulting to Christian phrases that sound "worshipful"—such as "Glory to God" or "Praise the Lord." Or maybe you're happy to say nothing at all and just let God speak through the songs.

Like all skills, speaking to others clearly and persuasively involves the hard work of preparation. We like to think spontaneous ramblings are more genuine than prepared thoughts, but that's hardly ever true.

When I arrived at Covenant Life, C. J. told me that if I wanted to grow in communicating effectively, I should write down what I wanted to say and keep it to a certain length. He assured me that the more I thought through my comments in advance, the more substantive they would be and the easier it would eventually be to prepare them. He was right.

It's easy to be content with speaking honestly and passionately. We're transparent about our failings, struggles, and sinfulness and speak with real emotion. That may help people relate to us, but God wants to change them through eternal truth and an unchanging gospel. That takes clear, theologically informed communication. And that's a skill we can grow in, by God's grace and for his glory.

Technology

Technology can help us communicate God's truth more clearly, or it can be a major hindrance to that end. It can be a valuable asset or a terrible taskmaster. The difference is in how skillfully we use it.

That means being familiar with current methods of transferring and downloading music (legal ones, of course), notating charts, using MIDI, producing music, amplifying sound, and projecting lyrics and images, to name a few.

If you don't have time to invest any study in this area, you can probably find people in the church who do. They don't have to be musicians. But they do need to understand they're more than techies. They're worshipers. They're using their gifts to help proclaim God's Word and celebrate the gospel of Jesus Christ.

SKILL MATTERS

Other areas of worship ministry also require skill and sensitivity to the Spirit's leading (for example, administration and pastoral care). I'm sure you can think of more. The important thing to recognize is that leading the church to worship God requires more than a sincere heart and good intentions. It requires skill. And that involves work, time, and preparation.

My prayer is that guys like Joe will see the light and give themselves to the diligent practice and careful attention necessary for biblical leadership.

Even more importantly, I pray that each of us will never substitute talent, gifting, ability, or skill for what God is really after—genuine worship that affects our entire lives.

chapter 5

MY LIFE:
WHAT DO I MODEL?

I've never thought of the apostle Paul as a worship leader. He apparently didn't strum a lyre in front of the church or keep time with a timbrel. He did lead an a cappella hymn-sing in prison at midnight after being beaten and thrown in the stocks. Not exactly the kind of worship context I'm used to.

Paul may not fit our image of a worship leader, but he can tell us how to live like one. Maybe he never led a worship band, but he consistently glorified God and exalted the Savior in the power of the Holy Spirit. His life and words have inspired millions throughout history to offer up God-honoring worship. More than any musician I've ever known, Paul shows us how to live like a worship leader.

If leading worship were merely a matter of what we did on Sunday morning, I wouldn't need to write this chapter. But leading worship starts with the way I live my life, not with what I do in public. It's inconceivable for us to see ourselves as worship leaders if we're not giving attention to what we do every day.

COUNSEL FOR A YOUNG MAN

In his first letter to Timothy, Paul gave him directions for leading the church in Ephesus. Timothy was probably in his thirties, younger than many of the Christians he led. Paul knew that his young age might lead people to question his authority or effectiveness. So he also told Timothy, "Let no one despise you for your youth, but set the believers an example in speech, in conduct, in love, in faith, in purity" (1 Timothy 4:12). Whether we're young or old, that's God's counsel for each of us. Is your desire to lead people in worshiping God? Then the example of your life will show it.

It doesn't matter whether we're leading a congregation, driving our car, or sitting alone in our bedroom. Everything we do should be governed by one goal—to see Jesus Christ praised, exalted, magnified, lifted up, and obeyed.

SET THE BELIEVERS AN EXAMPLE

Paul knew that a leader's spiritual life is never a private matter. Timothy was a leader, and people were watching him, studying him, and learning from what they observed. So Paul wisely charged him: "*Set . . . an example.*"

People are watching us as well. Not just on Sunday morning, but throughout the week. If we lead God's people in worship, we can't exempt ourselves from this biblical standard. Paul's charge to Timothy applies to us, too; *set an example*.

In my experience, this is rarely the emphasis among worship leaders. Godly example is too often assumed or ignored, while public gifting is highlighted and exalted. But Paul can't imagine a leader whose personal life doesn't commend his message.

This command to be an example touches every area of our lives. Let's consider the categories Paul brings to Timothy's attention.

In Speech

Every time we open our mouths, we're leading others. Not just when we're in front of people, but all the time. We're counseling them. Communicating what's important and what's not. Letting others know whose words matter more—ours or God's.

Of course, what we say in front of the congregation is important. But the words we use on blog posts, on church web sites, in articles, and in private conversations are equally as important. As a leader, every word we say has an increased potential to either confirm our example of genuine worship or take away from it. If our words are foolish, sensual, or sinful during the week, it's hard for people to take us seriously when our mouths are suddenly filled with God's praise on Sunday morning.

James gives us a sober warning:

But no human being can tame the tongue. It is a restless evil, full of deadly poison. With it we bless our Lord and Father, and with it we curse people who are made in the likeness of God. From the same mouth come blessing and cursing. My brothers, these things ought not to be so. (James 3:8–10)

He's right. "These things ought not to be so." But from the little I've heard and read, we seem increasingly comfortable with conversations that contain profanity and sexual innuendo. I've read blog posts by worship leaders that are slanderous and provocative. It could be an attempt to sound cool and relevant. Or it could be that we're just being foolish.

God wants our speech to be sound, gracious, truthful, and edifying,[1] no matter where we are or whom we're with. That includes the way we speak to our spouse, our children, our team, our pastor, and anyone else we happen to be talking to.

That doesn't mean there's no place for appropriate humor or informal conversation. It does mean taking responsibility for our words, written or spoken, and understanding that they influence others to fear God or ignore him. Jesus said we'll be held accountable for "every careless word" we say (Matthew 12:36). That's why he wants us to set an example for others in our speech.[2]

In Conduct

Worldly musicians can make great music on stage and live totally decadent lives—and no one thinks twice about it.

Worship leaders don't have that option.

God wants our conduct to be an example to others. If the way we live doesn't back up what we proclaim on Sunday morning, we're not only deceiving the church—we're misrepresenting the God we claim to be worshiping.

I don't ever want people who see me lead worship publicly to be surprised by the way I live privately. It's not my songs that define my worship; it's my life. So if your marriage is struggling, if your children are rebelling, if you're viewing pornography, if you're easily angered, if your speech is foul, or if you're engaged in a pattern of sin I haven't mentioned yet, get help now. If no one is aware of your sin, start by confessing it to those who can help you. "Whoever conceals his transgressions will not prosper, but he who confesses and forsakes them will obtain mercy" (Proverbs 28:13). We need the eyes of others who know and care about what we do with our free time, our money, our thought life, and our family.

The standard for leading worship isn't sinless perfection. But there has to be a consistent lifestyle of godliness. Areas of compromise not only weaken our example but call into question whether we should be leading at all. Sometimes the best way you can demonstrate the value of Jesus Christ to others is by stepping down. Remember, God can use us, but he doesn't need us. The world has seen enough leaders whose sin has dishonored the Savior and harmed the church. We're called to set an example for the church with our conduct. We need to pursue every possible means available to do that.

If you don't have people in your life who know you well and are helping you live a life worthy of the gospel, find them *now*. Temptation is too great, sin too deceptive, and the world too attractive to think we can live an overcoming life on our own.

In Love

We can't claim to fulfill the greatest commandment in song while neglecting the second greatest commandment in life.

God calls us to set an example in love. The love he calls us to is grounded in his character, not ours. It's more than our culture's idea of being tolerant or experiencing sexual attraction. Our love is fleeting, self-centered, and polluted. God's love is eternal, sacrificial, and holy.

God describes love as being "patient," "kind," humble, polite, thoughtful, forgiving, hopeful, and enduring (1 Corinthians 13:4–7). Are those your attitudes after a worship service where the mix was bad and the vocalists were out of tune? When members of the church criticize you, do you respond with blame-shifting and accusations, or do you respond with patience and humility?

How would your wife and children evaluate your example of love? Your pastor? Your church? Non-Christians? When we fail to set an example in love, our ability to lead others in worship is seriously compromised.

How do we grow in love? The best place to start is remembering the love that God showed to us through giving his Son for us at Calvary. "By this we know love, that he laid down his life for us, and we ought to lay down our lives for the brothers" (1 John 3:16).

"Let us not love in word or talk but in deed and in truth" (1 John 3:18). In that way, we'll be leading others in worship with our lives.

In Faith

Every Sunday morning I'm seeking to point people to God. My role isn't to direct people's eyes to me, but to the God in whom I trust. The primary way I do that is by making sure I'm looking to God myself.

For me to effectively lead others in worship, I need to exude a steadfast confidence in God and his promises. That doesn't mean I make presumptuous statements and never experience trials. It simply means I'm always seeking to grow in my trust in God. I'm not content to sing "Blessed Be Your Name" on Sunday and doubt the power and goodness of that name on Monday.

A lack of faith reveals itself in different ways. Do you regularly find yourself battling thoughts of discouragement and despair? Do you doubt God is going to be actively present as you gather on Sunday? Do you lose sleep over your finances or your future?

If faith means believing that God "exists and . . . rewards those who seek him" (Hebrews 11:6), we should bring those convictions not only into our worship leading but into every area of our lives.

In our consistent pursuit of faith and our constant practice of faith, God wants us to set an example for the church.

In Purity

God made it clear to Moses that everything associated with the tabernacle and Israel's worship was to be characterized by absolute purity and holiness. Nothing defiled or impure could draw near to God's presence in the Holy of Holies.

Various purification rites reminded the Israelites that they were set apart from the world and separated from sin. Sacrificial animals were to be pure and without blemish. To ignore these requirements for purity was to face exclusion from God's covenant people or even death.

Jesus came to purify his people once and for all through his atoning sacrifice (Titus 2:14). He fulfilled what ceremonial purification could only point to. But God's demand for purity hasn't changed. The Lord is still holy. So it's not surprising that God wants leaders in the church to set an example for the believers in purity.

Purity is the quality of being undefiled, unmixed, and undiluted, free from evil or contamination. The first area this applies to is our motives. God calls us to guard against being "led astray from a sincere and pure devotion to Christ" (2 Corinthians 11:3). Leading worship for financial gain or public recognition dishonors God. God wants our worship to be sincere, not hypocritical; willing, not forced; wholehearted, not distracted. In other words, pure.

God also calls us to model purity in the area of sexuality. Music in the world is filled with sexual innuendo, provocative dress, and sensuality. Music in the church should never be.

But signs of compromise aren't hard to find. Individuals on worship teams wear clothes that are too tight or revealing. Worship leaders sometimes use vocal inflections that sound alluring and sensual. Worship songs are described as "sexy." Ads for Christian bands and soloists are as visually seductive at times as their non-Christian counterparts. Music ministers commit adultery and continue ministering.

Given the holiness of God, his jealousy for the church, and the preciousness of Christ's body, our behavior is dangerous and inexcusable. There are few things as serious and destructive in the life of a leader as sexual impurity. The consequences are not only personally harmful but publicly dishonoring to the name of Christ.

We worship the Savior who "gave himself for us to redeem us from all lawlessness and to purify for himself a people for his own possession" (Titus 2:14). By his grace and for his glory, let's be who we've been saved to be, and set an example for the believers in purity.[3]

OUR ETERNAL OCCUPATION

The fact that you're reading this book says something about your desire to learn and grow in the ways I've been describing. You've tasted God's goodness and power, but you want more. You aren't content to simply lead songs on Sunday morning or be a great musician. You want your life to count for eternity. Worshiping God is an eternal occupation, and you know that we'll barely scratch the surface in this life.

I'm with you. That's why I started with these four areas—loving, believing, practicing, and modeling. These aren't merely preliminary or introductory chapters. They're foundational. If we aren't exemplifying a genuine yearning to bring glory to God that touches every aspect of our existence, then we have no business leading worship on Sundays.

I trust that bringing God glory *is* your desire . . . and I pray he will use this first section toward that end.

But there's more to cover. Having looked at what a worship leader is supposed to be, it's time to look at what a worship leader is supposed to do.

part two

THE TASK

chapter 6

SO WHAT DOES A WORSHIP LEADER DO?

If you were born after 1980, you probably don't remember when the term *worship leader* didn't exist. But that designation really didn't emerge until the early 1970s. I still remember my shock and delight the first time I heard the group Love Song. *They're singing to God. And they're a band!* I was hooked.

At that time Integrity's Hosanna Music was still a decade away, most churches were singing hymns, and Scripture choruses were one of the hottest things going. I don't think anyone back then had a clue how the thinking, structure, and practices of the church would come to be dominated by worship music and worship leaders.

Today it's hard to imagine the church without them. Their influence has been broad and often beneficial. They've made us more aware of the importance of praising God and engaging deeply with him as we sing. Churches all over the world are singing new, expressive, Christ-exalting songs. Many Christians have started to see themselves as worshipers for the first time in their lives.

Worship leaders are one part of a long line of musical leadership in the church. Cantors, choral directors, accompanists, soloists, music directors, song leaders, conductors, and organists have all played a part, with varying degrees of success. Churches have tried everything from a cappella singing to a single guitar to full orchestras with two-hundred-voice choirs. It hasn't always been awe-inspiring.

A low point occurred during the seventeenth and eighteenth centuries when some congregations employed the practice of "lining out." One author describes it this way:

> Each line of the psalm verse was recited—and often sung—by the leading voice, which the congregation would then follow. . . . Both leader and individual members of the congregation tended to take their own time (and a very long time indeed it was—perhaps half a minute for each line!). Where harmonization was attempted it was unsupported by any organ or instruments, probably improvised, and most unlikely to conform to the four parts of a printed book. The slow pace of the singing allowed the possibility of decoration and ornamentation of the melody by extra notes, though these might be spontaneously and simultaneously created by several singers at once. The result was a kind of semi-improvised chaos.[1]

We've come a long way.

SOME LINGERING QUESTIONS

As I've thought about and studied my role as a worship leader, I've had questions. I've wondered if "worship leaders" have become too significant.

"For many young people choosing a church," writes Gordon MacDonald, "worship leaders have become a more important factor than preachers. Mediocre preaching may be tolerated, but an inept worship leader can sink things fast."[2]

Music in the church is important. But is it more important than solid biblical teaching that helps me grow in knowledge of God and obedience to his Word? In a word, no.

So how important are worship leaders?

And what should they actually be *doing*?

These questions aren't as easy to answer as we might think.

First, it's hard to find a clear worship leader role in the Bible, especially in the New Testament. That alone should give us pause.

We can glean some important principles from Old Testament Levites such as Asaph, Heman, Jeduthun, and others who led in song at the tabernacle and temple (1 Chronicles 16:1–7, 37–42; 25:1–8). But we can't transfer everything they did then to what we do now. They foreshadowed the perfect priest, Jesus Christ, who fulfilled everything their ministry pointed to (Hebrews 9:23–28). They worshiped God at a physical temple, while we worship him through the perfect temple of Jesus Christ and are ourselves a temple for God's presence (John 4:23–24; Matthew 12:6; Ephesians 2:21).

They were specifically appointed by God to lead the nation of Israel, while now the entire church is "a royal priesthood" (1 Peter 2:9).

The Psalms tell us volumes about what corporate worship should say but aren't as clear on how it's led, other than saying it involves instruments. And some people question whether that still applies.

Second, the most important worship leader is Jesus. He reveals God to us and through his perfect sacrifice provided the only way into the Father's presence (1 Timothy 2:5; Hebrews 10:19–22).

We can't do what only Jesus does. But in a culture infatuated with musical experience and expression, worship leaders can be erroneously expected to lead us into God's presence, usher in the presence of God, or in some way make God show up. People can start to think of us as "musical high priests" who bring God near through sheer musical skill, or as it's often called, anointing.

Third, the term *worship leader* can be misunderstood. It can communicate that the only time we worship God is when a musician is leading us. Or that worship is the same as singing. Or that God commands us to have worship leaders.

None of those statements is true. Anyone who encourages others to praise God can be referred to as a "worship leader." Worship can involve music, but it can happen without it as well. And while aspects of the worship leader's role may be inferred from Scripture, there are no requirements to have one. A pastor or a team of people can serve together to accomplish these goals just as well as, if not better than, a single person.

MAKING THE MOST OF THE SITUATION

So why am I writing a book for worship leaders? Why not get rid of that term?

That's what D. A. Carson suggests:

> I would abolish forever the notion of a "worship leader." If you want to have a "song leader" who leads part of the worship, just as the preacher leads part of the worship, that's fine. But to call the person a "worship leader" takes away the idea that by preaching, teaching, listening to and devouring the word of God, and applying it to our lives, we are somehow not worshiping God.[3]

Carson makes a great point. If the individual leading the singing is the "worship" leader, it can imply we aren't worshiping God during the rest of the meeting. But activities such as praying for others, giving financially, and studying God's Word together are also acts of worship that bring glory to God.

So I've started using different names for the person who leads the singing, depending on the situation. Music minister. Worship pastor. Service leader. Corporate worship leader. Lead worshiper. Or one of my favorites, the Music Guy.

And while I agree with Dr. Carson's perspective, I don't think we have to lose the term *worship leader*. It succinctly communicates that our goal is to lead others in praising God. But neither should we exaggerate the significance of the phrase or attach a biblical authority to it.

Because Scripture is vague about the worship leader role, churches assign differing degrees of significance to it. Humanly speaking, the pastor is the worship leader. He is the one responsible before God for the corporate worship of the church (Hebrews 13:17; 1 Thessalonians 5:12–13). That includes what songs are sung, what is preached, what activities we engage in.

In other churches the worship leading task might be distributed among different individuals, such as a pastor, song leader, service leader, or elder.

But in most churches, designated worship leaders play a fairly prominent role. They can lead up to half the meeting and have a sizable influence on how the church practices and thinks about worshiping God. That can be good or bad, depending on who's leading.

That's why I wrote this book.

No matter how important we think the worship leader role is or isn't, every week those who lead congregational worship have significant opportunities to teach, train, and encourage God's people in praising him rightly and living for his glory. In that sense worship leaders follow in the footsteps of Old Testament Levites who taught the Israelites what God required in worship and how they could faithfully follow him.

A WORKING DEFINITION

As I understand it, a worship leader exercises various gifts listed in 1 Corinthians 12, Romans 12, Ephesians 4, and elsewhere. These include pastoring, leading, administration, and teaching. Under the oversight of the pastor, he combines those gifts with musical skill to care for, guide, and instruct God's people as they sing his praises.[4]

A few years ago I started crafting a working definition of a worship leader (with help from my good friend Jeff Purswell) to clarify my understanding of what God was calling me to do in the church.

Here's what I've come up with:

A faithful worship leader
magnifies the greatness of God in Jesus Christ
through the power of the Holy Spirit
by skillfully combining God's Word with music,
thereby motivating the gathered church
to proclaim the gospel,
to cherish God's presence,
and to live for God's glory.

Over the next ten chapters I'll unpack each phrase, trying to answer the questions "What do worship leaders do?" and "What are they seeking to accomplish?" Whether you're a worship leader, musician, worship planner, music minister, or pastor, I pray that these chapters will help you serve God's people more effectively as we all gather each week to worship him.

chapter 7

A FAITHFUL
WORSHIP LEADER . . .

In recent years worship has hit the big time. Ten of the top fifty Christian albums are worship projects. Chris Tomlin, Matt Redman, Paul Baloche, Tim Hughes, and other worship artists have become household names. The successful marketing of worship music inside and outside the walls of the church has changed what the church sings and how we understand worship.

Of course, in God's eyes true worship has always been big-time. But the growing prominence and commercialization of worship music, with all its benefits, has some drawbacks.

For me, it brings unique temptations to worship leaders in the local church. We read about well-known worship artists and their CD sales, concert tours, and media interviews, and we wonder if we're doing something wrong. We start to think we'd be more effective if we looked, sounded, and acted like the worship leaders everyone knows.

But the worship industry isn't the standard God has given us to determine our effectiveness. His Word is. And if we don't understand that distinction we could miss God's unique plan for our lives. We'll be tempted to surrender to discouragement. And we'll fail to see that God hasn't called us to be successful or popular—he's called us to be faithful.

THE CALL TO BE FAITHFUL

Whatever standards others might use to judge our ministry, God is concerned that we be faithful. Faithfulness means firmly adhering to the observance of a duty, keeping your word, fulfilling your obligations. It involves being loyal, constant, and reliable.

Being faithful means fulfilling the desires of another. *We* don't define our ministry; *God* does. And he hasn't left it up to us to determine the content and purpose of what we do. We're fulfilling a responsibility he has given us.

Paul elaborates on this thought in his first letter to the Corinthians:

This is how one should regard us, as servants of Christ and stewards of the mysteries of God. Moreover, it is required of stewards that they be found trustworthy. (1 Corinthians 4:1–2)

Although Paul was writing as an apostle, each of us is to be trustworthy with the mysteries of God—what God has shown us about himself, especially his character and works displayed in the gospel. We're called to faithfully proclaim what he's revealed.

POTENTIAL TEMPTATIONS

Countless temptations can keep us from being faithful and trustworthy. One of them is fame.

Harold Best observed, "Ministry and fame have become so equated with each other that it is nearly impossible to think of anything but fame if one contemplates a ministry in music."[1] That's not the way God intended it to be.

Some of the most godly worship leaders I know are people you've never heard of. They don't have a national ministry, and they've never recorded a CD. They remind me that leading worship on a best-selling worship project isn't a sure sign one way or the other that God is pleased with what we're doing. It just means a lot of people have bought our CD.

God puts people in the spotlight for different reasons. It may be to give a wider platform to those who have followed him faithfully. Matt Redman is one of many internationally known worship leaders who doesn't think of himself as a star but as a humble servant. He has a heart for theology and a deep love for his local church. I think that's why God has given him an international influence.

But sometimes an individual's popularity shows us the effects of indwelling sin and how in these last days people with "itching ears" will flock to leaders who "suit their own passions" (2 Timothy 4:3). Reaching the top of a best-seller list or music chart is no guarantee that someone actually has something worth saying or hearing. It may prove just the opposite.

We're also tempted to gauge how we're doing by the numbers, like how many people show up on Sunday. But people can be lured to come to church for all kinds of reasons—stunts, lavish multimedia productions, cutting-edge music. More people doesn't always mean we're pleasing God. It could just mean we're good at marketing. Like the disciples, we can have a hard time understanding a Savior who's more concerned about obeying his Father than about seeking out a large crowd (Mark 1:36–38).

We can also get sidetracked by importing a "concert mentality" into our Sunday meetings. We put together "worship sets," sing the latest worship hits, and overwhelm people with special effects. Technology becomes crucial and governing rather than secondary and serving. We can certainly learn from concert settings. They show us how sounds, lights, images, and music can be used for emotional impact or to focus attention. Concerts are intended to be intense, emotional, and multisensory. But on Sunday mornings we're not trying to emotionally stimulate people or provide a moving experience regardless of the source.

I once heard a woman describe how Bono and U2 taught her more about worship than any Sunday morning worship leader. That's an alarming statement. Our goal as worship leaders is unlike that of any concert and is far more significant. We're seeking to impress upon people the greatness of the Savior whose glory transcends our surroundings and technology.

Occasionally someone passes me after a meeting and calls out, "Hey, great worship this morning!" After thanking them and walking on, it hits me: I have no idea what they meant. Did they like the music? Was the kick drum extra-loud? Were they impressed by what I was wearing? Did the band sound tight? Was my voice lost in the mix? All I know is that something affected them. My job is to make sure I provide the opportunity for them to be affected by the right things. And that means being faithful to draw people's attention to the God we're there to worship.

FAITHFUL TO LEAD

Romans 12:8 says leaders are to lead "with zeal" (or "with diligence," NKJV). Leading people to praise God involves energy, intentionality, and thoughtfulness.

Although we never know exactly how people are going to respond during a meeting, we tend to reap what we sow.

If our leadership focuses on musical experiences, we'll reap a desire for better sounds, cooler progressions, and more creative arrangements. If we sow to immediate feelings, we'll reap meetings driven by the pursuit of emotional highs. If we lead in such a way that we're the center of attention, we'll reap a man-centered focus, shallow compliments, and ungodly comparisons.

On the other hand, if we sow to God's glory in Christ, we'll reap the fruit of people in awe of God's greatness and goodness. But to do that we must faithfully paint a compelling, attractive, biblical picture of the Savior.

God isn't hiding from us, waiting to see if we'll find the right combination to unlock his blessing. He is eager to work through us as we faithfully lead our church into a clearer understanding of his glory.

THE FRUIT OF FAITHFUL LEADERSHIP

Faithful leadership doesn't always result in being commended, applauded, or appreciated.

Sometimes we'll be criticized for doing what we believe is biblical. I have a friend whose pastor once asked him to stop using songs that mentioned "sin" because he thought non-Christian visitors might be offended. Fortunately, over time the pastor was persuaded that was a bad idea. Other worship leaders I know have been chastised by church members for putting a new melody to a hymn, using drums, or singing songs that mention God's wrath. If you're a faithful leader, you won't always be appreciated.

But experiencing opposition doesn't necessarily mean we're godly. It could be we're just dumb. We think we're being Spirit-led when actually we're being distracting or unwise. Like the worship leader who inserts a drum solo without running it by anyone in advance. Every criticism provides a fresh opportunity to examine our motives and actions and to respond as those who have received amazing mercy through the cross.

Ultimately, the fruit of faithful leadership is knowing we've pleased the audience of One. Our joy doesn't come from leading the perfect worship time, winning awards, or having a song on the worship charts. Our goal isn't success, popularity, or personal fulfillment. It's anticipating—by God's grace and for the glory of Jesus Christ—that we'll hear on that last day, "Well done, good and faithful servant" (Matthew 25:21, 23).

And that's a greater reward than anything this world could ever offer.

chapter 8

. . . MAGNIFIES THE GREATNESS OF GOD . . .

"Great is the LORD," David reminds us, "and greatly to be praised, and his greatness is unsearchable" (Psalm 145:3).

David shows the appropriate starting point for worship. It involves thinking about, magnifying, and responding to the glory and splendor of God.

Many of those we lead on Sunday morning are eager to join us and have been magnifying God's unsearchable greatness all week.

Others are distracted. It could be anything from the superficial to the serious—deadlines, unpaid bills, a friend's unkind comment, a lab test for cancer, the *thump-thump* noise the car is making, a rebellious child, some besetting sin. Or a million other details of life.

What size does God appear to be when our mind is preoccupied with all the cares, worries, and concerns of life? Very small.

But God is not small. He is great. Magnifying and cherishing his greatness is at the heart of biblical worship. As J. I. Packer reminds us:

> Today, vast stress is laid on the thought that God is *personal*, but this truth is so stated as to leave the impression that God is a person of the same sort as we are—weak, inadequate, ineffective, a little pathetic. But this is not the God of the Bible! Our personal life is a finite thing: it is limited in every direction, in space, in time, in knowledge, in power. But God is not so limited. He is eternal, infinite, and almighty. He has us in his hands; we never have him in ours. Like us he is personal; but unlike us, he is *great*.[1]

A worship leader echoes David's invitation in Psalm 34:3: "Oh, *magnify* the LORD with me, and let us exalt his name together!" The first priority of our time together is to magnify the Lord. I want to help people remember that God is bigger than their problems and joys, greater than their sorrows and successes, more significant than their tests and triumphs.

Because we lose perspective so easily, God needs to become bigger in our eyes. He never changes in size—it just seems that way.

It's like looking up at the stars. To the naked eye they appear like tiny pinpoints of light, barely visible against the black backdrop. Twinkling dots suspended in vast darkness. We can walk outside and barely notice them. But when we look through a high-powered telescope, we're awestruck by what they really are: massive spheres of raging fire, millions of times larger than the earth, brighter than our human eyes can bear. The stars haven't changed. Our vision has.

Our great privilege as worship leaders is to help people see through the eyes of faith how great God has actually revealed himself to be. He doesn't change. We do.

BE CLEAR AND SPECIFIC

Every time we lead people in singing God's praise, we stand before people who, just like us, tend to forget who God is and why he's so worthy of worship. We're called to clearly and specifically remind them what God has shown us about himself.

John Owen, a Puritan pastor of the seventeenth century, wisely wrote, "We must not allow ourselves to be satisfied with vague ideas of the love of Christ which present nothing of his glory to our minds."[2] Vague ideas of God don't serve us or the people we lead. If most of our songs could be sung by Buddhists, Muslims, or Hindus, it's time to change our repertoire.

Of course, songs aren't meant to be systematic theology. Songs are poetry. They include figurative images and creative metaphors. Trees clap. Oceans roar. But our songs don't have to be obscure or ambiguous. They should help us accurately identify and praise the only true God who has revealed himself in the Savior, Jesus Christ.

If our songs aren't specific about God's nature, character, and acts, we'll tend to associate worship with a style of music, a heightened emotional state, a type of architecture, a day of the week, a meeting, a reverent mood, a time of singing, or a sound. We'll think of all the things that accompany worship rather than the One we're worshiping. Worse, we'll create our own views of God, portraying him as we like to think of him.

Reimaging or renaming God isn't an option he's given us. He has told us who he is, and because of that he commands the kind of glad response that John Stott defines as true worship:

> All true worship is a response to the self-revelation of God in Christ and Scripture, and arises from our reflection on who He is and what He has done. . . . The worship of God is evoked, informed, and inspired by the vision of God. . . . The true knowledge of God will always lead us to worship.[3]

EXPLORING GOD'S GREATNESS

So how do we magnify the greatness and glory of God in the hearts and minds of those we lead?

God has given us the book of Psalms, sometimes called "God's hymnal," to help us. The Psalms explore the highs and lows of human emotions and demonstrate how to express them before a holy, sovereign, and loving God. They suggest three categories in which we can magnify God's greatness: his Word, his nature, and his works.

God's *Word* is his self-revelation to us. While we don't actually worship the Word of God, we come to know his greatness through it.

So the psalmist declares, "In God, whose word I praise, in the LORD, whose word I praise, in God I trust" (Psalm 56:10–11). The word of the Lord is "perfect," "sure," "right," "pure," and "true" (Psalm 19:7–9). The longest chapter in Scripture, Psalm 119, is a captivating meditation on how God's Word encourages and governs our lives, and near the end the writer concludes, "My tongue will sing of your word, for all your commandments are right" (v. 172).

No matter what we do with lighting, video, sound, or drama, our purpose isn't coming up with the best video images, the hottest musical arrangements, or the most creative props. We want people to leave in awe that God would speak to us—encouraged by his promises, challenged by his commands, fearful of his warnings, and grateful for his blessings. We want them to see God's greatness in his Word.

The Psalms also focus on God's *nature,* conveying the reasons he deserves our praise. We'll never reach the end of them.

> *The LORD is gracious and merciful, slow to anger and abounding in steadfast love. The LORD is good to all, and his mercy is over all that he has made. (Psalm 145:8–9)*

Praise the LORD, *all nations! Extol him, all peoples! For great is his steadfast love toward us, and the faithfulness of the* LORD *endures forever. Praise the* LORD*! (Psalm 117:1–2)*

Be exalted, O LORD, *in your strength! We will sing and praise your power. (Psalm 21:13)*

Let them praise your great and awesome name! Holy is he! (Psalm 99:3)

On this side of the Incarnation and Pentecost, we can also see God's greatness in his triune nature. We worship the Father, Son, and Holy Spirit who are eternally coexistent, coequal, and co-glorious. One God in three persons. In fact, worship is the triune God inviting us to share in the fellowship and joy he has known from eternity past. We've been chosen to join him in his eternal preoccupation: magnifying his endless glories, perfections, and beauty.

How could anyone ever think worshiping God is boring? There's no limit to his holiness, glory, and sovereignty, no end to his riches, wisdom, and righteousness. All his attributes exist together in perfect harmony, perfect balance, perfect cooperation, with no contradiction, no confusion, and no diminishing of their glory forever. He is the source of everything good and beautiful. No wonder Paul breaks into worship as he describes God's greatness: "Oh, the depth of the riches and wisdom and knowledge of God! How unsearchable are his judgments and how inscrutable his ways!" (Romans 11:33).

Magnifying God's greatness, as we learn from the Psalms, also includes drawing attention to his *works.* "Sing to him, sing praises to him; tell of all his wondrous works!" (Psalm 105:2). His works are different from but eternally linked to his character.

One of our problems is that we're often more impressed with what *we* do than with what *God* has done. We're like those who "do not regard the works of the LORD or the work of his hands" (Psalm 28:5). But the psalmist reminds us, "Great are the works of the LORD, *studied* by all who delight in them" (Psalm 111:2). Corporate worship should help us become freshly acquainted with what God has done, because we forget so quickly.

God created everything from nothing and spoke the universe into existence with a word (Psalm 148:5; Hebrews 11:3). He sustains all living creatures and non-living matter. His power holds all things together and keeps them from exploding or disintegrating (Colossians 1:17).

Psalm 111 is a condensed song of praise extolling God's works on behalf of his people. In this one psalm alone, God is praised as the one who provides for us, keeps his covenant with us, delivers us, rules us, and redeems us.

The Psalms resound with detailed praises of God's wondrous works. Our songs should as well.

The Psalms serve as our example in praising God but only point to the fuller revelation of God's glory in Jesus Christ. The greatest of all God's works by far is the giving of his Son at Calvary. It's only through Jesus' perfect sacrifice on the cross that we can draw near to God at all (Hebrews 10:19–22). In the cross we find a perfect reconciling of God's blazing holiness, holy justice, incomprehensible wisdom, omnipotent power, and unfathomable love.

What a God we worship! As the psalmist said, "There is none like you among the gods, O Lord, nor are there any works like yours" (Psalm 86:8).

These truths about God's Word and worthiness and works aren't just for seminarians pursuing a theology degree. God has revealed them to us for our comfort, correction, strengthening, protection, and joy. He has revealed them to us for our worship. That's why the books I typically find most profitable for leading worship aren't daily devotionals that bring God down to my level, but theology books that stretch my understanding of God. *Knowing God* by J. I. Packer, *Systematic Theology* by Wayne Grudem, *Knowledge of the Holy* by A. W. Tozer, and *The Pleasures of God* by John Piper are a few of many I'd recommend.[4]

LOVING GOD'S GREATNESS

Magnifying God's greatness *begins* with the proclamation of objective, biblical truths about God, but it *ends* with the expression of deep and holy affections toward God. We aren't simply reciting facts about God, like students reviewing their multiplication tables. God wants us to *delight* in him (Psalm 37:4). He is exalted when all our energies are directed to one end—being satisfied in who he is. "The engagement of the heart in worship is the coming alive of the feelings and emotions and affections of the heart," John Piper writes. "Where feelings for God are dead, worship is dead."[5]

Scripture repeatedly teaches and models the fact that truth about God invites a response. In fact, we're commanded to respond. "Rejoice in the Lord always; again I will say, Rejoice" (Philippians 4:4). "Love the LORD, all you his saints!" (Psalm 31:23). "Serve the LORD with gladness!" (Psalm 100:2).

The psalmists model numerous ways we can express our affections toward God to magnify his greatness, all of which can be reflected in our songs. I've summarized these ways as *delight, commitment, yearning,* and *trust.*

It glorifies God when we delight in him, expressing the joy of knowing him and being known by him, as in Psalm 18:1: "I love you, O LORD, my strength." Or in Psalm 34:8: "Oh, taste and see that the LORD is good!" Such expressions of delight point to God's worth.

Committing ourselves to follow and serve God also honors him. "So I will bless you as long as I live" (Psalm 63:4). "I will bless the LORD at all times; his praise shall continually be in my mouth" (Psalm 34:1).[6]

I've met Christians who feel dishonest or hypocritical when they sing words like "I'll always follow you," "I will worship you alone," or "I surrender all." But expressions like these help us align our hearts with God's work in us through the gospel, especially as we're aware of our need for God's Spirit to carry out those commitments. That doesn't mean we sing song after song about our commitment while living in unrepentant sin. With the cross in view, we can follow the counsel of Isaac Watts:

> We can never be too frequent or too solemn in the general surrender of our souls to God and binding our souls by a vow to be the Lord's forever: to love him above all things, to fear him, to hope in him, to walk in his ways in a course of holy obedience, and to wait for his mercy unto eternal life.[7]

Yearning to know more of God also brings him glory. "O God, you are my God; earnestly I seek you; my soul thirsts for you; my flesh faints for you, as in a dry and weary land where there is no water" (Psalm 63:1). "My soul longs, yes, faints for the courts of the LORD; my heart and flesh sing for joy to the living God" (Psalm 84:2).

Modern worship songs have made a significant contribution in this area. Some fault them for this very reason, deriding lyrics about wanting, desiring, needing, and being thirsty or desperate for God. Yet those phrases reflect the attitude of many Psalms, drawing attention to our need for God. We *do* need him! And saying so magnifies his greatness.

Lastly, we can express trust in God in times of trial, suffering, and discouragement. The Psalms deal with our condition in a fallen world. But in the midst of troubles and persecution, the psalmist never forgets that God is sovereign, God is faithful, and God alone can deliver.

Simply rehearsing our problems isn't worshiping God; recalling his character in the midst of them is. Asaph did that in his "day of . . . trouble" (Psalm 77:2):

> *Will the Lord spurn forever, and never again be favorable? Has his stead-fast love forever ceased? Are his promises at an end for all time? Has God forgotten to be gracious? Has he in anger shut up his compassion? (vv. 7-9)*

The apparent disconnect between Asaph's circumstances and what he *knows* to be true of God compels him to cast himself on his mercy. It should be the same for us. "Trust in him at all times, O people; pour out your heart before him; God is a refuge for us" (Psalm 62:8).

Magnifying God's greatness, then, involves proclamation and passion. Our responsibility as worship leaders is to make sure that in both ways—biblical truth and strong affections—people have every opportunity to magnify and encounter our great and awesome God.

chapter 9

. . . IN JESUS CHRIST . . .

In 586 B.C. the unimaginable happened: The Babylonians destroyed the temple in Jerusalem. The building that represented God's pres ence with his people—the building that ensured they would always have a way to worship him—was in ruins. God had used a pagan nation to punish the Israelites for their idolatry.

But the story was far from over.

THE MYSTERIOUS TEMPLE

The Israelites eventually returned to Jerusalem to rebuild their temple. And though its reality fell far short of the previous temple, it continued to serve as the center of Judaism's life and worship.

During the time of Christ, the Jews still viewed the temple in Jerusalem as the place where their sins were acknowledged and dealt with and where God revealed his presence to his people in a unique way. How shocking it must have been therefore to hear Jesus declare, "Destroy this temple, and in three days I will raise it up" (John 2:19). Jesus was proclaiming the arrival of a new temple. Jesus *was* the new temple.

This sheds light on Jesus' mystifying explanation to the Samaritan woman:

> *Woman, believe me, the hour is coming when neither on this mountain nor in Jerusalem will you worship the Father. You worship what you do not know; we worship what we know, for salvation is from the Jews. But the hour is coming, and is now here, when the true worshipers will wor-*

ship the Father in spirit and truth, for the Father is seeking such people to worship him. (John 4:21–23)

Jesus was saying that our meeting place with God would no longer be limited to physical structures, geographical locales, or specific times. It would no longer require animal sacrifices, Levitical priests, or holy places. In a single conversation he relocated the place of worship from the Jerusalem temple to himself.

As D. A. Carson comments:

> To worship God "in spirit *and in truth*" is first and foremost a way of saying that we must worship God *by means of Christ*. In him the reality has dawned and the shadows are being swept away (cf. Hebrews 8:13). Christian worship is new-covenant worship; it is gospel-inspired worship; it is Christ-centered worship; it is cross-focused worship.[1]

It's hard for us to imagine the impact of this reorientation. Our meeting place with God—the "place" we now worship—is the exalted Lord Jesus Christ. Not a temple. Not a church building. Not a sanctuary or auditorium.

Jesus is where and how we meet with God.

After he rose from the dead, the early Christians came to understand that Jesus' life, death, and resurrection had been the perfect and eternal fulfillment of all that the temple merely foreshadowed.

The implications are staggering. There's *nothing* about our worship of God that isn't defined or affected by Jesus Christ.

JESUS OUR MEDIATOR

One of the most significant passages for understanding the role Jesus plays in our worship of God doesn't even mention the word *worship*. "For there is one God, and there is one mediator between God and men, the man Christ Jesus" (1 Timothy 2:5). A mediator is a person who intervenes between opposing parties to help reconcile them. Without a mediator, there's no hope of the two connecting or being restored.

To magnify God's greatness in Jesus Christ means more than worshiping Jesus as God, extolling his example, and thanking him for his love. It involves drawing attention to, and trusting in, his specific work as our mediator and Savior.

Most people haven't spent much time considering their need for a mediator in their relationship with God. That's because we grossly under-estimate the gravity and offensiveness of our sin in light of God's infinite majesty, holiness, and justice.

As C. J. Mahaney explains:

> When you tell non-Christians, "God loves you," they aren't surprised, they aren't perplexed, they aren't stunned. Regrettably, the same is true among most evangelicals, who simply assume this gracious disposition of God—and therefore presume upon it. And we'll continue to do this until we learn to see our condition more fully from God's perspective.[2]

God is gracious, to be sure. But not in the way most of us think. To us, graciousness implies overlooking some petty offense. It means being polite when we could be rude. Maybe we resist slamming on the horn when someone cuts us off in traffic or hold the elevator door open for a frantic businessman. We view graciousness from *our* perspective—one sinner relating to another.

God's perspective is different. He faces an infinitely more difficult dilemma. How can he forgive those who have defied his good and holy laws without compromising the integrity of his just and righteous character?

When we sin against God, and all sin is against God, we aren't sinning against someone like us. God is perfect. He is all-good, all-powerful, sovereign, and holy. And with each sin, we raise our fists in defiance against him. We assert our authority over his. Because God is holy and just, he must punish sin. He can't simply "sweep things under the rug" or "forgive and forget." The entire Bible reveals God's unflinching commitment to the glory and honor of his name. We make a mockery of it when we sin.

For that reason, we need to be saved from God's justice. We need to be protected from his fierce jealousy for his supreme and unique glory.

And what we need has been provided for us in Jesus Christ.

Jesus served as our mediator when he willingly endured God's wrath against our sins at the cross, even though he himself was completely innocent. Jesus served as our mediator when he became our substitute to receive the punishment we deserved, after which the Father raised him from the dead, demonstrating the sufficiency of his sacrifice. Jesus was our mediator when he embraced the torment of separation from God so we could live with God forever.

This is the good news of the gospel. This is the means by which we can now worship God.

In the thirty-plus years I've been involved in leading congregational worship, I have never found a truth that more consistently, powerfully, or rightly calls forth the passionate praises of God's people than this: *Christ died for our sins to bring us to God* (1 Peter 3:18).

WHY THE CROSS IS CRUCIAL TO WORSHIP

The gospel is not merely one of many possible themes we can touch on as we come to worship God. It is the central and foundational theme. All our worship originates and is brought into focus at the cross of Jesus Christ.

Glorying in Jesus Christ means glorying in his cross. That doesn't mean looking at some icon or two pieces of wood nailed together. Nor does it imply that every song we sing has the word *cross* in it. It has little to do with church gatherings that are more like a funeral than a celebration.

The cross stands for all that was accomplished through the life, death, and resurrection of Jesus, the Son of God. It focuses on his substitutionary death at Calvary but includes everything that gave meaning to that act. His preexistent state in glory. His incarnation. His life of perfect obedience. His suffering. His resurrection. His ascension. His present intercession and reign in glory. His triumphant return.

It is Christ's atoning sacrifice for our sins that the New Testament writers continually return to as a main focus both for worship and for life.

For I decided to know nothing among you except Jesus Christ and him crucified. (1 Corinthians 2:2)

For I delivered to you as of first importance what I also received: that Christ died for our sins in accordance with the Scriptures. (1 Corinthians 15:3)

He himself bore our sins in his body on the tree, that we might die to sin and live to righteousness. By his wounds you have been healed. (1 Peter 2:24)

In this is love, not that we have loved God but that he loved us and sent his Son to be the propitiation for our sins. (1 John 4:10)

"Christ is to us just what his cross is," pastor and theologian P. T. Forsyth affirms. "All that Christ was in heaven or on earth was put into what he did there. . . . You do not understand Christ till you understand his cross."[3]

Nor will we understand worship until we understand his cross. Here's why.

For Our Access to God

Only Christ's work on the cross ensures our complete and immediate access to God.

When we approach God through Christ, "we have boldness and access with confidence through our faith in him" (Ephesians 3:12). For centuries prior to the coming of Christ, the high priest represented God's people once a year as he entered the Holy of Holies to make atonement for their sins. The holiest man from the holiest tribe offered the holiest sacrifice in the holiest place for the holiest people on earth. To attempt to draw near to God in any other way or by any other means would result in certain death (Leviticus 16:2).

Now Jesus has entered a holier place, the heavenly sanctuary, having atoned for our sins and having torn down the veil separating us from God.

> *Therefore, brothers, since we have confidence to enter the holy places by the blood of Jesus, by the new and living way that he opened for us through the curtain, that is, through his flesh, and since we have a great priest over the house of God, let us draw near with a true heart in full assurance of faith, with our hearts sprinkled clean from an evil conscience and our bodies washed with pure water. (Hebrews 10:19–22)*

Apart from Christ's finished work, we would have no access to God. It reminds me of when the words "Access Denied" appear on my computer screen when I forget a password to a web site. I can't get in unless I remember the right word or combination of letters and numbers.

As our High Priest and perfect sacrifice, Jesus is our "password" into God's presence. Without his substitutionary sacrifice we could never draw near to God. And, of course, we're not simply reciting a mantra or secret code but are exercising faith in what he has done. His access is sufficient and unique. Apart from Jesus Christ, we cannot approach God.

This makes a huge difference as we lead others to worship God.

I had a conversation once with a well-known worship leader who confessed that every time he leads worship, he experiences a degree of anxiety. Will people "get it"? Will they experience real worship? Will they be able to get close to God?

Biblically speaking, no worship leader, pastor, band, or song will ever bring us close to God. We can't shout, dance, or prophesy our way into God's presence. Worship itself cannot lead us into God's presence. *Only Jesus himself* can bring us into God's presence, and he has done it through a single sacrifice that will never be repeated—only joyfully recounted and trusted in.

We need to remember that our access to God is not based on last week's performance, today's practices, or tomorrow's potential. Rather, we're accepted "in the Beloved" (Ephesians 1:6) and need have no fear of rejection as we come before God's throne.

God poured out on his Son the cup of wrath we deserved. And Jesus drank the last drop. No wrath or judgment remains for those who have trusted in the substitutionary sacrifice of Jesus on the cross.

Mark Altrogge has expressed this thought well in his song, "Across the Great Divide":

There is no more fear of judgment;
The Father's wrath is satisfied.
You have brought us near, O Jesus,
Across the great divide.
There's a way beyond the curtain
Through our Priest and King on high.
You have brought us near, O Jesus,
Across the great divide.[4]

For Acceptable Worship

Christ's work on the cross also assures us that our worship is acceptable to God.

God could reject our worship for a number of reasons. He specifically condemns acts of worship associated with idolatry, unbelief, disobedience, and evil motives (Jeremiah 13:10; Exodus 30:9; 32:22–27; Jeremiah 7:21–26). Rehearsing this list makes me aware that our offerings of worship will never please God on their own. Try as hard as we can, our hearts and worship will always be tainted in God's sight.

The ultimate factor of acceptable worship is faith in and union with Jesus Christ. Our spiritual sacrifices are "acceptable to God through Jesus Christ" (1 Peter 2:5). It is his sinless offering of worship that cleanses and perfects ours.

Harold Best says it well:

There is only one way to God, through Jesus Christ. This means that God sees and hears all of our offerings perfected. God sees and hears as no human being can, all because our offerings have been perfected by the giver. The out-of-tune singing of an ordinary believer, the hymnic chant of the aborigine . . . the open frankness of a primitive art piece, the nearly transcendent "Kyrie" of Bach's B Minor Mass, the praise choruses of the charismatic, the drum praise of the Cameroonian—everything from the widow's mite to the poured-out ointment of artistic action—are at once humbled and exalted by the strong saving work of Christ.[5]

All our offerings are humbled by the work of Christ because they would be unacceptable to God without him. All our offerings are exalted because when they are joined to the atoning sacrifice of the Savior, God accepts them as though his own Son were offering them.

Nothing against skill, practice, complexity, nuance, musicianship, or sincerity, but only the finished work of Christ makes our offerings of worship acceptable in God's eyes.

What a relief!

That doesn't mean what we do in corporate worship is unimportant. But when we overemphasize our own actions in worship, we can inadvertently create the impression that our contribution makes our worship acceptable to God. We think God is persuaded to listen to us because of our sophisticated musical arrangements, our polished performance, or even our heartfelt sincerity.

It's not the excellence of our offering that makes our worship acceptable but the excellence of Christ. We cannot worship the eternal Father apart from the eternal Son. He was able to offer his own righteous life as a perfect offering because he had no sins of his own to die for (Hebrews 7:26). Even now he intercedes for us, saving us "to the uttermost" (Hebrews 7:25).

Our worship is accepted not on the basis of what we have done, but on the basis of what Christ has done.

It's not uncommon for us to "feel" accepted and loved by God when we're engaged in worship. But if that feeling isn't rooted in the gospel, it will be an elusive sensation. It's not enough to sing songs about God's love that produce warm feelings in our hearts. We need to glory in the reality of Jesus Christ, beaten and bruised for our transgressions, giving up his life in our place on the cross. There will never be a greater proof or demonstration of God's love.

If we help people focus on what God did two thousand years ago rather than twenty minutes ago, they'll consistently find their hearts ravished by his amazing love.

For God's Glory

Christ's work on the cross displays God's glory most clearly.

As we set our hearts and minds on worshiping God, his various attributes can begin to seem contradictory to our finite minds. He is merciful and gracious, compassionate, forgiving, abounding in steadfast love. But he's also pure, holy, and righteous, and he "will by no means clear the guilty" (Exodus 34:7). How do we worship this God in truth without minimizing any aspect of his nature?

We do it by worshiping him as he has revealed himself to us in Jesus Christ. God has given us "the light of the knowledge of the glory of God in the face of Jesus Christ" (2 Corinthians 4:6). Where do we find God's glory? "In the face of Jesus Christ." "He is the radiance of the glory of God and the exact imprint of his nature" (Hebrews 1:3).

It is in Christ, and specifically in his atoning work, that all the attributes of God shine most clearly and brilliantly. As John Owen wrote in *The Glory of Christ*:

> In Christ we behold the wisdom, goodness, love, grace, mercy, and power of God all working together for the great work of our redemption and salvation. The wisdom and love of God are in themselves infinitely glorious. But we cannot see how glorious they are except in the redemption and salvation of the church which is achieved only in and by Christ.[6]

In the cross we see the justice of God requiring a perfect payment for sins committed against a perfectly holy God.

We see the holiness of God acting to judge the sin that spoiled his creation by punishing his own Son.

We see the mercy of God in providing a substitute for those who should have been condemned.

We see the wisdom of God in providing a glorious solution to an impossible dilemma.

We see all this about God and more. So much more. As David Prior has written, "We never, therefore, move on from the cross of Christ, only into a more profound understanding of the cross."[7]

For Participating in Heaven's Worship

Christ's work on the cross is the focus of worship in heaven.

When Jesus appears as the Lion of the tribe of Judah in Revelation 5:5, he might have been honored for his moral perfection, his teaching, his miraculous healing powers, or his glorious resurrection. The host of heaven might have called attention to his role in creation and sustaining the universe. But they don't.

Heaven's worshipers join together to proclaim:

Worthy are you to take the scroll and to open its seals, for you were slain, *and by your blood you ransomed people for God from every tribe and language and people and nation, and you have made them a kingdom and priests to our God, and they shall reign on the earth. (vv. 9–10, emphasis added)*

Day and night the hosts of heaven cry out, "Worthy is the Lamb who was slain, to receive power and wealth and wisdom and might and honor and glory and blessing!" (v. 12). It seems that heaven itself never moves on from the cross. As Jim Elliff points out, "One is taken aback by the emphasis upon the Cross in Revelation. Heaven does not 'get over' the cross, as if there are better things to think about, heaven is not only Christ-centered, but cross-centered, and quite blaring about it."[8]

With so many clear references to the priority of Jesus and his atoning work, it's astounding how often we go through entire church meetings with only passing references to what he's accomplished through his life, death, and resurrection. And when we do mention him in our songs or prayers, we often fail to elaborate on what he's done.

The hosts of heaven never tire of extolling the Lamb who was slain. Should we?

HOW TO GLORY IN THE CROSS OF CHRIST

Worshiping God in spirit and truth involves magnifying the way God has shown his greatness in Jesus Christ and his glorious work of redemption. This doesn't happen automatically for us or for those we lead. I've learned I need to present these truths in consistent, clear, and compelling ways.

"To see what is in front of one's nose needs a constant struggle," George Orwell wrote.[9] Unless we consistently keep the cross within our view, we'll surely forget it.

Over the years I've tried to develop a "gospel radar" that's sensitive to any mention of the Savior's work in verses, songs, messages, and meetings. Otherwise I might leave it out. For instance, I'm aware that the third verse of the hymn "It Is Well" addresses my sin being nailed to the cross and my bearing it no more. On the other hand, "Amazing Grace" describes how I've been saved, found, and given sight, but it never actually articulates how that was accomplished through Christ's atoning death. That doesn't make it any less of a great hymn. But it does mean I'll want to do another song that's more specific about the cross. I think it also explains why "Amazing Grace" is so popular, even among non-Christians.

We must also be clear about what the cross actually means. Some worship songs leave the impression that the cross is about how important we are to God. One song claimed Jesus "would rather die than live without me." While it's true that God's love motivated him to send his Son to die in my place, the cross ultimately points not to the greatness of our worth but to the greatness of our sin. Yes, if I were the only person in the world, Jesus would still have come to die for me. But that's because my sins would require the shedding of his blood unto death.

Frederick Leahy cautions us:

> There is an error to avoid, the danger of seeing the loving obedience of Christ as primarily and exclusively for the sake of man, when, in fact, it was primarily out of love for God that he accepted the cross (Hebrews 10:7). . . . This is a truth too often overlooked, and it in no way detracts from the wonder that Christ loves each one of his people with all of his love.[10]

The cross sets us free from misguided self-love to passionately love the One who redeemed us.

Besides being consistent and clear, we also need to be compelling. The role of the cross in worship isn't merely a matter of singing the right lyrics. No facet of God's truth should move our affections more than the gospel. How could the death and resurrection of the Son of God ever seem irrelevant or be sung about in a dull, uninterested way? But it happens every Sunday. Because of our sin and negligence, we lose sight of the glories of Calvary. That's why pastors and worship leaders must make sure Calvary is always in our view. One of the most important aspects of biblical worship we desperately need to recover today is *a passionate, scripturally informed exaltation of Jesus Christ and his redemptive work*.

Every time we step up to lead our congregation, we should present a clear picture of "the glory of God in the face of Jesus Christ" (2 Corinthians

4:6). We come together to retell, remember, and respond to the gospel and all it has accomplished. We have been saved to trust in, love, desire, and obey the matchless One who is the only Savior of the world and the radiance of the Father's glory.

Therefore, one of our primary thoughts as we plan a Sunday meeting should be: Will our time together cause people's view of, trust in, and desire for God's glory *in Christ* and him crucified to increase?

For a worship leader's preparation, focus, and evaluation, no question is more important.

chapter 10

. . . THROUGH THE POWER OF THE HOLY SPIRIT . . .

Churches can faithfully magnify the greatness of God in Christ, yet fail to demonstrate the kind of empowered living and passion that the gospel should produce.

Why is that?

One common reason is this: We attempt to worship God apart from the power of the Holy Spirit. We trust in our own wisdom, plans, creativity, and skill. We forget that worship of the triune God includes the Holy Spirit.

Just as we can't worship the Father apart from Jesus Christ, worship is impossible apart from the Holy Spirit. Scripture describes the Spirit as the member of the Trinity who reveals the reality, presence, and power of Christ to us, for the glory of God. Paul proclaims that "through him"— through Jesus Christ—all believers "have access *in one Spirit* to the Father" (Ephesians 2:18).

It is the Spirit who initially opens our eyes to see our sin and causes our hearts to trust in the Savior for complete forgiveness. He causes our dead spirits to come alive (Galatians 5:25). The Spirit confirms to us that we are children of God and shows us what God has freely given us (1 Corinthians 2:12). He comforts us in our trials, enlightens us in our confusion, and empowers us for serving others, all for the Father's pleasure and the Son's glory. All this is part of the broad work of the Holy Spirit. As one author starkly put it, "If worshipers are not consciously dependent upon the Holy Spirit, their worship is not truly Christian."[1]

THE SPIRIT'S ROLE

One night I was leading worship in a gym for about fifteen hundred people. Somewhere around the third song, we lost power. Miraculously, our tech director traced the problem to a power line running up to the stage beneath the seats in the middle of the room. Enthusiastic worshipers had been jumping up and down on the cable, causing the connection to arc and overload the circuits. Fortunately the whole building didn't burn down.

We've lost power on Sunday mornings as well. It's an awkward moment. In the middle of a song the bottom suddenly drops out. It's obvious the congregation can no longer hear you. And if your drummer is playing electronic drums, it's particularly embarrassing.

Trying to lead worship without electrical power can be a humbling experience. Trying to lead without spiritual power is far more serious. But normally not as obvious.

Paul reminded the Philippians that "we are the circumcision, who worship by the Spirit of God and glory in Christ Jesus and put no confidence in the flesh" (Philippians 3:3). Part of his intention is to communicate our need to rely on God's power rather than on our own when we draw near to him. For years I thought Paul was referring to spontaneous singing, prophetic words, and heightened emotional experiences. I looked down on churches that followed a plan for their meetings and assumed Paul supported my position. My interpretation of worship in the Spirit wasn't particularly biblical or helpful.

But some Christians have so minimized the Spirit's role in worship that he's functionally irrelevant. Like a person's appendix—it's there, but we're not sure why. And if it was removed, we'd get along just fine.

However, I don't doubt that most of us believe we need the Holy Spirit's power when we worship God. But what does that mean? And how do we pursue it practically?

Three attitudes are indispensable in this area—desperate dependence, eager expectation, and humble responsiveness.

DESPERATE DEPENDENCE

A while back I was helping my daughter and son-in-law move into a new home and unwisely tried to carry a fairly large chair by myself. A few days later I was in significant pain and found I couldn't even get up from my chair after my morning devotions. I eventually rolled onto the floor and crawled upstairs. For the next few days my wife served me heroically, and I became aware how truly dependent I was on her and others.

I visited the doctor and expected to be told I had three herniated discs. After examining me, he gave me the diagnosis: garden-variety back strain. Oh well.

Of course, nothing I went through remotely compares to the dependent condition of those who are blind, hearing-impaired, or confined to a bed. Still, the sense of the dependence I felt during those days more accurately reflects my true state as I lead the church in worship.

I may not be incapacitated physically, but I am weak and needy every time I step up to lead. Sinful desires wage war against me in my heart (1 Peter 2:11). The world has been calling me to enjoy immoral pleasures, adopt ungodly attitudes, and live for passing rewards (1 John 2:15–17). The devil is prowling around "like a roaring lion, seeking someone to devour" through deceit and condemnation (1 Peter 5:8).

We are desperately dependent.

God has sent his Spirit to help us. We show our dependence by asking him to empower us by his Spirit. That's why we're taught to pray in and by the Spirit and to pray for the Spirit's working (Ephesians 6:18; Jude 20; Romans 8:26). He helps us in our weakness. Prayer is one of the primary ways we show that we're desperately dependent on God.

So, here's the question: How much do you pray? Do you pray for his guidance before you start planning for Sunday? What do you place more trust in—God's power or your performance? Do you toss up generic prayers like, "God, please bless our time today"? Or do you pray specifically, asking the Spirit to reveal Christ to everyone gathered, to help the congregation sing with understanding, and to bring forth fruit in people's lives?

Confessing our utter dependence on the Holy Spirit should produce a deep sense of gratitude, humility, and peace in our hearts. It should free us from anxious thoughts about how smoothly the service will flow, whether or not the sound system will feed back, and how people will respond to us. Of course, each of those items requires our attention, but our confidence isn't tied to them. After all, it's not our sufficiency that displays God's power but our weakness (2 Corinthians 12:9).

EAGER EXPECTATION

Acknowledging dependence on God's Spirit is one thing. Expecting him to act is another.

Do our actions communicate that we believe God is actually with us? Do we *expect* him to reveal his power as we worship together?

D. Martyn Lloyd-Jones once asked similar questions to a group of Welsh pastors:

> Here is the crucial matter. Do we individually and personally really believe that God still acts, can act and will act—in individuals, in groups of individuals, in churches, localities, perhaps even in countries? Do we believe that He is as capable of doing that today as He was in ancient times—the Old Testament, the New Testament times, the book of Acts, Protestant Reformation, Puritans, Methodist Awakening, 1859, 1904-5? Do we really believe that He can still do it? You see, it is ultimately what you believe about God. If He is the great Jehovah—I am that I am, I am that I shall be, unchanged, unchanging, unchangeable, the everlasting and eternal God—well, He can still do it.[2]

Yes, God can still do what he did in ancient times. He really does still act, and he really is unchanging. But do we really believe that?

Some of us believe in the Holy Spirit's empowering presence *theoretically*, but we don't seem to believe God is active when we meet. He's the Spirit of power in name only. Our focus is more on executing our plan than on expecting God to do anything through his Spirit. We move through a song list without considering what the Spirit may want to accomplish as we sing.

On the other extreme are those who expect the active presence of the Spirit but assume it will always be revealed in spectacular or unusual ways. If certain spiritual gifts aren't exercised or people don't appear visibly affected, then they conclude that the Spirit "hasn't shown up" or that he's been quenched or grieved.

The Holy Spirit is indeed present and at work every time the church gathers. We just need to understand biblically what that means. When people grasp something of God's glory, the Spirit is at work. When people are convicted of sin, the Spirit is at work. When people receive hope and strength in the midst of a trial, the Spirit is at work. The Spirit may also choose to demonstrate his presence through a prophetic impression, a healing, or a heightened awareness of his nearness.

God doesn't reveal his power in spectacular ways every time we meet. But we can expect him to reveal it in some way. And I'm fairly certain he wants to show his power much more often than we expect him to.

None of us should be satisfied with our present experience of the Spirit's presence and power. Paul's account in 1 Corinthians 14:24–25 challenges us.

> *But if all prophesy, and an unbeliever or outsider enters, he is convicted by all, he is called to account by all, the secrets of his heart are disclosed, and so, falling on his face, he will worship God and declare that God is really among you.*

When is the last time a non-Christian came to your church and fell down on his face, convicted and gloriously converted? When is the last time you really expected the Spirit to work that way?

No amount of technology, practice, planning, or ingenuity can produce that kind of fruit. It is a demonstration of the Spirit's power in our midst.

Whatever you believe about the continuation of prophecy for today, this passage at least implies that the Holy Spirit at times works in ways that are more spontaneous and dramatic in their effect. Do we expect him to work in such ways? Do we allow any room for him to do so?

I don't want you to misunderstand this point. I believe in Spirit-led planning. I plan every time I lead. And I've been deeply affected, and God has been honored, by meetings that we've organized down to the last detail. We should expect the Spirit to work powerfully through the normal means of preaching, sharing the Lord's Supper, singing, and other means of grace. But he can also interrupt our meetings with an exhortation, a Scripture, a call to prayer, or a spontaneous impression that has had an effect similar to what Paul describes in 1 Corinthians 14.

So expect him to keep his promise to empower our activities as we gather in his name. Trust his word that he is eager to give each of us manifestations of his Spirit for the good of his church (1 Corinthians 12:11). And listen and watch for the Spirit's leading and promptings, leaving room for him to work spontaneously.

HUMBLE RESPONSIVENESS

If we acknowledge our dependence on God's Spirit and eagerly expect him to be working in power, then we should be humbly responsive to what he is doing.

That first means fulfilling our responsibilities with joy, expectation, and faithfulness. No Sunday is a "normal" Sunday. No meeting is a "routine" meeting. Every time we gather, we can expect God to do the miraculous, transforming us into his image as we behold his glory (2 Corinthians 3:18).

A while back we had to begin offering two meetings on Sundays due to space limitations. We frequently remind ourselves that there are no identical services when we're depending on the Holy Spirit's power, and we need to pray just as earnestly for the second meeting as we do for the first.

Humble responsiveness also involves acting on impressions we receive while leading. What might the Holy Spirit "say" to us? We may feel led to emphasize a certain line from a song or repeat a verse that draws attention to a relevant theme. The Spirit might bring to mind a particular need or a reason to celebrate. He might direct us to a Scripture we hadn't previously thought of including.

It's important to add here that impressions like these will never replace our absolute confidence in God's written Word. The Bible is our only infallible rule for life, practice, and doctrine, and it remains the primary way God speaks to us and the standard by which any impression is tested. But spontaneous spiritual gifts serve to confirm God's active presence in our midst, to strengthen, encourage, and build up his people.

When God speaks to us subjectively through his Spirit, we want to be humbly responsive.

THE PROPER FOCUS

My roots are in the charismatic outpouring of the 1970s, a time when thousands were converted and powerfully filled with God's Spirit.

Since that time, the term *charismatic* has sometimes been associated with doctrinal error, unsubstantiated claims of healing, financial impropriety, outlandish and unfulfilled predictions, an overemphasis on the speech gifts, and some regrettable hairstyles.

Of course, many charismatics aren't characterized by any part of that list. However, it's not unusual for the term *charismatic* to be connected primarily with the gifts of tongues, prophecy, and miraculous healings, along with certain worship styles. But the Spirit's work isn't limited to particular manifestations. Scripture associates the Spirit's work with all aspects of the Christian's life.

That's why I've started to identify myself more often as a continuationist rather than a charismatic. That means I believe that all the spiritual gifts mentioned in the New Testament have continued to the present day and don't limit the Spirit's work to specific gifts. Ultimately, I'm not nearly as concerned about the label as I am about cultivating an active dependence on God's Spirit as he works in and through us for his glory.

Gordon Fee offers this biblical view of the Spirit's work in our midst:

[I]n Paul, power is not to be thought of merely in terms of the miraculous, the extraordinary. . . . Paul understood the Spirit's power in the broadest possible way.[3]

Let's not make the mistake of exalting certain manifestations of the Spirit's working over others, seeing them as marks of "true" spirituality. But let's also not err on the other side—failing to recognize our dependence on the Spirit in our worship and to desire his active presence when we meet. Let's pursue and enjoy all that God has for us.

Next Sunday, if the Spirit stopped empowering your worship, would anyone notice?

Would you?

I pray the answer to both questions is an emphatic, "Yes!" By God's grace, may people recognize that God's Spirit is really among us—actively working, empowering, encouraging, convicting—for the good of the church and the glory of the Savior.

chapter 11

. . . SKILLFULLY COMBINING GOD'S WORD . . .

"Come join us this Sunday for worship and the Word." I've heard that invitation more than once. It's an unfortunate dichotomy.

Most people understand it like this: Worship is when we sing and experience God's nearness, express our love for him, and allow his Spirit to move in our midst. All right-brain activities.

Hearing the Word, on the other hand, appeals to our left brain. It's mind food. It's for our intellects, designed to make us think, not feel.

Some Christians have so separated worship and the Word that they'll attend one church to experience the Spirit during the music, then visit another to get good teaching.

But singing and preaching aren't incompatible or opposed to each other in any way. Both are meant to exalt the glory of Christ in our hearts, minds, and wills. The whole meeting is worship; the whole meeting should be filled with God's Word. And the whole meeting should be characterized by the Spirit's presence.

Eagerly expecting the Spirit's power in our meetings goes hand in hand with a radical commitment to the authority and sufficiency of God's Word.

Does that sound like a paradox? It shouldn't. Our churches can't be Spirit-led unless they're Word-fed. A church that's dependent on the Spirit's power in its worship will be committed to the study, proclamation, and application of God's Word in its personal and congregational worship. The Word and the Spirit were never meant to be separated. In fact, God's Spirit is the one who inspired God's Word.

All Scripture is breathed out *by God and profitable for teaching, for reproof, for correction, and for training in righteousness. (2 Timothy 3:16)*

Not only did the Spirit of God inspire God's Word, he illuminates our hearts so we can understand it. God's Spirit and his Word go together.

But apart from being an evidence of the Spirit's presence and activity, there are other reasons why God's Word is central to our worship. Our relationship with God has always been characterized by the ebb and flow of revelation and response. If God hadn't revealed himself to us, we wouldn't know who to thank, who to obey, or who to serve. We wouldn't know how to worship him. But God does reveal his character, nature, and promises to us, and we respond with gratefulness and obedience. We respond with worship.

At least that's the way it's supposed to work.

WHY SHOULD WORSHIP BE WORD-CENTERED?

In Scripture, when the people of God gather to worship him, God's Word is at the center.

When Moses led the Israelites to Mount Sinai, God met them amidst thunder and lightning, thick clouds, and an ear-splitting trumpet blast. Quite the worship experience. But the most significant aspect of that encounter was God giving them the Ten Commandments, or more precisely, the "Ten Words" (Deuteronomy 4:2–12). God has always wanted us to know more of him than can ever be conveyed through impressions, images, and experiences, as powerful as they may be.

Probably no one exemplified God-pleasing worship more than David, the sweet psalmist of Israel. He was a skilled musician and a man of profound emotion. But when it came to worshiping God, it was his words, not his music, that God chose to preserve for us in Scripture.

Centuries later, when Israel returned from captivity in Babylon to restore Jerusalem, Ezra and the other priests sought to reestablish temple worship. We're told they stood up on a platform and read "from the Law of God, clearly, and they gave the sense, so that the people understood the reading" (Nehemiah 8:8). They wanted people to hear and understand what God had said to them. God's Word would provide the foundation for the expressions of repentance, gratefulness, praise, and celebration that followed.

The Word of God, clearly explained and understood, will affect us today in the same way.

In the New Testament, Jesus himself exemplified and commanded esteem for God's written Word. He rebuked the Pharisees and scribes for basing their worship more on the traditions of men than on God's commands (Matthew 15:3–9). His words were laced with references to and respect for the Old Testament Scriptures, for they all spoke of him (Luke 24:27).

The early Christians devoted themselves to the apostles' teaching (Acts 2:42). Paul encouraged Timothy to devote himself to the public reading of Scripture and commanded him to "preach the word" (1 Timothy 4:13; 2 Timothy 4:2). He also instructed us to "Let the word of Christ dwell in [us] richly" as we sing (Colossians 3:16).

Given the biblical history, God's commands, and the immeasurable benefits we receive from Word-centered worship, it's worth asking why worship today is so often focused on sensory experiences, inward feelings, and subjective encounters.

True worship is *always* a response to God's Word. John Stott has said that to worship God is "to 'Glory in his holy name' (Psalm 105:3), that is, to revel adoringly in who he is in his revealed character." Then he adds:

> God must speak to us before we have any liberty to speak to him. He must disclose to us who he is before we can offer him what we are in acceptable worship. The worship of God is always a response to the Word of God. Scripture wonderfully directs and enriches our worship.[1]

HOW CAN OUR WORSHIP BE WORD-CENTERED?

How can we ensure that the Word of God is central as we lead the church in worship?

By treasuring, singing, reading, showing, and praying God's Word.

Treasure God's Word

God wants the reading of his Word to be not only one of the highlights of our meetings, but one of our highlights every day. When we treasure God's Word, it means we'll love it more than the sports page, our favorite TV show, or time on the Internet.

A few years ago I began a quest to become better acquainted with God's Word so that my thinking, and ultimately my life, might more obviously proclaim his truth.

I read through the entire Bible for the first time and have continued to do so, seeking to understand the story line of the Bible, Christ and him crucified. I'm seeing connections, patterns, and parts of the story I never knew were there. I want to be able to say with the psalmist, "Oh how I love your law! It is my meditation all the day" (Psalm 119:97).

When we treasure God's Word, others will know it. Visitors to your church won't have the impression that the Bible is an optional extra or simply a handy reference book. They'll hear in your voice and see in your eyes that God's Word is your joy.

Referencing rock stars, funny stories, or lines from a recent movie can appear relevant and trendy. But in so doing we can leave people starving for what they need most to hear from God.

Treasuring God's Word means appreciating its inestimable value and transforming power. It means we look forward to spending the rest of our lives becoming more familiar with what God has said to us.

Sing God's Word

Songs are de facto theology. They teach us who God is, what he's like, and how to relate to him. "We are what we sing," one man said. That's why we want to sing God's Word.

One way of doing this is to use Scripture songs that quote specific passages of the Bible. A few years ago, as my church was going through the books of Philippians and Galatians, a group of us wrote and recorded songs taken from different verses. That enabled the congregation to sing many of the verses that were being preached.

Singing God's Word can include more than reciting specific verses in song. If the Word of Christ is going to "dwell in [us] richly" (Colossians 3:16), we need songs that explain, clarify, and expound on what God's Word says. We need songs that have substantive, theologically rich, biblically faithful lyrics. A consistent diet of shallow, subjective worship songs tends to produce shallow, subjective Christians.

That doesn't mean every song requires a seminary degree to understand, or that it needs seven verses. Simple songs can be just as biblical and helpful as complex ones, especially when they avoid overused or trite phrases. My friend Drew Jones says an amazing amount in these twenty-four words he calls "The Gospel Song":

Holy God in love became
Perfect man to bear my blame.
On the cross he took my sin;
By his death I live again.[2]

Too often we can be tempted to choose songs because of the music rather than the theological content. We need to realize that when words are combined with music we can be deceived. Music can make shallow lyrics sound deep. A great rhythm section can make drivel sound profound and make you want to sing it again.

That's why I typically read the lyrics before listening to a CD or playing a song from a songbook. If the words on the page are theologically shallow or vague, music won't add anything. It will only give the illusion that the words are actually substantive.

It's not that music is irrelevant. If great words are being sung to terrible music, no one will remember them or want to sing them. But according to the Lord's command, what should be dwelling in us richly is the Word of Christ, not musical experiences.

The words we sing should also be clear, not obscure or subject to personal interpretation. The Spirit of God wants to illumine our minds when we sing. We don't want to hinder that process through our songs. In congregational worship, poeticism and creative imagery have their limits. If you don't understand each line of a song you're singing, people in your church probably won't either.

British author Nick Page has written a short, insightful book called *And Now Let's Move into a Time of Nonsense: Why Worship Songs Are Failing the Church*. He writes:

> Worship songs are not solely vehicles for personal expression, they're invitations to corporate worship. If you want to write stuff that only you can understand then keep a diary, otherwise you have to cut the rest of us some slack; you have to help us understand.[3]

I should mention here that a skillful leader can fill in what a song might leave out. No song, traditional or modern, says everything we want it to. But just because a song is incomplete doesn't mean I can't use it. I can add spontaneous comments in between lines, say something in advance, or place other songs around it to supply the missing elements.

The bottom line is: Sing God's Word. Lyrics matter more than music. Truth transcends tunes.

Read God's Word

This is so obvious, one could assume I wouldn't need to include it. But I've learned otherwise.

In many churches today where the authority and sufficiency of Scripture are taught, very little Scripture is actually read publicly. But God has given us a specific command to *devote ourselves* to the public reading of Scripture (1 Timothy 4:13). Surely there must be a good reason behind this.

I can think of many. When we listen to God's Word being read, we're acknowledging our dependence on and submission to God's revelation. Children learn to respect God's Word when it's read with genuine respect and enthusiasm. Visitors see that we value the Bible. When Scripture reading is well planned, the congregation gets a balanced diet of God's Word. And for those who don't read their Bibles, it may be the only time they hear it.

Some traditional liturgies prescribe Scripture readings each week. Our church doesn't follow a plan like that, so we seek to make Scripture reading a priority in other ways.

After the meeting begins I might read a verse such as Psalm 111:1–2: "Praise the LORD! I will give thanks to the LORD with my whole heart, in the company of the upright, in the congregation. Great are the works of the LORD, studied by all who delight in them." That gives me the opportunity to explain what we've gathered to do—to delight in and study the works of the Lord. I try to avoid "worshipful" sounding verses that don't impact me personally, like, "Sing praises to the LORD, who sits enthroned in Zion!" (Psalm 9:11). In other words, don't use the Bible as filler. People should understand *why* we're reading a particular Scripture at any given moment.

We can also read Scripture between songs. Reading the Bible between songs doesn't necessarily break the flow or inhibit true worship; it feeds it. Reading a Scripture passage can help people understand why we're singing the next song, give a biblical basis for a line or verse from a song, or serve as a change of focus between two songs.

Sometimes we also intersperse verses of a song with Scripture. Once we had different vocalists read portions of Psalm 103 in between the verses of the hymn "Praise to the Lord, the Almighty." We were seeking to "ponder anew what the Almighty can do," as one verse says. The effect was an increasing faith and joy in our hearts as we sang each verse. On another occasion we read portions of Isaiah 53 in between verses of the song "Behold the Lamb" by Mark Altrogge. Doing so helped us freshly appreciate how Christ's sufferings fulfilled prophetic words written centuries before he was born.

God's Word can also be read responsively, as a leader and the congregation take turns reading through a passage or selected texts.

In whatever way we read Scripture, we want to do it with clarity, conviction, and power. People should be aware that the words they hear aren't ours, but God's.

Show God's Word

Scripture can be seen as well as heard. Sometimes we project verses on the screen during an instrumental break of a song or as an introduction to a song. If we plan it in advance, we can have a Scripture projected when the worship leader mentions it. That kind of visual reinforcement can help people better grasp the meaning of a passage being read.

If your church uses bulletins, you can also print relevant Scriptures on the front or inside.

At different times I've included a Scripture passage when sending the worship team the songs we were going to sing the next Sunday. My goal was to give everyone a sense of the theme and to remind them that everything we do is under the authority of God's Word and is meant to draw attention to his revelation rather than to our creativity or efforts.

Pray God's Word

More than once I've been involved in a meeting where the worship leader paused between two songs and began to pray like this: "Well, Lord, today, we uh, just wanna thank you, Father, for being with us here, Jesus, and for bringing us together, Lord, to worship you. You're incredible. We just wanna come into your throne room today, Jesus, and worship you like we've never worshiped you before, Lord, and that's what we're here to give you, Lord, by the Spirit of Jesus, Father, so that you'd be glorified. And, Lord . . ."

I know the worship leader is sincere. I know it because I've sincerely prayed that way many times myself.

But how much more helpful would it be to pray something like this: "Father, thank you that you've invited us to gather as your people to worship you. Thank you for Jesus, our great Savior. Because of his substitutionary sacrifice we're able to be here in your presence, unashamed and forgiven. We pray that your Spirit would open our eyes to see that we're dearly loved in Christ. Sanctify us by your truth, and work in us what is pleasing to you. Be glorified in everything we do this morning, Father."

Like everything else we do in worshiping God, prayer is an opportunity to be Word-centered. That doesn't mean we can't use our own expressions or thoughts. It just means they're shaped and informed—both in attitude and content—by what God has revealed to us in Scripture.

Prayers can be written, planned, or spontaneous. It's not a bad thing to use written prayers if that will enable a thoughtful, heartfelt, biblical response to God. I've tried it a few times and have been surprised at how free I am to focus on what I'm praying rather than trying to figure out what to say on the spot. And over the long run it will only make my spontaneous prayers more coherent and substantive.

You can make your public prayers more biblical by praying the Scriptures back to God privately. Psalms usually work the best. Read a verse, then begin praying the thoughts contained in it, applying them to certain situations or people in your life. Psalms 23, 33, 62, 86, 103, and 145 are good places to start. Over time you'll be amazed how your thoughts, attitudes, and words will be brought more in line with the way God thinks. Your prayers will take on a greater confidence. And your congregation will benefit from your example.[4]

A faithful worship leader combines the Word of God with music to magnify the greatness of God in Jesus Christ. We don't need music to hear God's Word. We don't need music to worship God. But the Bible connects music and worship often enough to persuade us that music might be an important aspect of our relationship with God. How important? That's the question I seek to answer in the next two chapters.

chapter 12

. . . WITH MUSIC . . .
(PART ONE: WHAT KIND?)

Music can be deceptive. I once heard of a Christian woman who spent time serving God in South Africa. While visiting a health clinic, she was deeply moved by the sound of the local Zulu women singing. Their harmonies were hauntingly beautiful. With tears in her eyes, she asked a friend if she knew the translation of the words.

"Sure," her friend replied. "'If you boil the water, you won't get dysentery.'"

Now if that doesn't make you want to worship, what does?

Being emotionally affected by music and actually worshiping God aren't the same thing, and no one should know this better than worship leaders. All by itself, music—even instrumental music—can make us cry, motivate us to cheer for our team, provoke us to protest, or fill us with joy.

It's part of the way God designed music to work in his creation. Now if we could only figure out how it works in worship.

A SAD HISTORY

Christians have been arguing about music in worship for centuries. And it hasn't always been pretty. Martin Luther, the Protestant Reformer, had strong opinions about music and wasn't afraid to express them. In an introduction to a sixteenth-century collection of chorale motets, he wrote that anyone who didn't appreciate the beauty of these multipart pieces and view them as a gift from God "must be a clodhopper indeed and does not deserve to be called a human being; he should be permitted to hear nothing but the braying of asses and the grunting of hogs."[1]

What Luther lacked in tact and diplomacy, he made up for in his commitment to congregational singing. But battles persisted long after Luther left the scene. Two hundred years later, churches in the American colonies were debating the relative merits of singing by ear and by note. At the same time, British churches argued about using hymns "of human composure," particularly by Isaac Watts. One hundred years after Watts died, people would still walk out of a meeting if someone started singing something other than a Psalm set to music.

Since then, the music wars have been fueled by Christian publishing houses, revivalism, charismatic outpourings, cultural shifts, sound amplification, electronic instruments, and of course, our own sinful hearts.

Does God even care whether or not we use music to worship him? Apparently so. The Bible's longest book is a collection of songs. God commands both instrumental and vocal praise in Scripture. Psalm 150 says we're to praise the Lord with horns, cymbals, and strings. Over fifty times in the book of Psalms we're told to sing God's praise. Psalm 47 is particularly clear: "Sing praises to God, sing praises! Sing praises to our King, sing praises!" (v. 6). The Bible is filled with references to music, from the dawn of creation to the final scenes in Revelation (Job 38:7; Revelation 15:3).

But if we don't understand God's purpose for music in worship, we can misuse it. Even worse, it can rob God of the glory we want to give him.

HOW MUSIC HELPS US

God wants us to use music to worship him in spite of the problems that can arise. Apparently God thinks it's worth the effort. Here are four reasons why.

Music stirs up and expresses God-glorifying emotion. Our deepest, strongest, purest affections should be reserved for God himself, and he gave us singing to help us express them. Halfhearted praise is an oxymoron. It doesn't make any sense. Listen to Jonathan Edwards on this:

> The duty of singing praises to God seems to be given wholly to excite and express religious affections. There is no other reason why we should express ourselves to God in verse rather than in prose and with music, except that these things have a tendency to move our affections.[2]

Some Christians repress their emotions as they sing. They fear feeling anything too strongly and think maturity means holding back. But the problem is *emotionalism*, not *emotions*. Emotionalism pursues feelings as an end in themselves. It's wanting to feel something with no regard for how that feeling is produced or its ultimate purpose. Emotionalism can also view heightened emotions as the infallible sign that God is present.

In contrast, the emotions that singing is meant to evoke are a response to who God is and what he's done. Vibrant singing enables us to combine truth *about* God seamlessly with passion *for* God. Doctrine and devotion. Mind and heart.

Music helps us reflect the glory and activity of the triune God. God is a singing God. We read in Zephaniah 3:17 that he will rejoice over us with singing. Jesus sang a hymn with his disciples on the night before he died (Matthew 26:30). And Ephesians 5:18–19 indicates that the Holy Spirit inspires songs in believers' hearts as he fills them. That's one reason we often sense God's presence in a more pronounced way when we gather to sing his praises. The Holy Spirit is in our midst, inspiring our songs.

It's a source of profound encouragement to realize that God gave us music to deepen and develop our relationship with him. The Father sings, the Son sings, and the Spirit sings. How can we keep from singing?

Music helps us remember truth about God. A year after we recorded a CD of Scripture songs from Galatians, a man in our church lost his memory due to a stroke. His wife e-mailed me later to say that though he had no memory of the sermon series, he remembered every song on the CD.

God himself used music as a means to help people remember his Word. As the Israelites were about to enter the Promised Land, God told Moses to teach them a song so that "when many evils and troubles have come upon them, this song shall confront them as a witness (for it will live unforgotten in the mouths of their offspring)" (Deuteronomy 31:21).

We remember what we sing, and nothing is more important to remember than God's Word. Music-produced feelings will fade, but God's living and active Word will continue working in our hearts, renewing our minds, and strengthening our faith.

Finally, *music helps us express our unity in the gospel.* In Scripture, the overwhelming majority of references to singing are corporate. People aren't singing alone but together. In the New Testament two of the most specific passages on singing refer to "addressing one another" and "teaching and admonishing one another" (Ephesians 5:19; Colossians 3:16). We've become a family, "a chosen race," "a holy nation," through the death and resurrection of Jesus Christ (1 John 3:1; 1 Peter 2:9). Singing glorifies God by expressing the unity we enjoy through the gospel.

Churches can potentially undermine this unity by offering different Sunday meetings based on musical preferences and styles. While it may mean numerical growth for the church in the short run, it also can separate families and tends to cultivate a consumer mind-set in the long run.

There are other options. Diverse music teams can take turns leading on a Sunday morning. Different styles of music can be brought together in one meeting. More importantly, the church can be taught that setting aside their musical preferences for the sake of others is obeying Philippians 2:4: "Let each of you look not only to his own interests, but also to the interests of others." Taking this path will probably require patient instruction, but over time the congregation will begin to see that the determining factor in our unity is not musical styles—it's the gospel.

WHAT KIND OF MUSIC?

God obviously wants us to worship him with music, but he hasn't given us as many details as we'd often like to know. Scripture doesn't come with an accompanying soundtrack. So we aren't sure what music from Bible times actually sounded like. Middle-Eastern folk music probably comes close, but I don't know any church—at least in America—that uses that style.

Some of the questions Scripture doesn't address include: How much music is too much? Should songs be passed down through the years, or should each generation write its own? Should our music be universal or more culturally localized? Should songs be liturgical or free-form? Should the singing be spread throughout our time together or happen all at once?

You might have a few questions of your own.

I won't be able to cover everything I'd like to here. But I can offer three overarching principles for making music in the church, with specific ways to apply them.

MUSIC SHOULD SERVE THE LYRICS

This e-mail came from a gentleman who had visited our church a few times:

> I'm one of those musician types who doesn't sing. . . . Being a musician type I tend to hear the music and most often miss the lyrics. That has not been my experience at Covenant Life. I would describe my experience at your church like this. I feel the music washing over me almost like a flood

even while my mind is captivated in meditation on the lyrics. I'm not only hearing, but also meditating on the lyrics. This is not like me. I see it as a good thing. My only question is, "How do you do this?"

I'm not quite sure how we "do this." Ultimately it's a work of the Holy Spirit. But we have been intentional about helping people focus on the lyrics as they sing.

We've taken to heart Gordon Fee's comment: "Show me a church's songs and I'll show you their theology." We know that people need songs that feed them, not simply songs that feel good.

Here are specific ways we've tried to serve the lyrics with our music.

Sing Songs That Say Something

The words to our songs should be as strong and memorable as the tunes we set them to or the arrangements we put behind them.

At times I've chosen not to do a well-known song because I thought the music was more impacting than the lyrics. The catchiness factor surpassed the weightiness factor. I'm tempted to list some of those songs here, but that's really a decision you have to make yourself. When in doubt, leave it out.

Songs can say something in different ways. *Objective lyrics* tell us something true about God that helps us know him better. Most, but not all, hymns from the eighteenth century tend to focus on objective truths.

Subjective lyrics express responses to God such as love, longing, conviction, or adoration. Don't assume that a song that uses a lot of first-person pronouns is man-centered. Psalm 86 uses the personal pronouns "I," "me," and "my" thirty-one times in seventeen verses. But you're never left wondering who the focus is. God delights in strong emotions that are a response to revealed realities.

Reflective lyrics describe what we're doing as we worship God. We bring our offering, we praise, we sing, we lift up our hands.

These three categories aren't hard-and-fast divisions, and many songs contain all three perspectives. All three can contribute to strong lyrics. But when we don't major on objective truth, our songs can quickly drift into emotionalism and self-absorption. We start to worship our own experiences.

Again, that doesn't mean all our songs need to be theological treatises. But if our primary criteria for using a song has to do with whether it's popular or enjoyable to sing, we're going to have a hard time persuading anyone that truth matters more than music.

Adjust Your Musical Arrangements and Volume

Most play-by-ear musicians think that being up front means you should always be playing. Wrong. Varying when we play, how loudly we play, and what we play affects how people hear the words.

The larger the team of musicians, the more each member should be listening to and making room for what others are doing. Believe me, this takes practice. Lots of it. If this is a new concept, try having one instrument accompany an entire verse alone. It could be an acoustic guitar, pianist, percussionist, or synthesizer player. It may seem unsettling at first, but the effect is often dramatic.

Try different combinations of instruments in rehearsal. Be clear in your direction, and insist at times that people not play. Help them see that their silence makes someone else's contribution more significant.

We can also monitor and vary the volume. The volume of the band (and vocalists) might be raised when we're leading a new song, when the church is singing loudly, when we're setting the tempo, or when we're giving directions. But the sound of the musicians shouldn't dominate or overpower the congregation. In the New Testament the predominant sound throughout the meeting is the singing of the congregation. *They* are the real worship team.

It's a good idea to check your volume by listening from out front, or ask someone you trust to evaluate it for you.

Use Instrumental Solos Wisely

The word *selah* appears frequently in the Psalms. Many scholars think it refers to a musical interlude for meditation or reflection. While that can't be proven, there are numerous passages where God commends instrumental music to praise him (for example, Psalm 33:3; 71:22; 150:3–5).

But a Sunday morning isn't a concert or recital, where an audience sits back to hear musicians use their gifts. We're not there to jam. The longer a band or music team plays, the more opportunity there is for the congregation to drift mentally or be more impressed with musical skill than with Jesus.

We've used instrumental solos as introductions, turnarounds between verses and choruses, or brief bridges. Be willing to forgo instrumental sections that only serve as filler or that delay congregational singing unnecessarily.

Focus on Projecting Lyrics

If your church doesn't use hymnals or songbooks, the person handling the projection of lyrics plays a crucial role in enabling people to engage with truth about God. If they're frequently late in putting up lyrics, show the wrong verse, leave a blank screen, or project misspelled words, that can counteract whatever good leadership you might be exercising. That's why I want that person to be humble, trained, and faithful. It also helps when they attend rehearsals.

Some churches never show more than one phrase of a song at a time, which can make it difficult to grasp the meaning of the lyrics. Imagine reading your Bible like that. People will understand the flow of thought better if they see lines in their context.

You might also consider projecting lyrics when people are learning songs, when a song is being sung by a soloist, or during an instrumental portion of a song. These are just a few more ways we can make music serve the lyrics.

Use Supportive Music

This has been done badly so many times, I hesitate to bring it up. But Scripture seems to make a connection between hearing music and being sensitive to God's voice. According to 1 Chronicles 25:1, those who led the worship at the tabernacle "prophesied with lyres, with harps, and with cymbals" accompanying them. Elisha was unable to speak the word of the Lord to the kings of Israel and Judah until a musician came and played for him (2 Kings 3:14–16; see also 1 Samuel 10:5–6; Ephesians 5:18–19). God seems to have established an undefined but discernible relationship between music and the way we hear his Word. As best as I can tell, music affects our emotions, which in turn can make us more receptive to, or at least aware of, the words we sing and hear. We can't speak dogmatically about this relationship, but neither can we deny it.

When I play piano softly behind a speaker, I'm listening carefully to what's being prayed, shared, or read. I seek to support, not distract from, the content. I rarely play a song that everyone can identify because that could easily draw their attention away from the speaker. I play sparsely and at times nothing at all.

We don't need to play music constantly or seek to manipulate people's emotions. Spoken words don't always have to be accompanied by a musical background. But in the right ways and at the right time, instrumental music can be an effective complement and support to the spoken word.

MUSIC SHOULD DISPLAY VARIETY

What did Paul mean when he encouraged us to sing "psalms and hymns and spiritual songs" (Colossians 3:16; Ephesians 5:19)? No one's completely sure. Most scholars agree he seems to be encouraging diversity in the songs we use to praise God. "Psalms" might be referring to the Psalter, "hymns" to songs that praise Christ, and "spiritual songs" to more spontaneous expressions. If that's the case, Paul is encouraging us to sing all our songs—short, long, fast, slow, old, new—with gratefulness to God.

Here are some ways that stylistic diversity pleases God, along with some ideas for how to pursue it.

Reflecting God's Various Attributes

Musical diversity reflects the varying aspects of God's nature. He is transcendent and immanent. He splits mountains and clothes the lilies. We worship him as our Creator and Redeemer, King and Father. How can anyone think that a single kind of music could adequately express the fullness of God's glory?

There are four Gospels in the New Testament, not one. God used the unique backgrounds, personalities, and education of Matthew, Mark, Luke, and John to bear witness to the Savior. Music can be used in a similar way.

There's a time for singing "Lo, He Comes with Clouds Descending" by John Cennick, another for singing "Because of You" by Paul Oakley, and yet another for singing "In Christ Alone" by Stuart Townend and Keith Getty. All three mention Christ's return in different but equally valid ways.

God is too great and the human experience too complex to think that one kind of music will always best express the dynamics of our relationship with a living God.

Hearing Familiar Words in a Fresh Way

Musical variety enables us to hear the same words with different effect. "Amazing Grace" has a different emotional impact when it's accompanied by a black gospel choir, a large orchestra, a sustained synthesizer chord, or a lone acoustic guitar.

Hymns are especially suited for innovative treatments that help us hear the words from a new perspective. Moving beyond traditional tunes and arrangements shouldn't bother us too much since most hymns were written without music, and a favorite tune only emerged over time.

At my home church, we regularly reharmonize songs or write original melodies for hymns to help people hear the lyrics in a different way. We also try singing songs just like they were sung centuries ago. Sometimes old is new. Sometimes old is *better.*

Recognizing God's Heart for All People

Musical variety communicates God's heart for all generations, cultures, and races. We don't use different music because we want to keep everyone happy or because we're aiming for a "blended" service. It's the gospel that blends us together, not music.

As Michael Hamilton reminds us:

> It is fruitless to search for a single musical style, or even any blend of musical styles, that can assist all Christians with true worship. The followers of Jesus are a far too diverse group of people—which is exactly as it should be. We need, rather, to welcome any worship music that helps churches produce disciples of Jesus Christ. We need to welcome the experimental creativity that is always searching out new ways of singing the gospel, and banish the fear that grips us when familiar music passes away.[3]

To demonstrate this point one year we used a different style of music every Sunday for an entire month. We called it, "It's Not About the Music." The first Sunday felt very much like a traditional Presbyterian service. I gave a message on the role of music in congregational worship, followed by the Lord's Supper and a benediction. The next Sunday focused on world music, using songs from a variety of cultures. We followed that with Hispanic Sunday, then Bluegrass/Country Sunday with banjo, fiddle, and harmonica. We finished up with a black gospel/R&B/rap Sunday, led by a choir. Although purists might quibble with the authenticity of each style, no one missed the message. Each musical style brought a different emphasis to the praise that God so richly deserves.

I realize that demonstrating musical diversity depends on a number of factors, including the size of your church, the training and talent of your musicians, and your budget. But in our rapidly shrinking world it's even more important that we at least teach on the importance of this diversity. Christ's command to take the gospel to the ends of the earth should inform and shape our theology of musical worship. It's unwise and unbiblical to think that churches in Bolivia, Indonesia, Uganda, and elsewhere must conform to an American's definition of "appropriate" worship music.

MUSIC SHOULD EDIFY THE CHURCH

When someone insists that we should only use the *best* music to worship God, I scratch my head. Is the best music simple or complex? Written or spontaneous? Short or long? Do they mean the best aesthetically, pragmatically, emotionally, or historically? We usually already have in mind what we mean by "best," and it often says more about our preferences than our theology.

As I understand it, the *best* music enables people to genuinely and consistently magnify the greatness of the Savior in their hearts, minds, and wills. That's a standard that will never change from culture to culture, generation to generation, church to church.

To flesh out this standard of excellence in your church, you'll probably have a musical center that effectively communicates to most people in the congregation. The songs sung in churches in rural Idaho, downtown Manhattan, Nottingham, England, and Bharuch, India are going to sound different. They should.

When it comes to innovations, remember that Scripture doesn't mandate that we push the envelope, artistically speaking, on Sunday mornings. Artists will always be searching for new and fresh ways to express their gifts, but congregations must be able to hear the message without being distracted by the medium. When we meet to worship God, we're not aiming to glorify creativity but the Creator.

And as a practical matter, edifying the church means using songs that everyone can sing. What's on my iPod isn't always the best place to start when I'm picking songs for congregational worship. I need to think through the musical level of the people I'm leading. I generally look for songs with melodies between a low A to a high D that are easy to learn and hard to forget. I also try to avoid complicated rhythms.

But churches can be taught to sing songs that are initially unfamiliar and even complex. I remember introducing Matt Redman's "Let Everything That Has Breath." The verses have an unusual rhythm that can be difficult to pick up, especially for older folks. But the song has a number of strengths. It passionately declares God's worthiness to be praised. It combines an outward focus ("calling all the nations to your praise") with an admonition to the church ("if they could see how much you're worth"). It also speaks to generations worshiping God together ("praise you when I'm young and when I'm old").

So we taught it. Over time the church learned to sing it together, and sing it well.

And now that we've introduced the topic of selecting songs, let's spend a whole chapter on it.

chapter 13

. . . WITH MUSIC . . .
(PART TWO: PLANNING
SUNDAY'S SONGS)

Every worship leader knows the feeling, the pain, the anxiety, the utter discouragement. Your song list for next Sunday is due in thirty minutes, and you have no idea what to do.

Or maybe next Sunday is tomorrow morning.

It's late. You're tired. You're staring at a blank computer screen surrounded by stacks of CDs, three hymnals, your worship songbook, and a list of what you've sung for the past five months. Nothing's helping.

You pray. And you start to wonder if even God knows what you should sing.

As you start to sweat, thoughts like these begin to influence your choices:

• This is my favorite new song from my favorite CD by my favorite worship artist. It's *hot*. And no one I know is doing it yet.

• No one got upset when I taught this song last month.

• I really like the way my voice sounds on this one.

• I can't do this one because it has three verses, and I'm into simple right now.

• I think I know all the chords on these three.[1]

Fortunately, we can do better when it comes to planning songs.

Here are ten principles that might help.

PLAN SELECTIVELY

We have more songs available to sing than anyone in church history. That means we don't have to settle for those that "kind of" say what we want, or songs that are boring, or songs whose music is more memorable than their lyrics. And we certainly don't have to use songs just because they're popular.

Great songs come from a variety of sources. We've used hymnals, worship web sites, independent band CDs, nationally known worship artists, quarterly song services, compilation CDs, and recommendations from friends.

We've also encouraged and used songs from budding writers in our own congregation.

When researching songs, I generally think of them in one of four categories.

"Don't Use" is for those with words that are unbiblical or unclear or just bad poetry.

"In Private" is for songs that I can listen to on my own but that wouldn't serve our church. The lyrics might include an obscure phrase or verse or be set to poor or complicated music.

The "Could Use" category is for songs that are a good choice for the congregation depending on the situation, need, and context.

And "Should Use" are songs like "In Christ Alone" or "Blessed Be Your Name." They communicate truth about God in such a compelling and clear way that I make it a priority to teach them to the church.

PLAN PEACEFULLY

There's a good chance you've heard another worship leader talking excitedly about some new song he recently introduced to his congregation. It's incredible, he says. Life-changing. Awesome.

You've never even heard of it.

Your heart sinks, and you start to panic as you realize how behind you must be. You just don't want to be out of the loop when it comes to what's happening in the worship world.

You can relax. Our peace comes from knowing we don't have to wonder if we're missing "the" song that's going to make all the difference on Sunday. Our confidence is never in any particular song but in a gracious

God. Though he can use new songs to impart an eternal truth in a fresh way, he isn't confined to them. He does amazing things with old songs too.

PLAN PRAYERFULLY

God is eager to help us as we prepare, but he wants us to ask him for that help. We don't simply plan for meetings; we plan for people. Ask God for songs that will serve those you're leading rather than ones you like or ones that will make you look good.

Every person walking in on Sunday morning has unique needs, specific sins he or she is battling, blind spots, and a tendency to forget the gospel. We have the awesome privilege of pointing everyone to the greatness, goodness, and grace of Jesus Christ. We need the Holy Spirit's power to be effective, as we'll never outgrow our need for his help.

And God is eager to answer our prayers for direction.

PLAN WITH OTHERS

"Two are better than one, because they have a good reward for their toil" (Ecclesiastes 4:9). I've found that to be true when planning songs. You'd think that after thirty years of leading worship I could do this by myself. But I don't want to. The results just aren't as good.

Planning with others involves a level of trust, developed over time. It also requires humility, because I'm acknowledging I'm not "Mr. Worship" with all the answers.

When I plan with my pastor, a team, or someone else I respect and trust, our different giftings of teaching, pastoring, or administration complement each other. We also benefit from different personal perspectives. Doctrinally rich songs may need to be balanced with simpler ones, familiar songs with new ones. We need to remember youth as well as senior saints, members as well as guests.

Communication can take place by e-mail or phone or in a face-to-face meeting. We've found that things go more smoothly when someone comes up with a suggested song list to work from rather than starting from scratch. And the earlier in the week we begin planning, the easier it is to make changes, notify the worship team, and pray through what we're planning to do.

Occasionally my pastor wants me to do a song I wouldn't choose. After I let him know my reservations, we dialogue about it, but I leave the final decision to him. I'm here to serve my senior pastor, and I want to follow his lead wholeheartedly.

PLAN THEMATICALLY

Our unchanging theme every week is the grand story of deliverance that God accomplished for his people through the life, death, and resurrection of Jesus Christ. We want to remember this, rehearse it, celebrate it, and respond to it.

But we also have the opportunity to highlight a specific aspect of how that glorious gospel reaches into our lives and affects us now. This provides a focus for both our songs and thoughts.

Themes can come from a variety of places. One common source is the sermon. Songs are chosen to highlight the theme of that week's message. But we've often found it more effective to use a particular point from the *previous* week's message. That reinforces the importance of last week's sermon and gives us an extended opportunity to meditate on and respond to a particular aspect of it.

Here's an example. One Sunday we wanted to teach Matt Redman's song "Nothing but the Blood." To introduce it, I shared something like this:

> "Last week, we heard how God sent Jonah to the people of Nineveh to warn them of the coming judgment. But Jonah ran away because he hated the Ninevites and was surprised that God was showing them compassion.
>
> "It's easy to be surprised when God shows compassion to certain people—people we think are beyond hope, offensive, and definitely objects of wrath. At least in our eyes. But whenever we gather as the church, God wants us to remember that at one time, we too were objects of wrath; we were his enemies, destined for destruction. Ephesians 2 tells us that God is rich in mercy, and 'because of the great love with which he loved us, even when we were dead in our trespasses, made us alive together with Christ.'
>
> "God showed his tender compassion to the Ninevites by sending them the prophet Jonah. He showed us compassion by sending his only Son. And through his blood shed for our sins, we can know his mercy and grace forever. We want to teach you a new song this morning that helps us recall the compassion that God demonstrated so clearly at the cross."

A theme might also arise from your personal devotions, from a memorable and powerful line in a song, or from a desire to teach a certain aspect of worship.

I'll often share a specific thought on the theme (or have someone else share it) after or during the first two songs. I want to discourage the impression that we have to warm up to worship. The sooner everyone's minds and hearts are engaged with the songs we're singing, the more benefit they'll see in their lives.

A theme can be woven throughout a group of songs, such as those that emphasize God's mercy or power. Themes can also be communicated through Scripture, a song, or a prayer.

The important thing is that at some point we give people a handle so they understand what they should be focusing on.

PLAN CONTEXTUALLY

The context for choosing your songs includes background details such as the sermons that have been preached, your congregation's demographic mix and level of spiritual maturity, plus weekly variables such as special occasions or events.

When planning each week, the first thing I want to know is how long we're supposed to sing. That tells me how many songs we can do well. Whether ten minutes or forty, I want to maximize the use of every song.

I also want to know what else is planned during our time together on Sunday. Are we opening with a call to worship, a prayer, or an instrumental piece? Are we sharing the Lord's Supper in the midst of singing? Is someone sharing a testimony after I finish leading worship?

One of the primary contexts will be what we're learning about. If the church is going through a particular sermon series, that will affect the songs I choose.

Circumstances that affect the entire church can also influence song choice. The size of your church is important here. In a church of three thousand, I can't allow something that affects a handful of people to determine my song choice. But if a well-loved teenager in a small congregation dies in a Friday night car wreck, I'll want to reconsider starting the meeting with "The Happy Song" or "Indescribable."

Context includes the songs we've been singing in recent weeks. I may want to repeat one that we've only recently learned or use one we haven't sung in a while.

By the way, if you want the church to sing a new song after the sermon, teach it in advance. People can have a hard time responding to the truths God just spoke to their hearts if they're learning a new song in the process.

PLAN PROGRESSIVELY

I've downloaded some great sermons to my iPod. But sometimes after listening to a message for about twenty minutes I'll think, *This guy isn't making sense. I can't understand his flow of thought, and his transitions are nonexistent.* Then I'll check my iPod. Oh. It's set on shuffle. That means I'm hearing five-minute tracks of the message out of sequence. No wonder I'm confused.

That's how some of us lead worship—on shuffle. We sing great songs, but they're unconnected and in no discernible order. That's why we need to plan our songs progressively.

By *progressive* I don't mean *cutting edge*. I'm referring to how things fit together, how a theme develops, how different portions of the meeting connect. Some people call it *flow*.

I know God can use even the most disjointed meetings to minister to people. He's certainly done it enough times when I've led. But a clear and connected progression of thought helps people fully benefit from our time together.

Since God hasn't given us in Scripture a detailed order for all our meetings, the progression can look different from week to week. We may even have multiple progressions in one Sunday.

The Revelation-Response paradigm is one approach. We determine at any certain moment whether God is speaking to us or we're responding to God.

Another helpful progression model is Exalt, Encounter, and Respond. We exalt God's greatness at the start, encounter him in our hearts and minds, then respond in appropriate ways.

Many churches follow the fourfold order of Gathering, Word, Table, and Dismissal.

Others find a basis for liturgical forms in passages such as Isaiah 6 and Psalm 95. Following the Psalm 95 emphasis, we enter with joyful thanksgiving, move on to reverential worship, then encounter God's voice.

Whatever pattern we follow, the church needs to know where we are at the moment and where we're going. That's planning progressively.

Once the songs or elements of a meeting are connected conceptually, we need to think about transitions—helping people understand how different elements connect.

Spoken transitions generally work best when they're brief and personal and are used strategically. You might explain why you're singing a certain song or point out the connection between two songs. Comments can bring clarity, inspire faith, sharpen focus, establish rapport, and teach. But if we don't think in advance about what we're going to say, we can sound aimless and confusing. And we almost always end up saying too much. Our words can become filler to cover up feelings of awkwardness or uncertainty. We gush with emotion but don't have any substance.

For years I printed out what I wanted to say on one page in 18-point bold Arial. That helped me be clear, biblical, personal, and brief, but it often lacked passion. It sounded like I was reading (because I was). Now I plan my comments in my mind and rehearse them until they're clear. That may take me thirty minutes. But I figure if I can't remember what I'm going to say, no one else will either.

Noticing how songs begin and end lyrically is another aspect of transitions. A word or thought that's repeated from one song to the next can build a sense of continuity and minimize the need to say anything. For instance, the last verse of "How Deep the Father's Love" ends with "his wounds have paid my ransom." You wouldn't need to say anything if you followed that with the chorus of "Jesus Paid It All."

Other questions to consider when thinking about lyrical transitions include who is being addressed (Father, Son, Spirit), whether we're talking to or about God (second- or third-person language), and whether the pronouns are individual or corporate.

Transitions can also be musical. Although a whole team can play a transition, using only one instrument provides greater flexibility and dynamic variation. A number of times I've watched a team flawlessly execute a transition they'd rehearsed. But because it was too long or excessively creative, the congregation became distracted and disengaged. Don't fall into the trap of thinking that worship in spirit and truth is dependent on musical interludes. They're tools, not masters.

Good musical transitions require a good understanding of tempos, keys, and mood. There's a common misconception associated with each of those.

First misconception: *Playing a song faster will make people worship God more passionately.* Not necessarily. Usually it just means they'll have a harder time thinking about the words. Try recording your version of an up-tempo song and comparing it with the recorded version. You'll see what I mean. Speed doesn't equal spiritual impact.

If you're not playing to a click track, take your time setting the tempo. The wrong tempo can hinder a song's effectiveness. Singing the chorus to yourself is usually a reliable way to remember how fast a song should be sung.

Second misconception: *For the best flow, songs need to be in the same key.* Again, not true. It's great when a song is in the same key as the previous one. But musical goals should serve, not dictate, spiritual goals. When two songs are in different keys, that just means we need to figure out how to modulate from one to the other. We typically use some variation of the V chord in the new key (for the key of D, that would be A, Asus, or G/A) or repeat a rhythmic phrase or harmonic progression from the old key in the new key. It's also possible just to end one song and sensitively start the next song in a new key. For slower songs, it's usually most effective to let one instrument carry the modulation.[2]

Third misconception: *We're trying to create a "worshipful" mood.* Wrong again. We're seeking to help people actually worship the Savior. They can do that with a loud song, a soft song, a fast song, a slow song, a modern worship song, or a hymn. However, we should be sensitive to the musical moods of songs and lead people naturally from one to the other. If I'm going to follow a quiet song with a rocker, I should be sure people know why and not simply allow the music to move their emotions.

Tempo, key, and mood are important in transitions. But unless we focus on the biblical truths we're seeking to communicate and respond to, they can distract us from the truth God wants to sow in our hearts.

PLAN CREATIVELY

Effective leadership involves more than coming up with a song list.

For one, we can vary the way songs are sung. A soloist can sing one verse or a whole song, we can use a choir, or the church can sing responsively with the leader or in groups. Singing congregationally isn't the only way of fulfilling God's command to address "one another in psalms and hymns and spiritual songs" (Ephesians 5:19).

We can also change arrangements, tempos, and song structure. Who says you have to do a song exactly the way it's written? Starting with the chorus or bridge might make a better lyrical and/or musical progression.

We can introduce nonmusical elements as well. Here are a few ideas we've tried or heard about from others:

• Pray for a specific need or situation, followed by a song that reinforces the prayer or draws attention to God's faithfulness.

• Have someone share a testimony of salvation or sanctification.

• Share the Lord's Supper, led by a pastor and followed by congregational singing.

• Have a pastor explain the theological meaning behind a word or phrase in a song.

• Change the setup of the musicians.

• Recite together a creed or the Lord's Prayer.

• Change the number and types of musicians. We've led with piano and djembe, full choir, band and string quartet, no drums, three acoustic guitars, band and brass quartet . . . you get the idea. Mix it up.

• Project Scriptures or names of God as you sing.

• Read Scripture before or during songs. You can do this yourself, assign it to your vocalists, have a pastor do it, or ask members of the congregation to read.

• Read a prayer from *The Valley of Vision*, published by Banner of Truth. It's a gold mine of biblical, honest, gospel-saturated prayers.

• Teach the congregation sign language for a familiar song. It's one more way of engaging our bodies in worshiping God.

• Begin with a scriptural call to worship.

• Read Scripture in different languages. One Sunday, to accent our unity in the gospel, four people read portions of Psalm 103 in Spanish, Mandarin, Swahili, and English.

• Confess sin corporately. This is usually a powerful time of specifically acknowledging our sins before a holy God, followed by a clear assurance of forgiveness through the atoning death of Christ.[3]

• Include the giving of tithes and offerings in between two songs to emphasize it as an act of worship.

Obviously this is a brief list just to get you started with your own ideas.

Planning creatively takes wisdom. It can easily become a distraction or the main event. Remember that creativity isn't something we *do*; it's a way we do *something*. That "something" is magnifying God's glory in Christ.

PLAN REALISTICALLY

One of our most common mistakes through the years has been underestimating how long portions of the meeting take. Worship leaders are notorious for losing track of time. (Pastors are guilty as well, but let's stay focused.)

Of course, we always go over our time for the "right" reasons. We really worked hard on the last song. We felt anointed. The Holy Spirit was just starting to touch people's hearts. People were finally worshiping God!

Staying within my allotted time isn't unspiritual, nor does it mean I'm quenching the Spirit. Actually, working within a time frame is a way of honoring your pastor, serving the church (especially children's workers), and pleasing the Lord.

I used to think the Holy Spirit didn't even show up until the fourth song. Nonsense. The Holy Spirit can be very efficient. More often than not, if we plan carefully and realistically, the Spirit has time to do more than we'd expect.

It's helpful to actually time how long songs take to sing. Listen to a recording of some of your meetings and find out. The general rule of thumb is: Assume you'll go longer than you think. It's better to sing fewer songs peacefully than more songs frantically.

I generally allow about five to six minutes per song for our meetings. Once you add in spontaneous contributions, a time of prayer, or a Scripture reading, four songs can easily fill thirty minutes.

PLAN FOR THE LONG HAUL

Most of us breathe a sigh of contented relief when Sunday's meeting is over. The band played well, people seemed to be engaged with God, and the new song went over great.

What we usually forget is that the clock immediately starts ticking for next Sunday. We put off that realization for as long as possible, especially if we're the only worship leader in the church.

But eventually it hits us: Sunday's coming. Again.

How do we break out of the rut of always feeling behind in our preparation?

The first thing we can do is place our faith in God's promises rather than in our preparation. He's the faithful one, and he's more concerned than we are about people worshiping him next Sunday.

But it also helps to keep the big picture in view. In that sense, worship planning is similar to preaching. The greatest effects are cumulative, not tied to what happens on any given Sunday.

One of the ways we've tried to keep the big picture in view is to keep (and regularly review) a record of the songs we sing. I've done this for years. I can do a quick search to see when we last used a song and how often. Software programs are available now that provide this information and more. But if you can't afford them, I've found that a Word document works fine.

Reviewing your songs can answer important questions:

• Are we aware of and emphasizing Christ's finished work each time we sing?

• Are God's character and works clearly proclaimed in our songs?

• Are the lyrics we sing biblically faithful and doctrinally sound?

• Are we worshiping a triune God in song, seeking to glorify the Father by honoring the Son in the power of the Spirit?

• Are we falling into a musical or thematic rut?

• Are we doing any songs too frequently or too rarely?

• Do we have a healthy blend of deep and simpler songs? (Simple songs are like dessert; trying to live on them can result in malnutrition.)

• Are there any songs we used to sing that we should start doing again? (It can help to keep a list of songs you'd like to bring back.)

Some songs are worth singing more than others. Since music is meant to help us remember God's Word, it makes sense to do the right songs often enough that they become a part of our collective memory. For that reason, when introducing a new song it's a good idea to repeat it once or twice over the next few weeks.

We've also planned ahead for two or more Sundays at once. This may seem like extra work, but in the end you actually save time. It allows us to schedule repeating songs, special creative elements, and songs we want to introduce.

When we sketch out multiple weeks, we refine the specifics as each Sunday approaches. We'll often plan more than we actually end up doing. But having a general idea of what we want to do makes the final planning easier and helps us keep the song diet of the church more healthy.

THE TWENTY YEAR RULE

A good measure of how we're doing in long-term planning is what I call the Twenty Year Rule. If someone was born in our church and grew up singing our songs over the course of twenty years, how well would they know God?

Would these songs give them a biblical and comprehensive view of God, or would they be exposed only to certain aspects of his nature and works?

Would they learn that God is holy, wise, omnipotent, and sovereign? Would they know God as Creator and Sustainer? Would they understand the glory and centrality of the gospel?

Or would they think worship is about music, and not much more?

May God give us grace to lead worship and choose our songs in a way that reflects his care, wisdom, and faithfulness.

chapter 14

. . . THEREBY MOTIVATING THE GATHERED CHURCH . . .

About fifteen years ago I was leading a small, unresponsive youth group in worship. About twenty of us were gathered in the home of one of the teens. It wasn't going well. No one seemed interested, and the singing bordered on dismal.

Setting an example as the "lead worshiper," I tried closing my eyes. When I opened them, I noticed no one followed my lead. I sang more loudly. That only caused a few of the kids to drop out altogether. I started a fast song everyone knew. Still no change.

Finally I stopped playing. That got their attention. I tried to cover my irritation but didn't do a very good job. In tense, measured tones, I said, "Do you have any idea who you're singing to?"

Pause.

"How can you stand there with your hands in your pockets and apathetic looks on your faces and claim to be worshiping God? This isn't worship. This is pathetic. You should be ashamed of yourselves. Now, let's see if we can't worship God the way he deserves."

Textbook leadership. As you might expect, this didn't exactly inspire any of them to a greater passion for God. But later I was inspired to ask their forgiveness.

A FEW WRONG WAYS TO MOTIVATE

What do you do when things aren't going well?

One of the greatest challenges worship leaders face is knowing how to lead people who seem unresponsive or unaffected. Before I share some things I've learned since that evening with the youth group, here are three ways we *don't* want to respond.

First, we don't want to demand that people worship God. "I want *every one of you* to raise your hands now. Come on, people! Sing louder. I can't *heeeeaaaar you*!"

These kinds of unwise, theologically uninformed comments don't inspire anyone. God never commands us to praise him without including reasons for doing so. Psalm 117 is just one example of many:

> Praise the LORD, all nations!
> Extol him, all peoples!
> For great is his steadfast love toward us,
> and the faithfulness of the LORD endures forever.
> Praise the LORD!

Sandwiched between two commands to praise the Lord are two distinct reasons for doing so: His steadfast love is great, and his faithfulness endures forever.

When I expect people to instantly respond to my directions without giving them biblical reasons, I'm expecting more than God does.

Second, we don't want to motivate people to worship God through manipulation.

I can try to manipulate them through music style (*That new reggae version of "Forever" will really get people on their feet*), insincere emotion (*Hold on a moment while I wipe this sweat, uh, I mean, tear from my eye*), mysticism (*Let's close our eyes and act like something really significant is happening, though no one's sure what it is*), and performance (*That electric guitar solo before the modulation on verse 4 is guaranteed to get people worshiping*).

Third, we don't want to project false guilt onto the church, as I did with those teenagers years ago.

I attended a conference once where the leader scolded us at a morning session. He said a window to heaven had been opened for us the previous night, and we didn't go through it. We came close but didn't succeed.

I don't think his desire was to make everyone feel like failures, but that was the net result. We just weren't doing enough to experience God's presence or to please him. Actually, I wasn't sure exactly what we were failing to do. I just knew I felt bad.

HELPING PEOPLE MAKE CONNECTIONS

I've been asked, "If you're leading worship and the people don't seem motivated to respond in worship, is that your fault?"

The ultimate answer is no. Every Christian is responsible to worship God regardless of what we're going through or who's leading us. A worshiper worships God.

But leaders can do things to make it easier or harder for them.

When people aren't responding to our leadership, our own response reveals what we're trusting in. If we merely raise our voices, turn up the volume, or flash the lights, we're no longer depending on the means God has given us to exalt him—the work of Christ and the power of the Holy Spirit. When I'm leading doctrinally rich, passionate songs, and people don't seem to be getting it, I need to help them understand how these truths relate to their lives.

Only God can illuminate a worshiper's heart. But he often uses means to do that. And three important means are my example, my exhortations, and my encouragement.

My Example

If I'm magnifying the greatness of God in Jesus Christ, I'm in the best place to motivate others to join me. They'll see it on my face, hear it in my voice, and observe it in my physical expression.

As we noted earlier from Psalm 34:5, "Those who look to him are radiant." When I'm anxious about whether a transition is going to work or worried about looking bad or wondering why the drummer is slowing down, it's going to show on my face. It will be obvious I'm not looking to the Lord.

Hopefully people aren't watching me the entire time they're praising God, but I never know when they'll happen to glance in my direction. When they do, I want my example to inspire them to look to the Lord as well.

The issue of example also applies to other musicians on the team. When they appear uninvolved or concerned only with the music, they miss an opportunity to encourage the congregation. That's why I ask instrumentalists to sing as often as possible. It helps them remember who we're focusing on.

The issue here isn't exuberance as much as authenticity. D. A. Carson put it like this:

> Some who publicly lead the corporate meetings of the people of God
> merely perform; others are engrossed in the worship of God. Some merely

sing; some put on a great show of being involved; but others transparently worship God.[1]

Which describes you? Are you simply mouthing lyrics? Do you only pretend to be engaged, moving your hands and bowing your head at the right moments to look "worshipful"? Or are you seeking to be a transparent worshiper—naturally, genuinely, and obviously demonstrating a desire to exalt Jesus Christ? If we want the church to be inspired by our leadership, we have to begin with an authentic example.

Exhortations

As a worship leader, I'm not simply playing music—I'm leading. So exhortations and other encouragements to worship play a vital role in what I do. I've found two kinds of exhortations helpful. The first is a more extended comment between two songs, as I described in the last chapter. The other is briefer and comes while we're singing a song, usually in between lines.

Have you ever noticed how easily your mind can drift when you sing? I can be belting out amazing, God-centered lyrics while thinking about what's for lunch, the movie I saw Friday night, or absolutely nothing at all. On the outside I appear to be fully committed to worshiping God. On the inside I'm doing anything but.

The same can be true for those we're leading. How can we help them focus on the words we're singing?

At the very least, I have to be thinking about them myself as I sing. So I ask myself questions like these: *Why is this true? What difference does it make? What if this wasn't true? What's not being said here? What does this word mean? Why does this line follow the last one?*

As I answer these questions specifically, it helps me interact more with what I'm singing and has a greater impact on my soul. As I lead, I'll simply share some of those answers with the congregation through words that I speak or sing.

For instance, Tim Hughes's song "Here I Am to Worship" opens with these lines: "Light of the world, you stepped down into darkness, opened my eyes, let me see." Then there's a pause. The words go on to explain what we now see: "Beauty that made this heart adore you." During that break I have some options. I may want to connect the lines by saying or singing, "You're so beautiful." I might be reminded of where I was before Jesus saved me and sing, "I was so blind." Or I could draw attention to *how* God opened my eyes and sing out, "Through the gospel" or "By your Spirit." In making these comments, I'm seeking to direct people's thoughts to the meaning of what we're singing by expanding on it.

Hymns are more challenging to add thoughts to because they have more words and fewer breaks between lines. But we can still encourage more thoughtful involvement through our comments.

One of my favorite lines in the hymn "Praise to the Lord, the Almighty" is this: "Ponder anew what the Almighty can do." What an invitation! We gather not only to remember what God *has* done, but to anticipate what he *will* do. So after that line I might call out a jubilant "Yes!" to accent what we're being asked to do. I might also say, "We trust you." Or "You're so good!" Or "Beyond all we could ask!"

Interjecting phrases like this takes thought and practice. It can easily be overdone, done poorly, or done in a way that draws attention to the leader. It requires finding open spaces in the song so you're not competing with the congregation. If they're singing while you're talking, they won't be able to hear you, and the effect will be minimal or counterproductive. But done well and with genuine emotion, brief exhortations can be an effective way to motivate people's devotion to the Savior.

Encouragement

If the people I'm leading are Christians, born again by the Spirit of God, I can be confident that somewhere in their hearts is a desire to proclaim and cherish the glories of God in Jesus Christ.

If I don't believe that, I'll be tempted to think I have to convince or coerce them into worshiping in spirit and truth. I'll be leading out of unbelief, not faith. My comments will lack grace. I'll be easily discouraged. Or if things go well, I'll be proud.

Many things can hinder a congregation's response. Some people went to bed at three A.M. Others had an argument with their spouse that morning or came expecting to be entertained. Maybe a few are about to lose their job or just found out they have cancer or can't resolve a conflict with a friend.

Whatever their situation, our goal is to impress on them what God has done in Jesus Christ, what he has promised to do, and what a difference this makes in their lives.

Thank God, we're not alone in this task. The Spirit is already working in every situation to expose their need for God's grace, mercy, and truth. The Holy Spirit is the one who makes us worshipers of God (1 Corinthians 12:3; Philippians 3:3). He has been sent to glorify Jesus and is actively working in our hearts to accomplish that goal (John 15:26).

If I trust the Spirit's activity, I don't have to be defensive, angry, or frustrated when people seem disinterested. Rather than focusing on their apparent lack of response, I can draw attention to what God is already doing.

I might say something like this:

"Some of us this morning are going through significant trials. You're hurting, discouraged, or depressed. And the truth is, it's difficult for you to sing these songs with any joy or meaning.

"But this is exactly where God wants you to be. He's arranged the circumstances of your life to make you aware of how much you need him and how eager he is to be your strength. He is so kind! He gave his Son to pay for your sins and bring you back to himself. He has shown you mercy instead of the wrath you deserved, and you've been adopted into his family. Now he's using everything you're going through to make you more like Jesus. He's a faithful Father who will never leave you or forsake you. Let's remember his mercy as we sing this next song . . ."

We'll never overcome self-centeredness, self-exaltation, or self-pity by staying focused on ourselves. That only exacerbates the problem. We're still the center of attention! But when we gather to worship God, he's the center of attention. And the more we encourage others that God is already working in us (Philippians 2:13), the more easily they'll remember.

THE GATHERED CHURCH

Over the years God has allowed me to lead worship in a variety of contexts, large and small. Living rooms. Auditoriums. Civic centers. Outdoor festivals. Each time it's been an immense privilege. I'm grateful that God uses events of every imaginable size and shape to bring glory to his name.

But nothing compares with leading worship in my local church.

Scripture tells us that the church is "God's building," God's "temple," the "body" of Christ, "the household of God." We are "living stones . . . being built as a spiritual house" (1 Corinthians 3:9b; Ephesians 2:21–22; 1 Corinthians 12:12; Ephesians 2:19; 1 Peter 2:5). All those metaphors certainly apply to the worldwide church. But their most immediate and practical application is to the local church—the Christians I'm joined with day by day, week by week, year by year. And gathering together with them should be one of the highlights, if not *the* highlight, of my week.

On Sundays God wants us to do more than sing songs together and have wonderful worship experiences. He wants to knit the fabric of our lives together. For many, church has become all about me—what *I'm* learning, what *I'm* seeking, what *I'm* desperate for, what *I* need, how *I've* been affected, what *I* can do. We see ourselves as isolated individuals all seeking personal encounters with God, wherever we can find them.

Sadly, this reflects our individualistic, me-obsessed culture. Rather than seeing ourselves as part of a worship community, we become worship consumers. We want worship on demand, served up in our own way, at our own time, and with our own music.

How do we counter that?

David Peterson tells us:

> Vitality and meaning will not be restored to Christian gatherings until those who lead and those who participate can recover a biblical perspective on their meetings, seeing them in relation to God's total plan and purpose for his people.[2]

Do you have a biblical perspective on your meetings? Are you helping people see how they relate to God's total plan and purpose for his people? In other words, are you attracting an audience, or are you building a worshiping community?

A worshiping community is made up of individuals whose lives are centered around the Savior they worship together each week. A worshiping community expects to encounter God's presence not only on Sunday morning but every day. A worshiping community recognizes that passionate times of singing God's praise flow from and lead to passionate lives lived for the glory of Jesus Christ.

In the next three chapters we'll look at how God wants to use you to build that kind of worshiping community for his glory.

chapter 15

. . . TO PROCLAIM THE GOSPEL . . .

Proclamation—declaring what's true about God—is often underrated. Why proclaim scriptural truths we've previously heard and already know?

Because we forget. We lose track of who God is and what he's done.

Proclamation helps set our minds and hearts right. It reminds us of the convictions and realities that should guide and govern our daily lives.

To proclaim is to announce something officially or publicly. We aren't keeping a secret. We want others to hear.

It also means declaring something important with the appropriate degree of emphasis. We're saying, *This* really matters. To me and to you. To everyone.

Biblical worship involves proclamation and leads to proclaiming God's truth with our lives. We're doing more than emoting or having a "worship experience." We're declaring why God is so great, what he has accomplished, and all that he has promised. We all need to be reminded, and proclamation helps us remember.

SAVED TO PROCLAIM

Peter tells us that we have been saved "that [we] may proclaim the excellencies of him who called [us] out of darkness into his marvelous light" (1 Peter 2:9). We're meant to fulfill this command both in our meetings and in our lives.

People come into our churches proclaiming all sorts of things with their words and actions. Through close-fisted giving, some are asserting how much their own personal wealth matters. Others, by their complaining, are declaring that personal comfort matters. Teens in the latest fashions may be proclaiming that being cool matters. Others confirm through their smiles or frowns that their musical preferences matter.

But we want each of them to leave proclaiming this: *The gospel of Jesus Christ matters.*

CONNECTING THE GOSPEL TO LIFE

God's Word commands us to "proclaim his salvation day after day" (Psalm 96:2, NIV). Proclaiming this salvation should be a daily practice and preoccupation for as long as we live.

If that's not happening in our churches, it could be because people don't understand how Jesus' dying for their sins affects the rest of their life. They're unclear on how to apply the gospel to their lives. Maybe they see the gospel as something only for unbelievers or new Christians. They're fine with singing about it in church, but they don't understand how it applies to the rest of the week.

It's our privilege to help people see how the gospel functions in every part of their lives. Here are some of those connections we can help them make as we worship God together.

The Gospel and Our Sin

> For I delivered to you as of first importance what I also received: that Christ died for our sins in accordance with the Scriptures, that he was buried, that he was raised on the third day in accordance with the Scriptures. (1 Corinthians 15:3–4)

What was "of first importance" to Paul is also of first importance to us and the people we lead each week: "*Christ died for our sins.*"

It's not enough to merely sing about Christ dying for our sins. We want to help people understand the benefits of what God accomplished through that act.

His Word tells us directly, "There is therefore now no condemnation for those who are in Christ Jesus" (Romans 8:1). If Christ died for my sins, that means I'm no longer under God's wrath. I don't have to live with the burden of low-grade guilt. I'm completely and finally forgiven. I have been declared righteous in the sight of God—not on the basis of my own works, but on the basis of Christ's righteousness that has been imputed to me.

This is what it means to be justified. There's nothing more we can do to earn God's forgiveness. God calls us to believe that the death of Christ was sufficient to pay for our sins. Every one of them. No matter how many times we're tempted to believe otherwise. Charitie Bancroft expressed it well in her hymn, "Before the Throne of God Above," set to music by Vikki Cook.

> *When Satan tempts me to despair,*
> *And tells me of the guilt within,*
> *Upward I look and see Him there,*
> *Who made an end of all my sin.*
> *Because the sinless Savior died,*
> *My sinful soul is counted free.*
> *For God the Just is satisfied*
> *To look on Him and pardon me.*[1]

The Gospel and Our Suffering

I've had the privilege of knowing families who have experienced chronic pain or severe trials and responded with humility and faith. I worship God with some of them every week.

There's Luke and Kriscinda, whose three-year-old son Micah finally succumbed to an aggressive brain tumor. There's Steve and Mary, whose son Ian was in a car accident on the way to work and has been in a coma for months. There's Ken, who lost his wife to cancer. There's Drew and Diane, who have cared for their severely disabled son Reid for over twenty years, feeding him and overseeing his every need.

I can't fully relate to all that these dear saints have gone through. But I know this: There are probably people in your congregation going through similar trials. And in the midst of their suffering, they'll be tempted to doubt God's goodness, question his sovereignty, and mistrust his wisdom.

But God has shown the greatness of his sovereignty, love, and wisdom in the cross. There at Calvary, God worked his sovereign purposes, even through the willful actions of evil men, to display the glory of his grace, resulting in the redemption of countless undeserving rebels.

Our sins have been forgiven. We've been bought by the blood of the Savior. We've become part of God's family, destined to become like Christ. God is now using our trials to accomplish his good and redemptive purposes in us (Romans 8:28–29).

That knowledge assures us that our suffering is never purposeless, blind, unfair, or random. God is working out his perfect plan for us, and he will never let us endure hardships without giving us the grace to endure them.

We can rejoice in our trials because we know that God is using them to prepare us for the glory to be revealed in us (Romans 8:18). We can be encouraged that our sufferings make us run to God for strength. We can thank God that in the midst of adversity he is working out his gracious plans for us (2 Corinthians 4:17–18).

It should also humble us when we consider that the Savior is the only innocent one to ever suffer. He's the only one without sin, without blemish, without fault. *We* deserved the punishment he received. The question in our hearts then won't be, "Why am I suffering?" but "Why don't I suffer more?"

The answer is that we have a Savior who "has borne our griefs and carried our sorrows" (Isaiah 53:4) forever. Jon Payne's song "Before the Cross" drives this truth home:

> *My Savior's sacrifice paid for all my sin*
> *So in my suffering I look to the cross again*
> *No need, no want, no trial, no pain*
> *Can compare to this*
> *The wrath of God, once meant for me*
> *Was all spent on Him.*[2]

The Gospel and Our Sanctification

How can singing songs of praise together help us become more like Christ?

By reminding us that it's the gospel that changes us. Peter tells us, "He himself bore our sins in his body on the tree, that we might die to sin and live to righteousness" (1 Peter 2:24). In the gospel, God has given us hope, motivation, and power for change.

The gospel assures us that not only have our sins been forgiven, but our bondage to sin has been broken. We have died with Christ and have been raised with him to new life. Therefore we can be confident that God will complete the work he began in us (Philippians 1:6). We've been freed to obey God in the power of his Spirit. We're no longer our own—we've been "bought with a price" (1 Corinthians 6:20).

Knowing our sins are forgiven through the gospel also persuades us of God's mercy and motivates us to live in obedience to his commands. How can we not want to please the one who became sin for us "so that in him we might become the righteousness of God" (2 Corinthians 5:21)?

Finally, the forgiveness we receive through the shed blood of Christ is the foundation for grace-enabled effort to pursue holiness. It protects us from legalism. C. J. Mahaney points out that legalism makes us think we can "achieve forgiveness *from* God and justification *before* God through obedience *to* God."[3] But we are already forgiven and justified through the substitutionary death of the Savior. All our hard work is now rooted in and fueled by the gospel. As we work and aim to do our best, we recognize that we can do this only because it's Christ who strengthens us. He redeemed us "from all lawlessness" to make us people "who are zealous for good works" (Titus 2:13–14).

Proclaiming this gospel of grace with faith protects us from placing false hope in our own efforts or thinking they'll in some way earn merit in God's eyes. I try to draw attention to this transforming grace in the song "Grace Unmeasured":

> *Grace abounding, strong and true,*
> *That makes me long to be like You,*
> *That turns me from my selfish pride*
> *To love the cross on which You died;*
> *Grace unending, all my days*
> *You'll give me strength to run this race,*
> *And when my years on earth are through,*
> *The praise will all belong to You.*[4]

The Gospel and Broken Relationships

We've been freed from the guilt and bondage of sin, but the presence of sin remains. Which means we'll eventually sin against each other.

And if we don't find people inside the church to fight with, there are plenty on the outside.

Most of the time we resolve our differences and move on. But occasionally a relationship goes sour and ends up consuming our thoughts, energy, and emotions. We spend countless hours replaying conversations, trying to assign blame, and thinking about our "rights." And all the time a knot of bitterness tightens in our hearts. We don't see how we could possibly forgive the person who has offended us.

Worshiping God together provides us with the opportunity to remember the One whom we *all* have offended.

We have sinned against an infinitely righteous God. The debt we've incurred is one we could never pay. We have fallen short of the glory of God—completely, consistently, willingly. We deserve God's just punishment.

Yet God designed a way to place our punishment on his Son. Perfect justice and perfect mercy kissed at the cross. We, the guilty ones, now stand forgiven through Christ's blood. How can we not forgive those who have sinned against us?

In Colossians 3 Paul describes the kinds of relationships God has called us to in the church. Relationships characterized by compassion, kindness, humility, meekness, and patience. And right before he instructs us to sing psalms, hymns, and spiritual songs to one another, he gives this command: "as the Lord has forgiven you, so you also must forgive" (Colossians 3:13).

The gospel powerfully reorients our view of relational conflict. No offense against us will ever be as serious as our offenses against God. If God has forgiven our great sins, how can we not extend mercy to those who have sinned against us?

PROCLAIMING THE GOSPEL TOGETHER

The world is constantly telling us lies: "God doesn't exist." "It's all about you." "Sin has no consequences." "This is all there is." "The more you own, the happier you'll be."

In the face of these lies, we gather as the church to proclaim the truth. We gather to declare—to ourselves, to each other, and to God—what we *know* to be eternal reality. There is one God, who is sovereign over the universe and every detail of our lives. We have rebelled against him. He sent his Son to die in our place for our sins. And through Jesus Christ we have forgiveness and peace with God.

There are many things we can proclaim during and after a time of corporate worship. God's glory is unending, and his perfections are infinite. But the fuel of our praise will always be the gospel of Christ who has redeemed us and brought us to God.

As we help people understand the relationship between God's love for us in Christ and our daily struggles and challenges, their love and appreciation for the gospel will grow. The result will be a joyful, gospel-centered community that demonstrates and proclaims the good news of God's grace to a lost and hopeless world: God's grace forgives! God's grace redeems! God's grace restores!

PROCLAIMING THE GOSPEL TO YOURSELF

As worship leaders, there's no more important or fruitful way we can serve our churches than this: immersing ourselves in the riches of the gospel every day. I begin most days by reminding myself of the gospel. I know that unless I bring to mind my need for redemption and God's provision for me in Jesus Christ, I'll be unable to help others value him above all else.[5]

"Preaching the gospel to yourself" is a phrase I first ran across in *The Discipline of Grace* by Jerry Bridges. And I've observed the reality of it for years in the life of my good friend C. J. Mahaney. In *Living the Cross Centered Life* he writes:

> Reminding ourselves of the gospel is the most important daily habit we can establish. If the gospel is the most vital news in the world, and if salvation by grace is the defining truth of our existence, we should create ways to immerse ourselves in these truths every day. No days off allowed.[6]

Is the gospel more precious to you now than the day you were converted? Or do you often find yourself taking off days, or even weeks, from it? Do you want to move on to supposedly more "advanced" elements of the Christian life such as discipleship, evangelism, spiritual warfare, and helping the poor?

Don't miss this. Nothing should ever displace or obscure the centrality of the gospel in our worship.

And nothing will bring us or the people we lead greater joy.

chapter 16

. . . TO CHERISH GOD'S PRESENCE . . .

Conversations about God's presence can be confusing. One web site I visited advertised a book that will teach you to "sing down the presence and power of God." Can we actually do that? What's the real connection between music and God's presence?

If God is present everywhere, why are we more aware of his presence at certain times?

Is congregational worship the primary setting where we should expect to encounter God's presence?

And how do we actually obey the command to "seek his presence continually" (Psalm 105:4)?

Inadequate answers to these questions can lead to emotionalism, superstition, discouragement, or worse. But wrong responses don't obscure the reality that God does indeed dwell in the midst of his people.

The reality is that if we understand God's presence rightly, it's something we'll enjoy, pursue, and anticipate. It's something we'll cherish.

ENJOYING GOD'S PROMISED PRESENCE

Scripture reveals the reality—both comforting and sobering—that God is present everywhere.

"Where shall I go from your Spirit?" David asks. "Or where shall I flee from your presence? If I ascend to heaven, you are there! If I make my bed in Sheol, you are there!" (Psalm 139:7–8). That pretty much covers it.

But while God is present everywhere, he also chooses sometimes to localize his presence, as he did so unexpectedly for Moses in a burning bush in the desert (Exodus 3:2).

And now, through his Spirit, he promises to be present in his people. Because of our union with Christ, the church is God's "dwelling place" on earth, the new "temple," the place where God lives (Ephesians 2:19–22). Because this temple is where the Lord chooses to reveal his presence, we should expect that when we meet in his name, he'll be with us.

And he is.

He has promised to be present in our fellowship. Jesus promised his presence "where two or three are gathered in my name" (Matthew 18:20).

God is also with us when we sing his praise. The Holy Spirit inspires our psalms, hymns, and spiritual songs that we sing with each other (Ephesians 5:18–19).

God reveals his presence when his Word is preached. The Bible isn't mere abstract truth. It is "living and active, sharper than any two-edged sword" (Hebrews 4:12). No doubt you've experienced the piercing effects of God's Word yourself.

At a conference a few years ago, I heard a message from 1 Timothy 4:16 on the importance of guarding our lives and doctrine closely. I felt as though God himself reached into my heart to convict me of laziness, unbelief, and pride. As the speaker finished, tears were streaming down my face. I didn't move. I wanted to freeze the moment to ponder the seriousness of God's call on my life.

No doubt about it, I thought. *God is definitely here.*

As a worship leader, I want to prepare people's faith for encountering God when the musicians sit down and the pastor steps up to preach. It's one of the most momentous events of our week.

God also has promised to be with us as we celebrate the Lord's Supper. What we're celebrating is more than a reminder or a mere symbol. The risen Savior is present with us through faith as we remember his work of reconciliation. In a profound way we're being freshly strengthened in our union with him and with each other.

These are just some of the times God has promised to be present with his people.

There are, of course, times when we become unexpectedly aware of the Lord's presence. Maybe a sudden wave of peace comes over us. Or an irrepressible joy rises up from the depths of our soul. Or we experience the sweet sting of the Holy Spirit's conviction.

In those moments has God's presence come down to us? Have we been led into God's presence? No. God was present from the beginning. We've just become more aware of it.

D. A. Carson observes how "we often *feel* encouraged and edified" as we engage in corporate worship activities. The result is that "we are renewed in our awareness of God's love and God's truth, and we are encouraged to respond with adoration and action." And he points out something we must not forget: "Objectively, what brings us into the presence of God is the death and resurrection of the Lord Jesus." He warns that if we start thinking it's our worship activities that bring God's presence near, "it will not be long before we think of such worship as being meritorious, or efficacious, or the like."[1]

A similar warning from Harold Best applies specifically to worship leaders:

> Christian musicians must be particularly cautious. They can create the impression that God is more present when music is being made than when it is not; that worship is more possible with music than without it; and that God might possibly depend on its presence before appearing.[2]

So what's the real difference between actually experiencing God's presence and simply being moved by a creative arrangement, a stunning vocal performance, a massive choir, or a beautiful melody?

It's hard to tell sometimes. God can use our musical gifts to affect people emotionally, but these never mediate his presence. Only Jesus can do that.

But the fact remains that God has promised to dwell in the midst of his people. And that's a reality he wants us to fully cherish.

PURSUING GOD'S ACTIVE PRESENCE

Pondering the reality of God's presence should lead us to consider the person and work of the Holy Spirit. Wayne Grudem shows from Scripture how one of the Spirit's "primary purposes in the new covenant age is to manifest the presence of God, to give indications that make the presence of God known."[3] And Gordon Fee adds, "For Paul, the presence of the Spirit, as an experienced and living reality, was the crucial matter for Christian life, from beginning to end."[4]

God reveals his presence not only through the means I've mentioned above but also through spiritual gifts, which we're told to "earnestly desire" (1 Corinthians 14:1). How do our spiritual gifts fit into the Holy Spirit's making God's presence an "experienced and living reality"?[5]

We're told in 1 Corinthians that the Spirit gives manifestations of his presence for "the common good" of the church (1 Corinthians 12:7). As we see and hear evidences of the Spirit's activity in our meetings, we become freshly aware that God is really with us and desires to build up, strengthen, and encourage the church through his people.

But as we saw in Chapter 10, we must be faithful to respond to whatever ways the Spirit empowers us to serve others. Don't hold back because you're afraid you'll fail or look stupid. If you mess up, you'll be humbled, which is a plus in God's eyes.

For many years I've sung spontaneous songs during corporate worship that I believe are a form of prophecy. They're similar to a spoken prophetic impression from the Lord, only they're sung, they rhyme, and they are often sung "from God to us." I've never believed for a moment that the words I sing are "word for word" from God. That's called Scripture. But these songs seem to consistently communicate in verse the Lord's heart for a particular individual, group, or situation.[6]

The effect over the years has been an increased awareness of God's care for his people. Early on I was nagged by questions that kept me from stepping out in this gift. *What if I get to the middle of a line and blank out? What if people think I'm trying to draw attention to myself? What if no one is affected?* Eventually I realized that my questions would keep me from ever responding to what I thought were the Spirit's promptings. Since I decided to simply be faithful, God has given me hundreds of songs to encourage his people.

Don't misunderstand me. You don't have to sing spontaneous songs to be used by God. God's Spirit is at work in a variety of ways. He might suddenly bring a thought or Scripture to mind that affects the direction of the meeting. You might be led to pause and lead in prayer for a particular category or need. We want to be listening in the midst of leading, "leaning forward" to hear what the Spirit might be directing us to do as we care for God's people.

We honor the Son and bring glory to the Father by allowing the Spirit to work powerfully through us.

It's important to realize that many spontaneous moments in public are the fruit of consistent preparation in private. As I study God's Word in my personal devotions, I'll be more prone to remember it in public. Praying over the lyrics before a meeting prepares me for listening more carefully as I'm leading the church.

Pursuing the Spirit's active presence means involving others as well. At our church any one of our pastors might offer a spontaneous impression. Often they do. We also encourage contributions from the congregation by placing a microphone at the front of the auditorium. This is overseen by one or more pastors who review each contribution for content, appropriateness, and attitude before it's shared.

When done responsibly and humbly, this is one more way we can lead the church in cherishing God's presence in our midst.

ANTICIPATING GOD'S UNVEILED PRESENCE

I've had the privilege of participating in meetings where the magnificence of God's glory, or a profound awareness of his mercy, made it difficult to stay standing. When that happens, I'm always aware of one thing: This is just the smallest glimpse, the faintest whisper, of what awaits us in heaven.

No meeting in this life will ever rival the splendor of heaven.

The Bible speaks of heaven as a place where God is uniquely present. "For Christ has entered . . . into heaven itself, now to appear in *the presence of God* on our behalf" (Hebrews 9:24, emphasis added). Although God is present everywhere, heaven is different.

Wayne Grudem writes:

> We might find it misleading to say that God is "more present" in heaven than anywhere else, but it would not be misleading to say that God is present in a special way in heaven, present especially there to bless and to show forth his glory. We could also say that God manifests his presence more fully in heaven than elsewhere.[7]

In the new heavens and the new earth, there will be no temple in which to worship God, no structure or locality that represents his presence more than another, because God and the Lamb will be the temple (Revelation 21:22). We will live, breathe, eat, sing, work, and rest forever in the Holy of Holies, where God's presence always dwells.

Heaven is our home, but we aren't there yet. The best is still to come. In this life our experience of God's presence is limited by what God shows us and what we can perceive. We sometimes recognize that God is near, but normally we don't experience it in any pronounced way. In heaven things will be very different. God's complete and immediate presence will be everywhere. And we will cherish it like never before.

Most of us don't have heaven in mind when we worship God on earth. You might look around on Sunday morning and think, "Well, my church sure doesn't *look* like heaven. Babies are crying, the musicians aren't play-ing together, and people seem bored." But the more we realize where we're headed, the more we'll want to look and act like heavenly worshipers.

Allen Ross points us in the right direction:

> If we even begin to comprehend the risen Christ in all his glory, or faintly hear the heavenly choirs that surround the throne with their anthems of praise, or imagine what life in the presence of the Lord will be like, then we can never again be satisfied with worship as usual. We will always be striving to make our worship fit for glory; and we will always be aware that our efforts, no matter how good and noble, are still of this world and not yet of that one.[8]

Very soon you and I will be standing before the majesty and glory of God. We'll take our place among the throngs of heaven, made up of people from every tribe, language, people, and tongue who have been purchased by the blood of the Lamb. We'll understand that our lives on earth were only the cover and title page to what lies ahead. We'll begin "Chapter One of the Great Story," as C. S. Lewis writes, "which goes on forever; in which every chapter is better than the one before."[9]

We don't know when that day will come. It might be tomorrow. It might be decades from now. But it *will* come. We'll close our eyes momentarily, then open them up again—and we'll be home!

> *And I heard a loud voice from the throne saying, "Behold, the dwelling place of God is with man. He will dwell with them, and they will be his people, and God himself will be with them as their God. He will wipe away every tear from their eyes, and death shall be no more, neither shall there be mourning, nor crying, nor pain anymore, for the former things have passed away." (Revelation 21:3–4)*

Amen. Come, Lord Jesus, come.

chapter 17

. . . AND TO LIVE FOR GOD'S GLORY

"Christians aren't perfect," the old saying goes, "just for-given." But that's only partially true.

Yes, there's unfathomable encouragement in knowing our sins have been completely paid for. But we're forgiven so that we might be different. We're justified so that we might be sanctified. Although we'll never be perfect in this life, God is committed to making us like Jesus (Romans 8:29).

Paul tells us:

And we all, with unveiled face, beholding the glory of the Lord, are being transformed into the same image from one degree of glory to another. For this comes from the Lord who is the Spirit. (2 Corinthians 3:18)

As we behold the Lord's glory, the Spirit of God is at work to *transform* us into the image of God's Son. This is one of the primary reasons we gather—to behold and be changed.

What change should we look for in the lives of those we lead? How do we evaluate whether our meetings are actually helping people? As we exalt the nature and works of God in our minds, affections, and wills, what should it produce?

I want to suggest six ways that worshiping God on Sunday should transform the way we live the rest of the week.

WORSHIPING GOD SHOULD MAKE US HUMBLE

If we see even a glimpse of the glory and splendor of God, it will produce a genuine humility in our hearts. That was the response of Moses, the Israelites, Isaiah, Jeremiah, Peter, the apostle John, and countless others in Scripture who beheld God's majesty. There's nothing about encountering God that should exalt *us*.

One reason we so often fail to be humbled by worship is that we focus on other things and end up obscuring God's glory. It would be like visiting the Grand Canyon and foolishly being enthralled with parking signs, souvenir shops, and the railings. We enjoy a picnic lunch, toss a football around, and leave—happy but unaffected by the glory of God's creation.

No one does that. We never allow the surroundings to distract us from the magnificent splendor of the canyon itself. And the effect is always the same. Suddenly we feel small, helpless, insignificant. As John Piper says, people never leave the Grand Canyon more in awe of themselves.

That's why it's so important that we worship God through the lens of the gospel. Nothing humbles us more than worshiping at the foot of the cross. No thought attacks the root of our pride like realizing that God himself had to pay for our rebellion against him.

I am a worshiper of God because Jesus died and rose to make me one, not because I earned the right to be one.

If worshiping God leaves us thinking more highly of ourselves, we've turned biblical worship on its head. Worship in general, and corporate worship in particular, is meant to make us humble.

We've found lyrics like these helpful for cultivating Christ-exalting, self-effacing attitudes in our hearts:

A debtor to mercy alone,
Of covenant mercy I sing.
I come with Your righteousness on,
My humble offering to bring.
The judgments of Your holy law
With me can have nothing to do;
My Savior's obedience and blood
Hide all my transgressions from view.[1]

WORSHIPING GOD SHOULD MAKE US SECURE

A few years ago the community where I live was terrorized by mysterious murders that took place in ordinary circumstances of everyday life. People were struck down by a sniper while they engaged in everyday activities such as filling up a gas tank, mowing a lawn, or catching a bus on the way to work.

For three weeks the fear and tension in the surrounding areas was palpable. People would zigzag as they walked through a parking lot, hoping no one could get a good shot at them.

Eventually the snipers were caught. Everyone breathed a sigh of relief.

As we planned for the Sunday meetings during that time, we wanted to specifically remind our church that God was in absolute control. More than that, we wanted them to know that God's Word, rather than the media, was the best way to find out how things were going. So we sang songs such as "Blessed Be Your Name" by Matt Redman and Edward Mote's "The Solid Rock."

After the terrible tsunami disaster in December 2005, I added a new chorus to William Cowper's hymn "God Moves in a Mysterious Way" to help the church not only proclaim the truth about God's sovereignty but to respond in faith to it:

So God we trust in you;
O God, we trust in you;
When tears are great and comforts few
We hope in mercies ever new;
We trust in you.[2]

The foundation of our security in God is not our preparation and plans, nor what others can provide for our protection. Our security doesn't ultimately rest in our alarm system, our military might, the police, or the stock market. Our security ultimately rests in the unchanging love of God, most gloriously displayed at Calvary.

One of the reasons Christians often question God's protection and love is that they fail to keep the crucified and risen Savior at the center of their worship. The comfort and strength that corporate worship instills in us is more than the result of soothing music or a familiar setting. It's the reminder that nothing in heaven, hell, or in between can "separate us from the love of God in Christ Jesus our Lord" (Romans 8:39).

WORSHIPING GOD SHOULD MAKE US GRATEFUL

There's a reason God commands us to "Enter his gates with thanksgiving, and his courts with praise!" (Psalm 100:4). "For the LORD is good; his steadfast love endures forever" (Psalm 100:5). And he has been unspeakably kind to us.

When people ask my friend C. J. Mahaney how he's doing, he typically brings God's kindness to mind by responding, "Better than I deserve." Someone might think he's just received an unexpected gift or he's an optimistic guy. It's much deeper than that. He's reminding himself of the gospel.

I've adopted that response at times and have received negative reactions. Some people thought I suffer from low self-esteem. I told them I have no problem thinking highly of myself, too highly in fact.

The truth is, we're *all* doing much better than we deserve. Because of our sin, we all deserve hell.

Yet many times people walk into our meetings unfulfilled, unsatisfied, and ungrateful. They've been thinking about others who are richer, more beautiful, more well known, stronger, more talented, or more godly.

Worshiping God rightly should open our eyes to God's amazing grace. We remember how in Christ Jesus we are redeemed and reconciled to our Father and therefore are enabled to abound in gratefulness and thanksgiving. Our greatest need has been taken care of at the cross.

For that reason, we're able to abound in gratefulness and thanksgiving. In fact, songs of gratefulness are one way Christianity is distinct from other faiths, as one author reminds us:

> The great faiths of the Buddhist and the Mohammedan give no place either to the need for the grace of reconciliation. The clearest proof of this is the simplest. It lies in the hymns of Christian worship. A Buddhist temple never resounds with a cry of praise. Mohammedan worshipers never sing. Their prayers are, at the highest, prayers of submission and of request. They seldom reach the gladder note of thanksgiving. They are never jubilant with the songs of the forgiven.[3]

When we gaze on the cross of Christ and truly recognize that *we* should be hanging there instead, what response can there be but overflowing gratefulness? Pat Sczebel's song is one expression of this:

The mystery of the cross I cannot comprehend,
The agonies of Calvary.
You, the perfect Holy One, crushed Your Son,
Who drank the bitter cup reserved for me.

Your blood has washed away my sin;
Jesus, thank You.
The Father's wrath completely satisfied;
Jesus, thank You.
Once Your enemy, now seated at Your table;
Jesus, thank You.[4]

WORSHIPING GOD SHOULD MAKE US HOLY

It is impossible for us to rightly consider God apart from his holiness—his wrath against sin, his steadfast opposition to injustice, and his righteous judgment of the wicked. These aren't exactly popular or seeker-sensitive topics, but they describe the God we worship. And the more we love to worship him, the more we will hate sin in all its manifestations. If God wasn't fiercely opposed to evil in every form, including our sin, he would not deserve our worship. He would not be good. He would not be God.

This is why those who bear his name and dwell in his presence are called to be holy like him: "You shall be holy, for I am holy" (1 Peter 1:16, quoting Leviticus 11:44–45).

Although holiness is typically mocked or misunderstood in our culture, it is precious in God's sight. And we should remind the church of that reality when we gather to worship him.

One way we've sought to increase our awareness of God's holiness is by occasionally confessing our sins before God together as a church. It's not that we enjoy morbid introspection. It's not that we've forgotten we're saved. Rather, we're seeking to counteract our continual attempts to justify, minimize, and ignore our acts of defiance against a holy God.

God is holy. As worship leaders we have the privilege of reminding the church that God has redeemed us to share in that holiness, for his glory. Mark Altrogge helps us do that in his song "In the Presence":

In the presence of a holy God
I'm so small and frail and weak
When I see your pow'r and wisdom, Lord
I have no words left to speak
In the presence of a holy God
There's new meaning now to grace;
You took all my sins upon Yourself
And I can only stand amazed.[5]

WORSHIPING GOD SHOULD MAKE US LOVING

When we gather for corporate worship, what should capture our attention, stir our affections, and elicit our adoration is God himself, revealed in Jesus Christ. But as we gaze upon his glory, our affection for those he created will be deepened as well. "If anyone says, 'I love God,' and hates his brother, he is a liar; for he who does not love his brother whom he has seen cannot love God whom he has not seen" (1 John 4:20).

Jesus left his followers with a clear command: "This is my command-ment, that you love one another as I have loved you" (John 15:12). He then gave the preeminent illustration of love by laying down his life for those he came to redeem. It's inconsistent to profess that we love God while with-holding love from those he came to save.

Not many of us enjoy hanging out with proud and selfish sinners. But as we worship the true God, we'll start to see our own faces in that description and will be amazed that God so loved us that he sent his only Son to save us (John 3:16). Experiencing and reveling in grace will cause us to extend it to others.

Good leaders recognize that extolling the gospel of Christ should moti-vate us to lay down our lives in love for others. Isaac Watts expressed that reality in his hymn "When I Survey the Wondrous Cross":

> *Were all the realm of nature mine,*
> *That were a present far too small;*
> *Love so amazing, so divine,*
> *Demands my soul, my life, my all.*

WORSHIPING GOD SHOULD MAKE US MISSION-MINDED

Mission-minded people are those who love sharing the good news of God's salvation with others through their words and their lives.

Worship leaders should make great evangelists. After all, it's our pas-sion to help people clearly see why God deserves worship, and we want as many people as possible to share in the joy of knowing him. We praise the God who desires all people to come to the knowledge of the truth and who doesn't wish that any should perish (1 Timothy 2:4; 2 Peter 3:9).

How can we not want our family, friends, neighbors, coworkers, and sometimes complete strangers to know about the magnificent Savior we worship? Why wouldn't we tell them about the source of all truth, life, meaning, and joy?

As we lead the church in meditating on these thoughts, we want to avoid singing songs that are high on the energy scale and low on the content scale. It's easy to be momentarily enthused about reaching the nations and fail to cultivate any desire to share the gospel with our neighbors.

Our church consistently and passionately preaches the gospel, offers evangelistic training, and provides meetings geared toward non-Christian friends. But we also encourage a clearer picture of God's heart for the lost through songs like these:

> *Give me a passion to see Your glory,*
> *A heart that worships You alone.*
> *Cleanse me, forgive me for my self-seeking,*
> *That I might seek to make You known.*
> *I want to serve You, I want to please You,*
> *My one desire is to*
> *See the name of Jesus lifted*
> *High above all things.*[6]

> *Your glorious cause, O God, engages our hearts.*
> *May Jesus Christ be known wherever we are.*
> *We ask not for ourselves but for Your renown.*
> *The cross has saved us so we pray*
> *Your kingdom come.*[7]

GENUINE WORSHIP CHANGES LIVES

In his insightful biblical theology of worship, *Recalling the Hope of Glory*, Allen Ross confirms the point I've been seeking to make in this chapter:

> If worshipers leave a service with no thought of becoming more godly in their lives, then the purpose of worship has not been achieved. If they walk away from an assembly without a conviction that they need to conform their lives to Holy Scripture, even if it means changing their lifestyle, then worship has been perverted somewhere. . . . The clear teaching of Scripture is that genuine worship is life changing.[8]

Do you really believe that? "Genuine worship is life changing."

If we grasp the implications of that statement, the way we think about and lead corporate worship will be dramatically impacted. We'll never again be content to simply prepare for a meeting. We won't be tempted to hope for merely "a good time of worship."

Our sights will be raised much higher. We'll be doing all we can to serve God's purpose for the church as we gaze on his glory.

We'll remember this:

And we all, with unveiled face, beholding the glory of the Lord, are being transformed into the same image from one degree of glory to another. For this comes from the Lord who is the Spirit. (2 Corinthians 3:18)

God intends to transform us into his image as we behold his glory.

The kind of change God wants to produce in us takes place in the context of the local church. As we glorify God together on Sunday morning, God works in us "both to will and to work for his good pleasure" (Philippians 2:13).

The joy is ours. The glory is his.

part three

HEALTHY TENSIONS

chapter 18

GUIDING PRINCIPLES

Sovereign Grace Ministries, the family of churches I'm privileged to serve, has its roots in the charismatic movement of the 1970s. Much of what we did in our early meetings was a reaction to the formal liturgies we'd grown up in.

But before we knew it, we developed our own liturgy. Of course, we never *called* it that. But a liturgy, which literally means "a public way of doing things," is simply a description of what a church does in corporate worship. And ours became fairly predictable.

Most meetings started with two fast songs, one medium song, then two or three slow songs. During that time (which lasted thirty to fifty minutes), people would contribute prophetic words or Scripture readings, and occasionally we'd pray for specific groups of people. After the "worship," we'd welcome guests, give announcements, and receive the offering. We might also dedicate babies or welcome new members. Finally we'd hear an hour-long message followed by a song and a time of prayer for anyone who wanted it.

Any Sovereign Grace church you visited would follow something close to that pattern.

As the number of Sovereign Grace churches increased, we had to ask some questions: Are we doing what we do on Sundays because it's biblical, or is it just our preference or simply what we've always done? Is there a scriptural or normal order of service that churches should follow?

GUIDELINES FROM OUR PAST

I realize we're not the first group of churches to ask these questions.

In the sixteenth and seventeenth centuries, congregational worship became a heated issue when the first Protestants sought to reform the unbiblical liturgical practices of Roman Catholicism. John Calvin and others developed what has come to be known as the regulative principle of worship.[1] This is the conviction that anything we do in a public meeting of the church must be clearly commanded or implied in Scripture. Occasionally the regulative principle is used to forbid instruments and the use of songs other than the Psalms in corporate worship.

Another approach is called the normative principle, practiced by Martin Luther and adopted by Lutherans and Methodists. Broadly stated, the normative principle holds that whatever Scripture doesn't forbid is allowed. This allowed Luther to keep much of the sacramental and liturgical practices of the Catholic Church.

In the centuries following Calvin and Luther, churches have split and new denominations have formed over what our meetings should look like. And the conflicts continue to this day.

Why is it so difficult to figure out what God wants us to do when we get together?

I can think of a few reasons.

First, although every generation and church is responsible to weigh its practices and traditions against the unchanging authority of God's Word, God hasn't been quite as specific in this area as some of us would prefer. The Bible doesn't give an order of service that applies to all cultures at all times. The Old Testament includes ample references to choirs, musicians, processions, priests, robes, annual celebrations, and instrumental praises. But how relevant are those things today, given the fact that the New Testament rarely mentions them? Should we enter God's presence with singing, dancing, and instruments, in line with Psalm 149? Or are those things excluded by the New Testament command to worship God "with reverence and awe" (Hebrews 12:28)? It depends on who you ask.

Second, we tend to read the Bible through the grid of our own practices and preferences. Charismatics open up the Psalms and find commands to clap, dance, and shout (as in Psalm 35:27; 47:1; 149:3). Presbyterians insist that Scripture should be read by ordained ministers (following the pattern in Nehemiah 8:2–7) and that everything is to be done "decently and in order" (1 Corinthians 14:40). Others will emphasize holistic worship (Mark 12:30), cultural relevance (1 Corinthians 9:22), and ministry to the poor (James 1:27). Whether a tradition is three hundred, thirty, or three years old, the danger is the same. We start with Scripture but eventually invest ultimate authority in our own traditions or views.

Third, some Christians think God hasn't said anything about how we should worship him. I call this the Whatever Principle. It says that we can worship God any way we want. The emphasis is on our own ideas and personal expression. The problem with this line of thinking is that God has given us a number of examples and commands in Scripture that clearly communicate what he wants us to do when the church meets. We're to pray together (1 Timothy 2:1–2). Pastors are to preach and explain God's Word (2 Timothy 4:2). We're to sing praises to God (Colossians 3:16). In addition, Paul specified how many consecutive prophecies could be given in any meeting and spelled out the proper way to participate in the Lord's Supper (1 Corinthians 14:29; 11:17–34).

God hasn't told us everything, but he certainly hasn't been silent on the subject.

THREE PRINCIPLES

With deep respect for those who've gone before us, in our church we attempt to follow three principles for ordering our services:

1. Do what God clearly commands.
2. Don't do what God clearly forbids.
3. Use scriptural wisdom for everything else.

We recognize that God hasn't given us a prescribed order of service that defines biblical worship. But we seek to faithfully apply biblical precepts and examples.

We also understand the crucial role that faith plays in corporate worship. So we never want our way of doing things to replace an active trust in the finished work of Christ to make our worship acceptable.

That's why we'll always be learning, always improving, always seeking to learn from others how we can more effectively magnify the greatness of God in Jesus Christ when we gather.

WHAT CAN WE LEARN FROM OTHERS?

A few years ago I asked Mark Dever, pastor of Capitol Hill Baptist Church in Washington, D.C., to speak at our biannual worship conference.

Sunday meetings in Mark's church look *very* different from ours. His service is formal, ours more free-flow. Capitol Hill's congregation is pretty reserved in physical expressiveness, while visitors to Covenant Life encounter everything from raised hands to dancing to bowing down on the floor. Mark plans out song choices months in advance, while we normally focus on the next one or two Sundays. His church sings mostly from a hymnal; we project lyrics on a screen. Their music team consists of two guitars and a few vocalists. We use a full band and sometimes add a contemporary choir. Capitol Hill is a Southern Baptist church. Covenant Life is a nondenominational church that believes all the spiritual gifts in 1 Corinthians 12 are still available today.

So what could Mark possibly teach us about worship?

Quite a bit, actually.

With all our differences, we've had great discussions about worship and what we've observed in each other's church. I've benefited greatly from his insights and perspectives, and hopefully Mark has gained something from my thoughts as well.

What enables us to carry on a dialogue like this?

For starters, we agree on the most important issues. The Bible is our authoritative and sufficient standard for everything related to life and doctrine. God alone determines how we approach him, what we call him, and how we relate to him. Jesus is the only Savior, who died and rose for all who would ever turn from their sins and trust in his atoning sacrifice for forgiveness. Worshiping God is impossible without the enabling power of the Holy Spirit. These are nonnegotiable truths that aren't open to discussion.

But as I noted earlier, there are several aspects of worship that we view, or at least practice, differently. Rather than just endlessly discussing disagreements, we try to learn what the other might have that we don't. We're trying to embrace what I call the healthy tensions of worship.

HEALTHY TENSIONS

One year on our annual family vacation, I tried to set up a volleyball net by myself. Fortunately no one had a video camera. I set up the first pole with guidelines attached to stakes in the sand. Then I ran as fast as I could to the other side before the first side fell down. I didn't make it. I tried again. I repeated that process three times before realizing I was an idiot. Yes, it took me that long.

I needed someone's help because the net could be set up only when there was a healthy tension between both poles.

It's like that with worship. One church argues for reverence, another for celebration. One rightly claims worship is about God, but another points out all the verses on edifying the believers. Isn't there a way to appreciate both perspectives—in tension together? Shouldn't we think of these as both/and issues rather than either/or?

The next several chapters will discuss nine healthy tensions related to worship. I'm sure you can think of many more.

My goal in examining these tensions is not so much to become balanced as it is to understand, pursue, and enjoy all the ways God has enabled us to worship him.

You may be completely unaware of some of the healthy tensions I'll outline here. You might think, *What's the big deal?* Maybe you're part of a church whose liturgy has remained consistent for years (and remember, every church has a liturgy), and you assume your church's approach is *the* biblical pattern for worship. If that's the case, I pray you'll hear my suggestion that we can humbly learn from other Christians whose corporate worship traditions differ from ours.

On most of these issues discussed in the coming chapters, our default setting is to prefer one side over the other. It requires a consistent submission to God's Word and a humble dependence on his Spirit to make sure both poles are standing.

Examining these tensions in light of God's Word may reveal the need for changes in your church. If so, remember that change takes place over time by God's grace. Truth must be patiently and humbly taught, retaught, and modeled. Your church won't change overnight. Mine won't either. Allen Ross says:

> There is no reason for individual churches to change everything they have been doing; but there is every reason for all congregations to evaluate everything they are doing to see how they can do it better.[2]

That's our goal—to evaluate everything and see where we can do something better.

May our meetings and churches be places where God is truly worshiped in spirit and truth, where people exalt God without having to choose sides, and where the glory of Jesus Christ is clearly seen in all we do.

chapter 19

TRANSCENDENT AND IMMANENT

I grew up in a religious environment characterized by solemnity, reverence, and silence. Jokes, fooling around, and loud noises were completely out of place on Sundays. A parent or some other authority figure was usually close by to make sure we didn't do anything inappropriate. We were in God's house, and we should act like it.

Such reverence is totally understandable in light of who God is. He is transcendent. He transcends, or surpasses, all our ideas, thoughts, and opinions about him. While some think of transcendence as God's being "unknowable," that can be misleading. God is unique from us, but he can be known.[1] He has been speaking to us about himself for as long as we've been on the earth.

Transcendence means that God is independent from and superior to his creation. As we worship God, we must recognize that he is not us. He is the sovereign King, infinitely majestic and glorious. His righteousness is like the mountains, and no one is holy like the Lord (see Psalm 36:6; 1 Samuel 2:2). God is God, and we are not. That's one of the most helpful attitudes we can cultivate when we meet to worship God.

THE REASON FOR REVERENCE

Our appropriate response to God's transcendence is reverence, honor, and respect.

In the Bible, when various people encountered God's presence, they were never flippant or casual. At Mount Sinai the Israelites "were afraid and trembled, and they stood far off" (Exodus 20:18). Seeing God's throne, Isaiah cried out, "Woe is me! For I am lost; for I am a man of unclean lips, and I dwell in the midst of a people of unclean lips; for my eyes have seen the King, the LORD of hosts!" (Isaiah 6:5). When John encountered the risen Christ in his vision of heaven, he "fell at his feet as though dead" (Revelation 1:17).

Reverence is essential to worship. Because "our God is a consuming fire," we are to "offer to God acceptable worship, with reverence and awe" (Hebrews 12:28–29).

Formal liturgies can sometimes help us worship in this way, with every word carefully chosen, devoutly said, and designed to draw our attention to God's majesty and transcendence.

Cathedrals do the same. Their lofty ceilings, towering stained-glass windows, and cavernous halls help make us more aware of our smallness before Almighty God.

Hymns like "Holy, Holy, Holy" by Reginald Heber impress the reality of God's uniqueness and transcendence upon us. We've sung it a cappella at times, and the effect has been heightened:

> Holy, holy, holy!
> Though the darkness hide Thee,
> Though the eye of sinful man
> Thy glory may not see;
> Only Thou art holy; there is none beside Thee,
> Perfect in power, in love, and purity.

Worship that approaches God casually loses sight of this truth. In our sincere desire to help others view God as approachable, we must not forget that God is wholly unlike us. He is the one "who alone has immortality, who dwells in unapproachable light, whom no one has ever seen or can see" (1 Timothy 6:16). He is holy, and we are sinful. He declares: "I am God, and there is no other; I am God, and there is none like me" (Isaiah 46:9).

NEAR AND NEARER

But God is not only transcendent—he is also *immanent*, which means he's near to us. He doesn't stay distant or isolated from his creation. "In him we live and move and have our being" (Acts 17:28). Though we may feel at times like God is a million miles away, he never is. He's right here.

One of the most amazing demonstrations of his immanence is the Incarnation, where God took on flesh and blood and became one of us. He laughed, ate, slept, talked, and interacted with those he'd created. Can God get any nearer?

Yes.

God's immanence takes on radical new meaning for Christians: God is not only with us—he actually dwells *in* us. The ascended Christ has now sent the Holy Spirit to live inside us. "Or do you not know that your body is a temple of the Holy Spirit *within you*, whom you have from God?" (1 Corinthians 6:19). The transcendent God has taken up residence in his people for his glory. And that knowledge is a constant source of wonder, gratefulness, and comfort.

God is immanent. He's our brother, shepherd, and Savior. His mercies are "new every morning," and he is able to sympathize with us in all our weaknesses (Lamentations 3:23; Hebrews 4:15). He is Immanuel, God with us (Matthew 1:23, quoting Isaiah 7:14).

A cathedral doesn't communicate God's nearness very well. Think instead of a downtown storefront church, rubbing shoulders with the poverty, crime, and need that so often characterize the inner city.

Many of the praise choruses of recent decades have emphasized God's immanence. They help us sing not only *about* God but *to* him. From "As the Deer" to "Breathe" to "Hungry," there's an emphasis on God's desire for us to know his nearness. He's not only the transcendent God; he is our friend.

That last statement needs some clarifying. Sometimes a song refers to God or Jesus as our friend in a way that makes God sound like our buddy or a sensual lover. That misses or distorts the biblical perspective. The Bible does affirm that we're friends of God:

> *You are my friends if you do what I command you. No longer do I call you servants, for the servant does not know what his master is doing; but I have called you friends, for all that I have heard from my Father I have made known to you. (John 15:14–15)*

But D. A. Carson makes the point that "not once is Jesus or God ever described in the Bible as our friend. Abraham is God's friend; the reverse is never stated. Of course, in one sense Jesus is the best friend a poor sinner ever had. Nevertheless, that is not the terminology of Scripture, almost as if the Bible is reluctant to descend into the kind of cheap intimacy that brings God or Jesus down to our level."[2]

Given this scriptural pattern, we must be careful never to refer to God in a way that dishonors his transcendence and uniqueness. Matt Redman has modeled this care in his song "O Sacred King," which masterfully captures the immanence and transcendence of God:

> O sacred King, O holy King.
> How can I honor You rightly,
> Honor that's fit for Your name?
> O sacred Friend, O holy Friend,
> I don't take what You give lightly,
> Friendship instead of disgrace.
> For it's the mystery of the universe.
> You're the God of holiness,
> Yet You welcome souls like me,
> And with the blessing of Your father's heart
> You discipline the ones you love.[3]

These lines are the essence of a healthy tension. John Piper has described it as "gravity and gladness."[4] It's what the psalmist means when he says we are to "rejoice with trembling" (Psalm 2:11).

MAINTAINING THE HEALTHY TENSION

There are a number of ways to keep God's transcendence and immanence in healthy tension.

One option is to recognize that different services can reflect different themes. One Sunday might focus on God's greatness, while another might focus more on his immanence.

We can also intentionally lead the church in appropriate responses to God's transcendence and immanence, not being casual when we should be weighty or somber when we should be warm.

But the best way to maintain this tension is to continually meditate on the gospel. God's transcendent holiness and justice required the sacrifice of the Son of God to be satisfied. At Calvary we stand in awe of perfect righteousness, holy justice, and unerring judgment. We can offer no excuses or justification for our sin. We're completely at the mercy of our sovereign Creator and King.

Yet the gospel assures us that our sins have been completely atoned for. We're no longer God's enemies. We're his adopted children.

This news is almost too good to believe, but it's true! We've been made into a dwelling place for his Spirit, joined to one another for his glory. He's with us, near us, in us—all made possible through the life, death, and resurrection of our glorious Savior.

God is *both* transcendent and immanent, as this passage affirms:

> *For thus says the One who is high and lifted up, who inhabits eternity, whose name is Holy: "I dwell in the high and holy place, and also with him who is of a contrite and lowly spirit, to revive the spirit of the lowly, and to revive the heart of the contrite." (Isaiah 57:15)*

Our corporate worship should reflect this distinction. Charles Spurgeon once said:

> I can admire the solemn and stately language of worship that recognizes the greatness of God, but it will not warm my heart or express my soul until it has also blended therewith the joyful nearness of that perfect love that casts out fear and ventures to speak with our Father in heaven as a child speaks with its father on earth. My brother, no veil remains.[5]

Yes, our God is a consuming fire. And yes, no veil remains.

chapter 20

HEAD AND HEART

When we helped start a church in Charlotte, North Carolina, we often heard the same complaint from visitors. It went like this.

There are two kinds of churches in town. The first loves expository preaching, Bible study, and theology. But there's no life. People seem cold and unaffected by the teaching.

The second kind is warm and friendly and sings passionately. But there's no truth. Scriptures are often taken out of context, and spontaneity is everything.

Obviously, I knew people were exaggerating. But churches can have a hard time connecting the knowledge of the mind with the passions of the heart. Yet they're integrally related. And both are crucial to biblical worship.

USING OUR HEADS

Every time we lead the church in worship we're doing more than singing songs. We're leading believers in a battle for the truth. The world has been trying to squeeze us into its mold, allure us with its smiles, frighten us with its frowns. Our flesh tells us that following God isn't worth it; he can't be trusted. We're constantly tempted to believe lies.

That's why worshiping God with our minds matters. God wants us to wrestle hard with apparent contradictions in Scripture and life, not simply ignore them or adopt the world's complacent attitude of "it's all good." He wants us to set our *minds*, not just our emotions, on things above (Colossians 3:2).

Leading worship involves more than helping people "lose themselves" in God or find a "safe place." God wants our worship to be intelligent and informed. He wants to stretch our minds to the limits as we consider the greatness of his being and the wonder of his works. That means some of our songs may require more than one hearing to fully comprehend, and may not fit on one page.

Helping people worship God with their minds also means using songs that go beyond the tired Christian clichés to which we've grown accustomed. Not new truth, but new ways of speaking and presenting truth. To lead worship in a way that makes God seem dull is a sin. But it's not creativity and production values that will help us. It's helping people clearly apprehend the character and works of God.

We can also explain the meaning of any words, biblical phrases, or terms that might be unfamiliar or too familiar. Words like *justified*, *Zion*, *grace*, and *glory*. Unbelievers, new Christians, children, and regular members can benefit from knowing what they're singing about.

Obviously, intellect can become an end in itself. We can become more impressed with our doctrinal formulations than we are with Jesus. We can end up leading a theologically orthodox but emotionally dead church. God receives no glory from that combination.

USING OUR HEARTS

But I don't think overemphasizing doctrine and truth is the problem in most American churches. If anything, we're drifting away from a clear proclamation of God's unchanging revelation in his Word.

And yet, not many churches excel in passionate worship from the heart either. Congregations muddle through meetings unresponsive, unaffected, and unengaged.

The Puritan pastor Jonathan Edwards considered it his duty to "raise the affections of my hearers as high as I possibly can, provided they are affected with nothing but truth, and with affections that are not disagreeable to the nature of what they are affected with."[1] That's our duty as well.

The affections we're seeking to stir up are more than fleeting, shallow, self-induced emotions. We aren't trying to excite people for the sake of excitement. We aren't leading a pep rally for band. Godly affections are deep and long-lasting. They're the result of focusing on what God has done and who he is.

A clear picture of the living God moves our hearts. His transcendence causes us to feel awe. His holiness evokes sorrow for our sin. A view of his mercy leads to gratefulness. The knowledge of his sovereignty brings great peace. Meditating on the price the Savior paid to reconcile us to God leaves us lost in wonder, and rightly so.

God is particularly interested in our joy. He tells us, "Be glad in the LORD, and rejoice, O righteous, and shout for joy, all you upright in heart!" (Psalm 32:11). When the church gathers, the sense of confident joy in God should be pronounced.

When we fail to demonstrate delight and satisfaction in God, we're not only dishonoring God, we're disobeying him. More than anyone else on earth, Christians have a reason to celebrate.

KEEPING EMOTIONS IN CHECK

As valuable as emotional engagement is, it's possible for feelings and experiences—rather than God himself—to become our goal. We come hoping to get a good feeling from worship and aren't as concerned about what produces it or how we express it.

Expressing our emotions in unclear or inappropriate ways can cause problems.

A while back, Chuck Colson took aim at contemporary Christian music in an article in *Christianity Today* called "Soothing Ourselves to Death." He said that much of the music written for the church (and especially what is played on Christian radio) has moved from worship to entertainment. He expressed a particular distaste for the song "Draw Me Close to You." Here are the lyrics:

> *Draw me close to you, never let me go.*
> *I lay it all down again, to hear you say that I'm your friend.*
> *You are my desire, no one else will do.*
> *'Cause nothing else could take your place, to feel the warmth*
> *   of your embrace.*
> *Help me find the way, bring me back to you.*
> *You're all I want. You're all I've ever needed.*
> *You're all I want. Help me know you are near.*[2]

My personal history with this song goes back to the mid-nineties, when I used it quite frequently. I specifically recall a time when my wife Julie and I listened to the song through tears as we reflected how futile it is to seek joy in anything other than God himself.

The song's strengths are evident. It expresses a longing for God's nearness and confirms "there is nothing on earth that I desire besides you"

(Psalm 73:25). It expresses a sincere dependence on God. The music is beautiful and allows appropriate time for reflection.

But over time I stopped using it. The intensely personal lyrics allow room for different interpretations, not all of them helpful. The overall impression of the song is one of uncertainty rather than faith. It seems to ask, "Will God let me go? Is he near?" The line, "No one else will do" can come across as too casual, almost saying that other options for fulfilling my relational desires are legitimate but just don't work for me.

Because nothing else in the song balances it out, the phrase "to feel the warmth of your embrace" can sound as though God simply wants me to feel soft, warm, and cozy. Others have alluded to the potentially sensual overtones of the words and music. (I say "potential" because the song doesn't affect everyone the same way.)

In general, I typically avoid songs that overuse words such as *intimate*, *embrace*, or *intoxicating* that our culture often associates with romantic love. As C. J. Mahaney reminds us, "When describing our relationship with God, or when communicating our passion for him in prayer or worship, it's right to use a vocabulary of love. But this language should never include anything erotic."[3] We are corporately, not individually, the Bride of Christ.

I think "Draw Me Close to You" may be symptomatic of a larger problem in Christian worship music. For more than a hundred years we've favored emotional, response-type songs over songs that magnify the nature, attributes, and works of God. We tend to favor devotion over doctrine. That order needs to be reversed, without losing either. We need more songs that help us think deeply about God and help us respond with wholehearted emotion.

This issue is far more than hymns versus contemporary choruses. Some hymns are sentimental and feeling-oriented; some contemporary songs are rich with theological content. The real issue is pastors and worship leaders taking responsibility for what their churches are singing, leading them wisely into truth-based affections, and making sure good fruit is being produced.

Most of all, God intends for us to remember that neither biblical truth nor deep emotion is out of place when we worship God; they're meant to go together. Let's keep the healthy tension strong.

chapter 21

INTERNAL AND EXTERNAL

When someone says, "Susie's a real worshiper," they usually mean Susie is expressive when she sings.

But there are several possible explanations for that expressiveness. Susie might be naturally demonstrative. She may come from a family of extroverts. She could be drawing attention to herself, trying to impress others with her spirituality. Or she may be worshiping God biblically.

We'll never know if Susie is a worshiper by observing her from the outside. We have to know what's going on inside.

Likewise, God looks upon the heart (1 Samuel 16:7), and he rebukes those who think that outward compliance compensates for internal coldness. God-pleasing worship involves heart engagement and an active faith in the existence and goodness of God (Hebrews 11:6). Jesus dismissed those who thought words of devotion were a sufficient measure of true worship: "This people honors me with their lips, but their heart is far from me; in vain do they worship me" (Matthew 15:8–9).

The state of our heart is of primary importance because "from it flow the springs of life" (Proverbs 4:23). In Scripture the heart encompasses everything from what we think to what we feel to what we choose. That's why we can never be satisfied that people simply attend meetings. We need to ask what is happening in the realm of their desires, thoughts, and feelings.

While heart worship is most important, what we do with our bodies isn't irrelevant or unimportant. It's not enough to say, "I'm worshiping God in my heart, and he knows it." If I told my wife, Julie, that I loved her, but never looked glad to see her, never hugged her, and never demonstrated my affection in any concrete way, she wouldn't be too impressed. We wouldn't have much of a marriage either.

LEADING YOUR CHURCH TO GOD-HONORING EXPRESSIVENESS

Biblical praise is normally expressed, spoken, and observable. That's why David says, "My heart is steadfast, O God! I will sing and make melody with all my being!" (Psalm 108:1). That's why the Psalms are filled with exhortations not only to proclaim God's greatness but to express his greatness with our bodies.

From talking to pastors and worship leaders, I know this internal versus external topic is a tricky one.

All kinds of questions emerge: How much physical expression is too much? How much can we encourage physical responsiveness without feeling like a cheerleader? What if a church is reserved, conservative, and unemotional? How do you move a congregation to broader physical expressions in response to God's glory?

Here are four guidelines to consider as you lead your church in this area.[1]

Direct People's Attention to God and the Gospel

We don't help people simply by telling them, "Sing it like you mean it!" or "Let's party!" Our goal is to direct people's gaze toward God's glory in Christ. Moving our church into greater expressiveness that's not rooted in a clear view of God's glory as revealed in the gospel will hinder, not help, true worship.

Our bodies naturally respond to what affects our souls. I open my arms wide as my daughter runs to greet me. I jump up from the couch with my hands in the air when my team scores the winning touchdown. I lunge when a glass of milk is about to be knocked over. I gratefully applaud heroic acts of unselfishness. I cry when a friend's child dies. No one has to teach us those responses. In a similar way, God-honoring expressiveness in corporate worship begins with clearly seeing the One we worship.

When we grasp the majesty of God, the mercy of the Savior, and the meaning of our salvation, we'll be more inclined to respond with physical expressions of worship.

Teach about the Appropriateness and Limitations of Physical Expression

God created our bodies to glorify him (1 Corinthians 6:20). The Greek and Hebrew words we most often translate "worship" contain the idea of bending over or bowing down. If we are to love God with all our heart, soul, mind, and strength, that certainly includes the bodies he's given us.

Some Christians are simply unaware that physical responsiveness to God in worship is encouraged and modeled throughout Scripture. Various physical actions can bring God glory, including clapping, singing, bowing, kneeling, lifting hands, shouting, playing instruments, dancing, and standing in awe (Psalm 47:1, 6; Exodus 12:27; Psalm 95:6; 134:2; 33:1; 150:3–4; 33:8).

These expressions don't all have to be evidenced every time we gather. But neither should we insist that these expressions were cultural and can be ignored today or that we can observe them spiritually ("I'm shouting in my heart"). The crucial question is this: Is there any physical expression of worship that God has given us in Scripture that I've never displayed? And if so, why?

Singing, shouting, dancing, lifting hands, bowing, kneeling—all these and others can honor God when done from the heart as an expression of gratefulness for God's grace. And they should be an overflow of the worship we give to God throughout our daily lives.

However, physical expressiveness alone is no sure sign that biblical worship is happening. People have been exuberant in corporate worship while living in adultery. Some Christians exhibit little physical expression on Sundays but have a profound love for the Savior, an exemplary life, and a thorough knowledge of Scripture.

A genuine response to God can't be measured by raised hands, dancing feet, and loud shouts. We might just be caught up in the enthusiasm of a large crowd. I still remember the first time I raised my hands to worship God. I was at an outdoor Jesus festival in the mid-seventies and saw everyone around me raising their hands. So I did too. But my arms felt like they weighed about fifty pounds. And I'm not sure much genuine praise was happening in my heart. I was too concerned about what everyone around me was thinking about me (as if they were).

Scripture gives numerous examples of times when physical expressions in worship actually offended God. Although raised hands can express dependence, gratefulness, or celebration, God once told Israel, "When you spread out your hands, I will hide my eyes from you; even though you make many prayers, I will not listen; your hands are full of blood" (Isaiah 1:15).

The hands we lift to worship God must be "holy hands" (1 Timothy 2:8)—made holy through our humble trust in the atoning work of Christ and dedicated to his purposes.

Outward expression in worship may say a great deal—but not everything.

Address Hindrances to Physical Expression in Worship

If your church is generally unexpressive in corporate worship, there could be a number of reasons that you or your pastor can address.

Some restrict their responses to God because they're afraid of what others might think. They wonder if their image as a "respectable" Christian will be tarnished. They're concerned that their actions might be seen as undignified or immature. That may be the fear of man (Proverbs 29:25). Our responses to God are based on his worthiness, not on some image or reputation we may be trying to protect.

Some godly Christians have too narrow a view of what constitutes an appropriate response to God. They emphasize "reverence and awe" as aspects of worship (Hebrews 12:28) and rightly encourage attitudes of sobriety and solemnity. It's true that reverence and awe are essential to biblical worship. But it's impossible to ignore the multitude of examples and commands in Scripture that emphasize celebration, passion, delight, and exuberance, all expressed through lifted hands, raised voices, and dancing feet.

Another group holds back on outward expressiveness because of a thoughtful concern for others. They don't want to do anything that will distract people from focusing on the glory of Christ. That leads to a final point.

Teach Consideration of Others

Expressiveness has its limitations. Our highest priority when we gather with the church is not our own personal expressiveness but the privilege of serving others (1 Corinthians 14:12; 13:1–8). Individuals should be following your example and direction in the area of expressiveness, not breaking into loud shouting and enthusiastic dancing just because they feel like it. We're to be concerned about "the interests of others" (Philippians 2:4). At the same time, more reserved members shouldn't assume that expressive individuals are hypocritical, seeking attention, or rude. They might want to consider what they can learn from the unhindered and sincere expressiveness they see.

It's a pastor's responsibility to gently and privately talk to anyone whose physical expressions are distracting or inappropriate. I'd begin by encouraging them about their apparent love for God, then ask if they've ever thought about the effect of their actions on others. Usually a conversation will help someone realize that God isn't honored by everything we "feel" will honor him, if we're failing to consider the effect on others.

So what might Christ-exalting expressiveness look like in your church?

As we sing, "No power of hell, no scheme of man can ever pluck me from his hand,"[2] people might raise their hands in gratefulness that God's plans can't be thwarted.

As we sing, "My sin, oh the bliss of this glorious thought! My sin, not in part but the whole, is nailed to the cross, and I bear it no more," some might kneel in grateful adoration that *all* their sins have been paid for.

After singing, "Crown Him, ye kings, with many crowns, for He is King of all," we might hear joyful acclamations of praise to the all-powerful, reigning Savior.

People in your church will learn the most from what is modeled by you and the other leaders. Churches rarely rise above the level of their leaders in expressiveness and genuine engagement. That's the way God designed the church.

If I had no other choices, I'd rather be sitting in the midst of a quiet congregation singing rich, doctrinal truths than jumping around with a lively congregation belting out shallow, man-centered songs.

But God never intended for us to have to choose. We're to pursue theological depth *and* passionate expression.

At the end of the day, no one physical expression will ever be adequate to fully express our amazement that God would graciously draw us to himself through the Savior. Our responses will look different at different times, in different churches and different cultures. But there's no question that we must help our congregations understand that God is worthy of our deepest, strongest, and purest affections. And that our bodies should show it.

chapter 22

VERTICAL AND HORIZONTAL

I don't need to convince you that worship, from beginning to end, is about God. But what does that mean? And why is it true? Imagine what it was like at the very beginning.

I'm not talking about Adam and Eve in the Garden. I mean before that. What was it like when there was nothing but God? "Before the mountains were brought forth, or ever you had formed the earth and the world, from everlasting to everlasting you are God" (Psalm 90:2). Father, Son, and Spirit. Supremely happy, perfectly content, delighting in each other's glory (John 17:5) and dwelling "in unapproachable light" (1 Timothy 6:16).

We can't imagine what it was like because we're not God and we weren't there. But one thing's certain: God didn't create the world because he was lonely.

THE VERTICAL ELEMENT OF WORSHIP

So what engaged God's heart before "the morning stars sang together" for joy at the dawn of creation (Job 38:7)?

God.

What brings the greatest joy, fulfillment, and delight to God?

Being God.

What will be the focus of heaven and the object of our affections throughout eternity?

God.

But doesn't God care about *us*? Yes. God's nature is to give—lavishly, graciously, and eternally—and he created the world so we could share in the joy of knowing him, ultimately for his glory.

That's what Paul draws our attention to in his letter to the Ephesians:

Blessed be the God and Father of our Lord Jesus Christ, who has blessed us in Christ with every spiritual blessing in the heavenly places, even as he chose us in him before the foundation of the world, that we should be holy and blameless before him. In love he predestined us for adoption as sons through Jesus Christ, according to the purpose of his will, to the praise of his glorious grace, with which he has blessed us in the Beloved. (Ephesians 1:3–6)

God chose us before the foundation of the world because he loved us. But why did he choose us? Not so that we might endlessly reflect on ourselves, but for the "praise of his glorious grace." When we worship God, we join an activity that began in eternity and will continue forever—the triune God valuing his beauty and worth above everything else.

John Piper, as usual, says it much better than I can:

From all eternity the ever-existing, never-becoming, always-perfect God has known himself and loved what he knows. He has eternally seen his beauty and savored what he sees. His understanding of his own reality is flawless and his exuberance in enjoying it is infinite. He has no needs, for he has no imperfections. He has no inclinations to evil because he has no deficiencies that could tempt him to do wrong. He is therefore the holiest and happiest being that is or that can be conceived. . . . To share this experience—the experience of knowing and enjoying his glory—is the reason God created the world.[1]

Why do we need to be reminded that worship begins and ends with God, is about God, and is for God? Isn't it obvious?

Apparently not. Most of the time when we think about worship, we start with what *we* do. Our intentions are noble; we come with our songs, our prayers, our offerings, and our lives to tell God how great he is. But we assume that acceptable worship ultimately depends on our efforts, sincerity, or gifts.

It doesn't. It never will.

In human relationships, when someone is sincerely and accurately praised, their "value" is increased in the eyes of others. That's why ads for movies report how many Academy Award nominations they received.

And why I pursued endorsements for this book. And why, if a politician's approval rating drops, his staff starts plotting how to boost the numbers. Public opinion matters to us.

God has never had that problem. It's true that the honor given to God is magnified when more people gather to proclaim his greatness, but this adds nothing to his intrinsic glory. He doesn't command us to worship him because of any deficiency in him but because of a deficiency in us. We *need* to worship God.

God also commands us to worship him because his moral perfection requires it. It's idolatrous to worship anything other than what is superior to everything else. And only God is in that category.

Worship is God's gift of grace to us before it's our offering to God. We simply benefit from the perfect offering of the Son to the Father through the power of the Spirit (Ephesians 2:18). Worship is our humble, constant, appropriate, glad response to God's self-revelation and his enabling invitation.

Apart from this perspective, leading worship can become self-motivated and self-exalting. We can become burdened by the responsibility to lead others and can think that we might not be able to deliver the goods. We subtly take pride in our worship, our singing, our playing, our planning, our performance, our leadership. Ultimately we separate ourselves from the God who drew us to worship him in the first place.

That's why biblical worship is God-focused (God is clearly seen), God-centered (God is clearly the priority), and God-exalting (God is clearly honored).

Gathering to praise God can't be a means to some "greater" end, such as church growth, evangelism, or personal ministry. God isn't a genie we summon by rubbing the bottle called "worship." He doesn't exist to help us get where we *really* want to go. God *is* where we want to go.

So God's glory is the end of our worship, and not simply a means to something else. In the midst of a culture that glorifies our pitiful accomplishments in countless ways, we gather each week to proclaim God's wondrous deeds and to glory in his supreme value. He is holy, holy, holy. There is no one, and nothing, like the Lord.

THE HORIZONTAL ELEMENT OF WORSHIP

But this all-encompassing, God-saturated emphasis can produce unbiblical distortions.

More than once I've heard someone say that God saved us for his glory, not for our happiness. Or that singing about what God has done for us makes worship man-centered. Or that we worship God because he's worthy, not because we as worshipers get something out of it. Or that spending time ministering to each other isn't worship. These are unfortunate and unnecessary dichotomies.

One of the primary ways we worship God is through proclaiming his glories, perfections, and works. But another equally significant way we worship God is through building one another up through encouragement and blessing. Different activities, but the same end.

Yes, we gather to worship God. But how do we do that? It's not just through songs and words directed to God.

The New Testament Christians gathered in large part to strengthen each other for the purpose of glorifying God in their daily lives. Hebrews 10:24–25 exhorts us about "not neglecting to meet together" so we can "stir up one another to love and good works." We're to be "encouraging one another."

Paul sounds a similar note to the Corinthians: "When you come together, each one has a hymn, a lesson, a revelation, a tongue, or an interpretation. *Let all things be done for building up*" (1 Corinthians 14:26). Everything in our time together has that same purpose: "building up."

Even our songs of praise are a way we minister to each other for God's glory. That's evident from Ephesians 5:19, where Paul says we're to be "*addressing one another* in psalms, hymns and spiritual songs," while at the same time "singing and making melody *to the Lord.*"

We aren't having our own little worship experiences independent of each other. As Donald Whitney reminds us:

> The thought that the Church at worship is an accidental convergence in one place of a number of isolated individuals who practice, in hermetically sealed compartments, their own private devotional exercises, is foreign to the New Testament picture.[2]

When we sing, we're "teaching and admonishing one another" (Colossians 3:16). To express that reality, I'll often open my eyes and look out at the congregation as I sing certain lines. I want to remind myself and the church that we're affirming truth together.

But the horizontal aspect of worship can be even more direct. We might take time to pray for those battling life-threatening illnesses. Someone may share a prophetic impression for older saints. We might honor an individual or specific group in the church for their faithful service or godly example.

If we pursue honor and edification for their own sake, we quickly lose sight of the One we're seeking to please. Meetings become all about what we're doing for each other, meeting people's needs, and making sure everyone is happy.

But done in a way that draws attention to God's grace, we're simply fulfilling the commands to "Outdo one another in showing honor" (Romans 12:10) and give "honor to whom honor is owed" (Romans 13:7). And we bring glory to God in the process.

David Peterson has helpfully pointed out that "edification and worship are different sides of the same coin." Then he adds, "This does not mean that prayer or praise is a means to an end, namely edification. We worship God because of who he is and because of his grace towards us."[3]

That's why we need to keep this healthy tension tense—so that God will be worshiped and his people will be built up, all for his glory.

chapter 23

PLANNED AND SPONTANEOUS

Back in the late seventies I led worship for an inner-city church in Philadelphia. It was quite the adventure.

We rarely rehearsed. I guess we figured the Holy Spirit would be freer to move that way. I usually came about five minutes before the meeting began and occasionally had even planned an opening song.

After that, it was pretty much a free-for-all. Occasionally someone in the congregation would start a song, which meant we had to be flexible and be able to play in whatever key they started in. If they were a quarter tone flat, we just endured it.

Fast-forward thirty years. At my current church about six or seven people meet on Tuesday to plan the following two Sundays. That group includes our senior pastor, technical director, music director, an assistant, and a few other pastors. At the end of the week, an e-mail is sent out letting everyone know who's doing what, how long each section of Sunday's meeting should take, any special announcements and events, what songs we're singing, and more. On Saturday night we rehearse for two hours, plus forty-five minutes more early Sunday morning.

I don't show up five minutes beforehand anymore. Those days are long gone.

These two scenarios highlight another healthy tension: planning and spontaneity. Some leaders like every detail planned or rehearsed in advance. Others prefer doing things on the fly. I'm definitely in the latter category.

Of course, in some churches technology leaves no options. I once visited a megachurch where any changes in the script would have to be communicated to twenty-four different people. Not much room for improvising.

The bigger your church, the more critical consistent planning and rehearsal become. But even when you're small, it's wise to develop the practice of planning. It's *not* unspiritual to determine ahead of time when things will take place, where transitions should be explained, how many songs to sing, what creative elements to include, or how the meeting will end. We've found that the Holy Spirit's most important guidance often comes before the meeting even begins.

As important as planning and rehearsals are, there are some things they can do and some things they can't. It helps to know the difference.

WHAT PLANNING CAN'T DO

Planning can't replace dependence on the Holy Spirit.

A few years ago Josh Harris, our senior pastor, took our pastoral team through a study on prayer. One of the effects was realizing how little we sought the Lord's help to establish our steps. Since then we take more unhurried time to express our need for God's wisdom and strength when we meet to plan the details of a meeting. The key word here is *unhurried*. Prayer is meant to be more than a perfunctory duty. We really need God. A number of times in our planning, Josh would start praying when we hit a roadblock. His example has been a great reminder of how we can do nothing apart from the Savior. Time after time the Lord has answered our prayers within a few minutes of our asking for clarity.

Planning doesn't substitute for listening to the Holy Spirit during the meeting either. Our goal should be to plan wisely, humbly, and prayerfully, fully expecting that God may provide fresh and unexpected guidance during the meeting. The Holy Spirit may have helped us, but that doesn't mean we've heard everything he wants to say.

Nor can planning ensure that everything will go right. You've probably figured that out. Making plans doesn't mean everyone will follow them or that you'll be immune from disruptions, errors, or disasters.

One Sunday my good friend Doug planned to start a song on his guitar and add the rest of the band on the downbeat of the verse. The effect would be dramatic.

It was. Doug's capo was in the wrong position, and the band came in a half step higher. Beautiful. That went on for about half a verse, the band frantically stumbling around behind him. Finally Doug stopped, laughed nervously, and started over. (Yet one more reason to thank God I'm a keyboard player.)

Planning also can't ensure we've made the *right* plans. We can have an incredible arrangement worked up for the wrong song. Or prepare an extended musical intro that effectively quenches what the Holy Spirit is doing and turns Sunday morning worship into Sunday morning performance.

There's nothing sacred about our plans. We shouldn't give them divine authority.

WHAT PLANNING CAN DO

Plans are meant to serve us, not rule us. And they can serve us in many ways.

Planning can make us aware of our need for God before the meeting. As we sit down and ponder what God wants to accomplish on Sunday, we may start to feel very needy. People will be walking in confused, empty, and bitter, facing financial worries, life-threatening illnesses, and family struggles. We know that God is sovereign, wise, and good and that he cares for them. But they've forgotten that. We have God's Word, four or five songs, and thirty minutes to help them see that God is bigger than their problems and that Jesus Christ is a magnificent Savior. How can we arrange this time so people are best positioned to hear from God and receive his grace? What can we do to serve the church most effectively?

I'm never immediately sure. That leads me to pray.

Planning can cause us to clarify our goals and how to meet them. A few years ago a number of new people in our growing church didn't seem to have a biblical understanding of physical expression in corporate worship. So we wanted to equip the church in this area. For a month we took extended time each Sunday to explain how physical expressions are signs of a worshiping heart. On various weeks we clapped and lifted our hands, or danced and jumped with our feet, or shouted and sang, or knelt and bowed down. Planning enabled us to choose songs that mentioned those actions and to prepare comments that connected praising God with serving him in all of life.

Planning has helped us use different musical styles, diversify the racial mix of our team, and use God's Word more consistently in our times of singing.

Planning can also help prepare all the team members for their contributions. Adequately rehearsing musicians in advance enables everyone to focus on worshiping God when they lead rather than being absorbed in their music.

I used to play through whole songs during rehearsal without giving much direction. We had a great time but didn't really accomplish much in terms of preparing anyone for the meeting.

To maximize rehearsal time, I try to make sure I cover these elements:
• chords and lyrics
• dynamics
• how songs begin and end
• who starts each song
• when to lay out and when to enter
• how to repeat a chorus
• when someone should play or sing a solo

Planning can also prepare people for sharing personal testimonies. We've found it's preferable to have folks share them from notes. The drawback is that these can sound a little impersonal or stiff. But the benefits far outweigh the disadvantages. Besides being able to edit their thoughts in advance for clarity and content, people are less anxious, less apt to change what they're supposed to say, and more likely to stay within their allotted time. They can deviate briefly when appropriate, yet still have their written notes to return to.

THE BENEFITS OF SPONTANEITY

If planning is classical music, spontaneity is jazz. Both are important for serving the church faithfully with our gifts.

Pursuing spontaneity isn't simply about breaking our routine or being creative. We want the Spirit to manifest his power through us in as many ways as possible so people's hearts and lives can be affected. Spontaneity can be a means to that end.

From passages such as 1 Corinthians 12 and 14 we see that the early church exercised spontaneous spiritual gifts that were "the manifestation of the Spirit for the common good" (1 Corinthians 12:7).

Martyn Lloyd-Jones encouraged preachers in such Spirit-directed spontaneity, and his comments can easily be applied to those who lead congregational worship:

> Do you expect anything to happen to you when you get up to preach in the pulpit? . . . [S]eek His power, expect this power, yearn for this power; and when this power comes, yield to Him. Do not resist. Forget all about

your sermon if necessary. Let Him loose you, let him manifest His power in you and through you.[1]

Spontaneity gives us the freedom to respond to present needs and promptings. Earlier I mentioned leaving room for spontaneous contributions that increase our awareness of the Spirit's active presence. This could include an unplanned comment, a prayer, a Scripture reading, or a prophecy. Smaller churches may be able to do this more frequently, but even in a large church we can make room for unplanned moments. Whether your church is big or small, it's important that contributions are evaluated by a pastor. Valuing spontaneity doesn't negate the need for godly leadership.

GROWING IN SPONTANEITY

Charles Spurgeon shared these wise thoughts about spontaneous impressions:

> I have been the subject of such impressions myself, and have seen very singular results. But to live by impressions is oftentimes to live the life of a fool and even to fall into downright rebellion against the revealed Word of God. Not your impressions, but that which is in this Bible must always guide you.[2]

However, "to live by impressions" is different from simply being receptive and responsive to them. If our feet are firmly planted in the sufficiency of God's Word, we are then more prepared to benefit from listening for the voice of the Spirit as we lead.

Here are a few practices and principles that have helped me grow in spontaneity, both spoken and musical, over the years.

Don't plan to do too much. Why do we try to squeeze eight songs into twenty-five minutes? Either we sing really short songs, we were on caffeine when we timed them, or we're not expecting to do anything but sing them straight through. Whatever the reason, this limits interaction with the Spirit and the congregation. We can't repeat songs or parts of songs for emphasis, and we certainly don't expect anyone to have time to actually think about what we're singing.

Practice musical spontaneity alone. In the seclusion of your own home you can try any of the following:

• Sing your prayers, using a familiar melody or one you make up.

• Sing Scripture. These Psalms are a good place to start: 23, 63, 84, 95, 100, 117, 121, and 145.

• Sing a line from Scripture, then respond to it in song. This develops your ability to interact with God's Word.

• Sing your own words and melody over a simple chord pattern.

• Make up a new melody to a familiar or a not-so-familiar hymn.

If you play an instrument, learn how to improvise at the end of a song rather than just ending it. That opens up opportunities for people to sing freely or to reflect on the truths they just sang. Here are some possibilities:

• Repeat the song's last harmonic progression.

• Borrow a harmonic progression from an earlier part of the song.

• Play a new, simple progression in the same key. For instance in the key of D, you might try these:

D—Dsus—D—Dsus

D—G/D—A/D—G/D

D—Bm7—Em7—G

Work on spontaneity with your team. First of all, make sure your team can easily see and hear you as you lead. Take time to do a relaxed monitor check. If sight lines are blocked, rearrange the setup of the musicians.

Work out with the team how and when to listen for your direction. Some musicians do this naturally; others don't have a clue. I ask my musicians to look my way near the end of every verse and chorus. I'm glad they're engaged with the songs we're singing, but they'll serve the church more effectively if they're also engaged with me at the right moments. They don't have to look over at me in a dramatic or sudden way; a casual glance works fine.

About two to four measures before the end of a section I generally give a verbal cue so everyone knows what's coming. I've also developed a few hand signals to communicate with the musicians on the fly:

• *chorus:* forming the letter *c* with my hand

• *verse:* upheld fingers to indicate which one

• *a cappella:* point to my throat

• *fade out or play softly:* touching my thumb to my other fingers

• *tag or special section:* crossed fingers, signifying I hope everyone remembers what this means

• *I want you to play a solo:* pointing at someone

• *end the song:* an upheld closed fist

These will be a little difficult for guitar players, and in any case you might have your own set of cues. Whatever you do, give your cues briefly and discreetly.

Unless I've directed them otherwise, our team knows to stop playing at the end of a song even if I keep playing. At times a well-meaning guitarist has tried to accompany what I'm doing. That limits any harmonic or tempo changes I might want to make.

Practice spontaneity in your rehearsals. Rather than simply rehearse songs, I try mixing things up in rehearsal. I'll repeat a line or a verse unexpectedly or sing a chorus a cappella. If the band doesn't follow me, we might have a monitor problem. At the very least, it reminds the musicians to be watching me for possible changes in direction.

Playing spontaneously gives us one more musical tool to help people see the glories of our great God and Savior. It may be as simple as playing a brief interlude to transition between two songs or repeating the last line of a song to savor the truth we're singing. It may be as complex as composing a song on the spot so the congregation can respond to a message. In either case, being able to play spontaneously enables us to respond at any moment to ways the Holy Spirit might be directing us.

Of course, the Spirit can also use us in powerful ways as we play notes we've practiced for hours during months of rehearsals. But isn't it helpful to be able to do both?

chapter 24

ROOTED AND RELEVANT

For years I thought of religious traditions as a hindrance to biblical spirituality. I associated repeated prayers, reciting creeds together, public confessions of sin, Scripture readings, church calendars, and orders of service with legalism and bondage.

I was on a mission to start from scratch in my thinking about corporate worship. I would look only to Scripture rather than depending on anything people had done in previous centuries. I thought I was being original.

Actually, I was simply being ignorant—and proud.

BENEFITS OF BEING ROOTED

If you came into my office today, you'd see old books on my desk. One is a 1798 copy of *Discourses on the Love of God* by Isaac Watts. I also have a 1721 copy of his sermons. The pile includes hymnals from the nineteenth century and Thomas Gibbons's biography of Watts, published in 1780.

People often ask me why I keep them on my desk, and I always give the same answer: I never want to forget that my generation isn't the first to think about and pursue biblical worship.

When we decide what form our Sunday meeting will take, we aren't starting in a historical vacuum. Projection, lighting systems, and sound amplification don't mean that everything from previous centuries is irrelevant or unhelpful. Although technology changes many things, it doesn't change the gospel we proclaim or our need to be humble.

How can we become more rooted in what God has done in the past?

We can start by opening our eyes. I didn't grow up singing classic hymns.

To remedy that problem, I spent one summer singing my way through a hymnal in my devotions. I was shocked. Such truth, such profound theology, such poetic beauty, such passion! Where had these songs been? Sitting on the pages of hymnals everywhere. But in my arrogance I'd never opened one to learn them.

As grateful as I am to God for the outpouring of modern worship songs, I think the riches of hymnody far outweigh what we've produced in the last thirty years. They cover a broader range of topics, are more dense and theologically precise, and are often brilliantly crafted. And that's not a surprise. The hymns we sing today have been tested for centuries, causing the best ones to rise to the top.

There's richness for us as well in liturgical forms from the past. Christians through the ages have sought to articulate what's most important for Christians to hear and say when they meet. A repeated liturgy that's biblically based can help people rehearse and remember the story of redemption each time the church gathers. That's the reasoning behind a corporate confession of sin followed by an assurance of forgiveness through Christ's atoning death.

Throughout history, liturgies have helped regulate the theological diet of a congregation and protect them from the winds of errant doctrine that sweep through every generation. Good liturgies can also keep a church from conforming to culture or compromising its faith. Following a church calendar enables a church to sound all the right notes in the symphony of redemption each year.

That doesn't mean we have to incorporate everything from different liturgical traditions. But we shouldn't completely ignore them either.

For some, the whole idea of repeated liturgies is frightening. But as I've said before, we all have a liturgy. It may be the liturgy of "never doing anything twice." If so, we may discover that rather than helping people hear the gospel, we're hindering them.

We share a common heritage with saints who've gone before us. Actually, it's stronger than that. When the church gathers, we aren't alone. We join with "the assembly of the firstborn who are enrolled in heaven" (Hebrews 12:23), made up of those whom Christ has redeemed from every age. Reusing hymns and liturgical forms that go back hundreds of years is one way of affirming that we follow in a long line of worshipers who have sought to bring glory to God.

That doesn't mean hymn melodies are sacred, are the best they could ever be, or should never be altered. As I mentioned earlier, most hymns were written as text without music. They were joined to various tunes until one became more popular than all the others. But we're just plain arrogant when we think that all the great melodies have been written in the last twenty years.

As with any healthy tension, there's a drawback to focusing excessively on one side of it. Too much emphasis on traditions and roots can cause us to depend on them. Many traditions began as an earnest attempt to protect the truths of the faith, but over time they became separated from faith, resulting in dead orthodoxy. They now practice a form of godliness but lack true spiritual power. There will never be a perfect liturgy or tradition that ensures the continued faith of future generations.

THE RIGHTNESS OF RELEVANCE

The greatest traditions in the world are meaningless unless they effectively communicate God's truth to the people who come to our meetings. In every age the church must fight the tendency to grow mechanical in its worship as the Spirit-inspired practices of previous generations become the dead, unexamined practices of the next. That means we need to ask whether the songs, words, arrangements, visuals, expressions, and traditions we're using are saying the things we want them to say—and whether people actually understand what we're saying.

That's why we pursue worship traditions that are flexible and suitable for the present culture. We want to proclaim the unchanging gospel in ways our culture can comprehend, ways that will make it easy for people to perceive who Jesus Christ is and how he has changed us.

One application of this is avoiding verses from old hymns with lyrics whose meaning is unclear (or making them more relevant by altering a few words or phrases). "Come, Thou Fount of Every Blessing" is filled with biblically based images and aspirations, but the beginning of the second verse can raise eyebrows: "Here I raise mine Ebenezer; here by thy great help I've come." Why are we suddenly singing about a character from Dickens's *A Christmas Carol*? Some have argued that keeping the original words provides an opportunity to teach the story of God's faithfulness behind "Ebenezer" in 1 Samuel 7. That's true, if we do it well. But I think there are other alternatives that don't require an explanation each time we sing it.

We shouldn't expect everyone who walks in on a Sunday morning to be able to comprehend every word to songs we've sung for years. But we should consider whether the lyrics we're singing sound like a foreign language to anyone outside the family.

Another application is using relevant visuals. Being the church is no reason to be thirty years behind in decorating styles, graphics, and technology. But our goal is to communicate clearly, not to distract or overwhelm. I heard recently of one pastor whose media team had planned a video image to be shown behind him as he spoke. When he came in, he saw that the video was flickering very slightly. He made the decision right then to put a curtain over the screen. He didn't want anything to detract from what he was saying. That shows more wisdom than the constantly changing backgrounds that sometimes accompany lyric projection.

Relevance looks different from one geographical area to the next. One church will become more informal, another more ordered. A large church in the city might add a jazz band and use the Internet for all its communication, while a church in rural Tennessee may add a dobro to the worship team and stick with a Sunday bulletin.

But every church should make sure that the story of God's redemption can be clearly understood and experienced by those they're seeking to reach with the gospel.

THE DANGERS OF PURSUING RELEVANCE

We can't assume that we can adapt anything the world does and trust God to use it for his glory. The medium can affect and even obscure the message.

For instance, communication in our culture today has become more image-driven and less text-driven. But an overuse of video imagery in our churches can lessen the impact of the Word and fuel a desire for more images.

As I've heard it said, what you win people *with* is what you generally win them *to*.

Relevance can also be an idol. We become convinced that some fresh, different, culturally hip idea will make our worship more powerful or appealing. Maybe it's lighting or candles or creative videos or "interactive artistic worship activity."

But we may find ourselves on the treadmill of cultural change. We keep moving, but we're not making any progress. What's worse, we can't stop. We forget that what was once contemporary is now traditional. Blink, and today's newest musical style or liturgical form is so *yesterday*.

Os Guinness wrote:

> By our breathless chase after relevance without a matching commitment
> to faithfulness, we have become not only unfaithful but irrelevant; by our

determined efforts to redefine ourselves in ways that are more compelling to the modern world than are faithful to Christ, we have lost not only our identity but our authority and our relevance. Our crying need is to be faithful as well as relevant.[1]

One of the benefits of rooted traditions is their ability to immunize us against the relentless changes in our culture and make us more attuned to faithfulness.

The church is set apart from the world. That difference will at times be repulsive, at times attractive. We shouldn't be surprised when unbelievers who visit our meetings don't understand everything that's going on. "The natural person does not accept the things of the Spirit of God, for they are folly to him, and he is not able to understand them because they are spiritually discerned" (1 Corinthians 2:14).

When evaluating ways we could become more relevant, our questioning should include a focus on the theological basis for our actions. (What biblical truths are we seeking to communicate more clearly through these changes?) Plus a careful examination of our motives. (Do we just want to be on the cutting edge?) And a realistic anticipation of the consequences. (What will we have to *stop* doing in order to *start* doing this?)

FIRST THINGS FIRST

When it comes to forms of worship, any form that facilitates and encourages worship in spirit and truth by a particular gathering of people, at a particular time in history, in the context of a particular culture is pleasing to God. That implies that no one form can fully express the vastness of God. No given time, culture, or generation can give God the honor he deserves.

This understanding keeps first things first. Cultures change, styles change, traditions change, times change. God remains the same.

Through wise leadership and a faithful example, let's train our people to draw upon the rich heritage of the past, while at the same time seeking to communicate the eternal gospel in ways our culture can understand.

chapter 25

SKILLED AND AUTHENTIC

Here's a quiz. Which is more pleasing to God?

(a) A hundred-voice choir singing Handel's *Messiah* accompanied by a full orchestra.

(b) An average guitar player sincerely leading his church in a passionate rendition of "Amazing Grace."

The answer depends on whether we define excellence from our perspective or God's.

Certainly (a) involves more people, hours, and preparation than (b). But that doesn't automatically mean God is more pleased. All the musical skill in the world won't substitute for a genuine heart of worship.

But (b) isn't a safe bet either. Churches that minimize the need for skill can tend toward sentimentalism, sloth, and pride in their "genuineness."

God wants us to pursue both skill *and* heart, like the craftsmen who built the temple. "Moses called Bezalel and Oholiab and every craftsman *in whose mind the* LORD *had put skill, everyone whose heart stirred him up* to come to do the work" (Exodus 36:2).

Since I addressed the issues of skill and heart engagement earlier, I'm going to take this chapter to answer specific questions that arise as we seek to keep these in healthy tension.

Can we pursue skill too much? Is it possible to worship God and lead skillfully at the same time? And how important is excellence on the worship team?

CAN WE EXPERIENCE SKILL OVERKILL?

When we worship God skillfully, we offer him what is excellent, our very best (Exodus 23:19a; Numbers 18:29–30). But taken to the extreme, an emphasis on skill and excellence can drift toward arrogance, formalism, and art worship.

The religious landscape today is filled with churches offering incredibly beautiful music, worthy of a concert hall, played and sung by musicians who don't know Christ as their Savior. Those same churches often have preachers who are great orators, trained in rhetoric and public speaking. Unfortunately, they have no good news to preach, only their own opinions and moralistic platitudes. Artistic excellence has replaced God as the object of worship.

Reggie Kidd, in *With One Voice*, pinpoints the problem:

> In some churches the quest for "excellence" is an idol, regardless of whether "excellence" is defined by standards of so-called "classical" culture or of "pop" culture. Such "excellentism" needs to be replaced with the quest to pursue the likeness of Christ crucified and him alone. As good as it gets this side of Christ's return, we're never going to get it completely right. There will always be a flat tenor, a broken guitar string, an overly loud organ, or a poorly placed hymn. But it's okay. The cross means it's covered.[1]

Does that mean we don't need to be concerned about how we play, whether we're in tune, or what songs we use? Of course not. God commends musical excellence (Psalm 33:3; 1 Chronicles 15:22; 2 Chronicles 30:21–22). Years ago my degree in piano performance taught me (painfully) something about the value of musical skill and excellence. But in congregational worship excellence has a purpose—to focus people's attention on God's wondrous attributes and acts.

In corporate worship, then, skill and excellence are functional. They have more to do with edification and encouragement than musical standards. I want to be the very best I can be so that I can serve others more effectively for God's glory.

A basic standard to achieve is playing well enough that I won't distract those I'm seeking to serve. It means I might play fewer notes so people can hear the words. It means sacrificing my ideas of musical "excellence" to make the truth more musically accessible to my congregation. It means I might not play at all, so the congregation can hear their own voices clearly ringing out in praise to God.

Musical excellence, understood correctly, is a worthy pursuit. But like all idols, it makes a terrible god.

TO LEAD OR TO WORSHIP—IS THAT THE QUESTION?

Earlier I mentioned that I'm often asked how it's possible to lead worship and at the same time focus on magnifying the Savior in my heart. One conference speaker said we should "sacrifice" our worship for the sake of the congregation. I don't agree.

Is it possible to effectively lead people in worship, give musical cues, play the right chords, and still worship God? Absolutely.

Assuming I have sufficient skill, do I have to sacrifice my worship of God in order to facilitate the worship of others? No. The only thing I have to sacrifice is my narrow understanding of what worship is.

Worship isn't just about what's happening between me and God—it concerns *us* and God. As I help people extol God's greatness through song, I'm contributing to praise for God. As I give a well-timed verbal cue, notice how people are responding, or communicate with the band, I'm wanting people to see and celebrate the supreme worth of God. That's leading worship. If that's *not* why I'm doing those things, I wasn't worshiping God to begin with.

Effective leadership and worshiping God are two sides of the same coin. They were never meant to be opposed to each other. And, of course, the more skillful I am in practical areas, the easier it will be for me to worship God through the songs we're singing. The point is, I do everything to magnify the greatness of God in Jesus Christ. That's worship.

QUALITY OR QUANTITY?

As your church grows in size, your team will too. One day you may find you have multiple players on each instrument and fifteen vocalists. Scheduling has become a nightmare. You know something has to change, but you're not sure what.

Looking at your roster, you think some are definitely "A" players and vocalists. They have character and gifting, and they're faithful. They're also rare. Most of the others are "B" musicians—genuine worshipers of God, but not as skilled. You even have a few "C" vocalists who were on the team when you came to the church three years ago (including the pastor's wife).

Do you reduce the size of the team and make your life easier but risk offending some people? Or do you just let things continue as they are, valuing the genuine desire of people to worship God with their musical gifts, however limited they might be? Are there other options?

The first thing to do is to ask God for wisdom and grace. You'll need it.

Romans 12:3–6 gives us fundamental truths about the gifts God gives us and how we're to view them. It provides biblical principles that can help us manage a growing team of musicians. We're reminded that we're not to think of ourselves more highly than we ought, "but to think with sober judgment." It tells us that "the members do not all have the same function," that we're "one body in Christ," that we're "individually members one of another," and that we have "gifts that differ according to the grace given to us."

In line with those truths, we don't have to apologize for using the most gifted musicians. "Members do not all have the same function." As we read in 1 Chronicles 15:22 (NIV), Kenaniah led the singing "because he was skillful at it."

Our first responsibility is not to make a specific individual happy but to serve the congregation with the gifts God has placed in the church. God gives those gifts to build up the church, not to fulfill the aspirations of various members. We ask our most outgoing members to be greeters, and people who are administrative to handle the finances. Those with a leadership gift head up serving teams, and people with an evangelistic gift serve in the follow-up ministry. So no one should think it odd that we want musically skilled people to serve on the music team (assuming we're not valuing skill over character—both are important).

We also shouldn't equate someone's *desire* to serve with *giftedness* to serve. We are to think of ourselves "with sober judgment." *American Idol* has shown us how deceived musicians can be about their talent. Wanting to sing doesn't mean someone is called or gifted to sing. I once had a woman in our church tell me repeatedly that she would be *thrilled* to serve on our *awesome* worship team. Unfortunately, I learned she had a strong vibrato and sang slightly off-key. It was obvious that the music team wasn't the best fit for her. I encouraged her to find another ministry to serve in, but she ended up leaving. As a leader I have to be willing to graciously redirect less musically gifted people to serve in other ways, aware that I might lose them in the process.

It's always a good idea to meet with your team to explain your qualifications for membership. At the very least those should include godliness, musical skill, and natural expressiveness. Make it clear that as the church grows, new members might surpass them in those areas. When that time comes, we want to make room for those new members.

I always stress that being on the music team is an opportunity to serve, not a right to protect. In fact, if we're humbly pursuing God's will for our lives, we'll be the first ones to encourage others' involvement. That means present members might end up serving less or in another ministry. But that doesn't lessen their importance to the team now.

If you don't know everyone's skill level, you may want to set up brief music interviews and adjust how you schedule your musicians accordingly. Communicate to less skilled musicians that they may not be scheduled as often, but they're still valuable to the team. Athletic teams typically have many more players than are actually playing at any given moment, but every player is needed. Your "B" musicians need to be the best "B" musicians they can be. When your main soprano gets laryngitis, when your guitarist cuts his finger, when your best drummer has a scheduling conflict, a less skilled player's stock goes up.

In *Music Through the Eyes of Faith,* Harold Best defines excellence as "the process of becoming better than I once was." God used that definition to help our team realize we're called to develop the gifts God gives us, not to be better than others.

If there are individuals who shouldn't be on the team because they lack gifting, I'd talk with them personally, thank them for serving, and help them find another ministry in which to serve. At times it might be necessary to involve a pastor in this conversation.

Another option is to schedule less talented musicians with more gifted musicians so they can support and learn from them. We've encouraged our best musicians to meet with less skilled members outside of rehearsals. Everyone benefits. If no one on the team is available to teach, you can also recommend private lessons.

For vocalists who aren't soloists, consider putting together an ensemble. Choirs and ensembles not only involve more people but also contribute to a bigger sound, more exuberant expressiveness, and more creative arrangements. You might use them only once a month, but it's one more way for more people to use their gifts to bless the church.

Some leaders opt for smaller teams with a higher skill level. That approach can serve the church more effectively, contribute to a tighter team dynamic, and shorten rehearsal time.

I typically use a larger team that involves more people musically, allows skilled players to take time off, and facilitates training others. Whatever you choose to do, don't compromise either skill or authentic worship.

When people understand that their gifts are from God, that gifts are different, and that they're all for God's glory, they'll have an easier time understanding why they don't sing or play as often as they'd like or as often as someone else. As we encourage and help people serve with "the measure of faith God has assigned," they'll be able to do so with joy, no matter when, where, or how.

chapter 26

FOR THE CHURCH AND FOR UNBELIEVERS

We love having people over at our house, whether it's a spontaneous party on Saturday night, lunch after church on Sundays, or a worship team crab feast.

A sign on the wall next to our kitchen table tells everyone what to do: "Sit long—talk much—laugh often."

But no matter how many people stop by or how often, we never get confused about who lives with us. Julie and the kids and I care for everyone who comes into our home, but not in the way we care for each other. Because we're family.

Our responsibility to the church is similar. Every week we have guests and visitors. Some have been brought by members of the church, some are visiting from out of town, and others just drop in. Occasionally people attend for months without getting involved. I want to serve each one of them.

But my greatest concern is for those God has joined to my particular congregation. They're my spiritual family, and together we are living stones that make up this temple (1 Peter 2:4–5). If they're not growing in grace and godliness, our demonstration of the gospel is out of step with our declaration.

A DEFINED WORSHIPING COMMUNITY

The church isn't made up of anyone who happens to be in the building on Sunday morning. It's the people God has joined together in a specific locality through the blood of his Son and the power of his Spirit (Ephesians 2:19–22).

The New Testament makes it clear that the church is a defined community. The Lord's Supper is shared by those who are part of that body (1 Corinthians 11:27–29). Paul instructed the Corinthian church to remove from their midst a man in unrepentant sin (1 Corinthians 5:2). Jesus himself provided a procedure for expelling someone from the church community (Matthew 18:15–17). First Corinthians 14:24 speaks of "outsiders" coming into our meetings. That means there must be insiders.

Churches view membership in different ways. Some take it pretty lightly. You can become a member on your second Sunday. Others, like ours, take it pretty seriously. People who want to become members go through a multi-week course where they learn of our doctrinal distinctives and practices, meet with a pastor, are presented to the church at a members' meeting, and join a small group.

However your church might view or practice church membership, we have a particular responsibility to shepherd those who are walking their Christian life with us. The first priority of our Sunday meetings is strengthening the church. We're God's covenant people who have gathered in his presence to be built into "a spiritual house" through the gospel (1 Peter 2:5).

God doesn't intend for the people we lead each Sunday to remain perpetually immature. He wants them in every way to grow up into Christ. So as leaders our job is to support our pastor in his role of insuring that the church is growing in maturity.

But that maturing can be hindered when we focus primarily on non-family members. When the entire church program revolves around drawing new people, when all your musical choices are geared to the tastes of non-Christians, it becomes difficult, if not impossible, to provide the teaching and nourishment the church needs.

One pastor confessed that he'd been marketing his church for years, offering "human enrichment rather than eternal and powerful truth." The unfortunate result is, "I have grown a church of baptized pagans."[1] Unless we focus on the genuine need of the members in our church to consistently sing, hear, and apply gospel-centered, biblical truth, we may have the same result.

Imagine the effect if *church growth* referred to churches growing in their understanding of the gospel, personal godliness, involvement in the church, and their heart for the lost rather than simply numbers. That kind of growth must take precedence over worship that is simply meant to draw crowds. And it will have more impact on the world than anything else we can try or think of.

KEEPING UNBELIEVERS IN MIND

But what happens when unbelievers show up at our meetings? Do we care if they feel confused by our "Christianese"? Are guests thrown off by actions and responses that are completely foreign to them? Do we ever acknowledge their presence or even consider them when we plan? Will unbelieving guests sense a spiritual pride in us that keeps us from remembering what it means to be a sinner saved by grace?

Hopefully not. But such are the dangers of forgetting the non-Christians who might be with us and are vulnerable to confusion.

Paul challenges the Corinthians to take unbelievers into account when they gather. He insists that they keep the unbeliever in mind as they exercise spiritual gifts (1 Corinthians 14:23–25). Your church may not believe in the present-day use of tongues, but to many non-Christians, that's exactly what some of our meetings sound like. Whether it's raised hands, formal liturgies, or unspoken standards, we need to see them through the eyes of an unbeliever.

Being aware of the presence of non-Christians in our meetings causes me to say things more simply, explain common Christian phrases or words, and occasionally address those with us who don't know the Savior.

It was fashionable for many years to take surveys of communities to find out what non-Christians liked and didn't like about churches. Churches then developed advertising strategies and meetings that reflected the expressed desires of their unbelieving community.

But that's a problem. Non-Christians are aware of their wants but not of their true need to be reconciled to God. And what meets that need can be found in any gathering of thoughtful, Christ-exalting worshipers.

Contrary to the surveys, here's what we've seen affects unbelievers most when we gather.

Authentic passion. We have an enthusiastic church. I've read the studies that say you can't sing for any longer than seventeen minutes, that messages shouldn't go longer than twenty, and that people are put off by expressiveness. That hasn't been our experience.

When unbelievers visit our church, they find people who are awestruck and amazed by the kindness and mercy of God. And we seek to make it clear that God's grace is what has affected us so deeply. We don't meet just to talk about God; we're encountering his gracious presence. And we aren't reluctant to express outwardly what has so affected us inwardly. People show demonstrative emotion all the time at rock concerts and basketball games and no one ever questions it. Why do we think guests will be surprised to see it in people who claim to have the greatest news the world has ever heard?

Love. One of the most significant ways of impacting non-Christians at our meetings is through the way we reach out to them. We've experimented with different ways of identifying visitors. We always come back to having them stand while we thank them for coming through our applause. This gives those around them an opportunity to introduce themselves, invite them to our guest reception designed just for them, and often invite them out to lunch. We want to overwhelm them with our love.

Time and time again visitors have commented not only on the genuine love they've received but on the love they've observed between members of the church. That's what Jesus said would happen. He prayed for our unity "so that the world may believe" that the Father had sent him (John 17:21). As we encourage believers in the church to serve each other in practical ways, not only are we fulfilling biblical worship, but people notice and are drawn to the Savior.

The gospel. The best way to maintain the healthy tension of building the church and reaching out to unbelievers is by proclaiming and expounding on the gospel—Jesus Christ was crucified for our sins to bring us to God.

The gospel, clearly proclaimed and faithfully applied, will speak to unbelievers because it is "the power of God for salvation to everyone who believes" (Romans 1:16). We have no better way to serve non-Christians than to help them hear, understand, and experience the grand story of God's redemption in Jesus Christ. The gospel will also speak to Christians because we're to "continue in the faith, stable and steadfast, *not shifting from the hope of the gospel that you heard*" (Colossians 1:23, emphasis added).

We don't have to adopt atheological, man-centered methods with uncritical, wide-eyed wonder. D. A. Carson, in *The Cross and Christian Ministry*, writes:

> If the church is being built with large portions of charm, personality, easy oratory, positive thinking, managerial skills, powerful and emotional experiences, and people smarts, but without the repeated, passionate, Spirit-anointed proclamation of "Jesus Christ and him crucified" we may be winning more adherents than converts.[2]

Let's not ignore non-Christians when we gather to worship God. But let's not allow them to dictate our direction, methods, and values either. Those have all been determined and modeled by the risen Savior who now invites us to celebrate as a family and to invite others to join in on the feast.

chapter 27

EVENT AND EVERYDAY

Years ago I attended a retreat for those in our church who
lead small groups. During one meeting I found myself overwhelmed with
a sense of God's love for me while I sang to him. For a few moments I was
completely undone. Oblivious to everyone around me, tears flowed freely
down my cheeks.

I wasn't sure what was going on, but I knew I wanted more of it. Earthly
pursuits suddenly seemed unimportant, and I had an all-consuming desire to
spend all my time worshiping and serving the Lord who had redeemed me
for his glory. *This is what I was made for*, I remember thinking.

Over the next few days, praise flowed constantly through my heart. I
went to bed singing and woke up with a song on my lips. God even gave me
grace to sing worship songs in the middle of the night when I was rocking
our newborn son, Jordan, back to sleep. I was carried along by an overflowing joy. Whenever I worshiped God with a group, I jumped high and sang
with all my heart. I was committed to being a 24/7 worshiper.

But worshiping God full-time had its drawbacks. Like when I walked
through a shopping mall and the Muzak blared over the speakers. "Don't
they know I'm trying to worship God? How can I glorify God if I can't even
sing a worship song?"

It wasn't long before I realized something was wrong. Either God didn't
expect me to worship him all the time, or my understanding of worship was
deficient.

I figured out it was the latter.

WORSHIP IN ALL OF LIFE

Like many people, I thought *worship* meant singing worship songs. You and I know it doesn't, but we often make comments like these:

- After the sermon we'll go back to worship.
- Who's doing the worship this morning?
- We only have twenty minutes for worship next week.

If we said anything like that to first-century Christians in Rome or Ephesus, we'd get some odd looks.

Although there are several Greek words in the New Testament that we translate "worship," none of them mean "singing." Kind of odd, don't you think?

Even in the Old Testament, God never intended that his people confine worship to sacrifices at the temple. Worship that pleased God couldn't be restricted to certain actions, forms, or rituals. Those were meant to encourage and express a life devoted to honoring God in all respects. The laws Moses recounted in Deuteronomy encompassed every aspect of life, not merely a specific time of "worship." Most of the Hebrew words that we translate "worship" refer to gestures, attitudes, and actions that could happen anytime, with or without singing.

In the New Testament there's an even stronger move away from identifying meetings and rituals as essential to our worship. Jesus made it possible for all of life to be experienced as worship in spirit and truth. Through his once-and-for-all offering, everything we do can be offered up as a sacrifice of praise to God (Hebrews 13:15).

In fact, the New Testament writers consistently take Old Testament words related to worship—words such as *altar, sacrifice, priest, temple*—and apply them to life in general.

Evangelism is worship. Paul spoke of how he served (worshiped) God "with my whole heart in preaching the gospel of his Son" (Romans 1:9, NIV).

Serving others is worship. "Do not neglect to do good and to share what you have, for such sacrifices are pleasing to God" (Hebrews 13:16).

Giving is worship. Paul referred to financial gifts as "a fragrant offering, a sacrifice acceptable and pleasing to God" (Philippians 4:18).

Romans 12:1 is one of the most familiar passages that connects worship to all of life: "present your bodies as a living sacrifice, holy and acceptable to God, which is your spiritual worship." The sacrifices that please God are no longer bulls, rams, and sheep but our very lives, indicated by Paul's intentional use of the word "bodies."

The phrase "spiritual worship" can also be translated "understanding" or "reasonable" worship. It was a term that Greek philosophers used to describe worship acts that were supposedly more rationally based than the animal sacrifices of their day. The Greeks valued internal worship, expressed in silence before an impersonal deity. In contrast, Paul emphasizes not only presenting righteous lives to God, but doing so on the basis of the one atoning sacrifice of Christ.[1] That means our worship is revealed not simply in a meeting but in the way we live every day. We worship God by seeking to obey 1 Corinthians 10:31: "So, whether you eat or drink, or whatever you do, do all to the glory of God."

So what does it look like to worship God all the time?

It's doing everything to draw attention to his greatness and goodness. It's doing the things God commanded us to do and avoiding the things he has forbidden, all with a heart that seeks to please and reflect the Savior whose sacrifice rescued us from eternal damnation. It's loving our spouse and children, serving others, spending our money, helping the poor, driving our car, going to school, and working at our jobs in ways that bring glory to the Savior whose praise will never cease.

Biblically speaking, there's no sacred/secular distinction in our lives. Every moment is an opportunity to worship God. Church buildings aren't sacred, and family rooms aren't secular; both are places where God can be worshiped in spirit and truth.

Many churches begin their meetings with a "call to worship." They're announcing that the church has gathered at God's invitation to remember and respond to his grace. We're taking time to focus all our energies on declaring, magnifying, and savoring the riches of God in Christ through song, prayer, and the Word.

But Harold Best suggests we should think of these instead as a call to *continue* worshiping.

> There can only be one call to worship, and this comes at conversion, when in complete repentance we admit to worshiping falsely, trapped by the inversion and enslaved to false gods before whom we have been dying sacrifices. This call to true worship comes but once, not every Sunday, in spite of the repeated calls to worship that begin most liturgies and orders of worship. These should not be labeled calls to worship but calls to continuation of worship.[2]

WORSHIPING WITH THE GATHERED CHURCH

So if we're worshiping God throughout each day, how important is it that we meet as the church on Sunday?

Very.

The early Christians are almost always seen worshiping, evangelizing, praying, singing, and living *together*. As in the Old Testament, the overwhelming focus is on the people of God, not on the isolated individuals of God.

Corporate worship is more than a good idea. It's crucial to God's purposes for his people. The spiritual fervor of Israel under leaders like David, Josiah, and Nehemiah was accompanied by a commitment to authentic corporate worship. The same attitude will be true of the church today.

We saw earlier that God demonstrates his presence in a unique way when we gather and that our meetings provide opportunities for mutual edification. Here are a few more reasons why we gather weekly as the church:

We need the encouragement and support. A few years ago we took our first two-week vacation as a family. While I enjoyed the extra week together, there was a definite downside. In spite of extended family time, days on the beach, reading books, and personal devotions, I felt a drag in my soul. I missed meeting with the church.

The truth is, we can study our Bibles, read Christian books, sing worship songs, pray, and commune with God in the privacy of our own homes. And we should. But we're easily deceived by our sinful hearts. God has so designed the church that it's impossible to grow in godliness and know the fullness of his grace apart from the church. That's humbling. It flies in the face of our self-sufficient and self-reliant tendencies. That's why we need the church. It also gives us an opportunity to be a means of support and encouragement to others.

God receives greater glory. God's inherent glory never increases or diminishes. But as Donald Whitney explains:

> When a football team wins the national championship, it gets more glory if the game is shown to millions throughout the country than if no one but you were to see it individually on closed-circuit TV. . . . Public glory obviously brings more glory than does private glory. Likewise, God gets more glory when you worship him with the church than when you worship him alone.[3]

No public gathering can substitute for private devotion, which honors God. No public gathering can replace individuals showing the love of Christ to others and proclaiming his truth in their schools, workplaces, and neighborhoods. Without those accompanying private actions, public worship will eventually drift toward shallowness and hypocrisy. But when we come together to "pour forth the fame of [God's] abundant goodness" (Psalm 145:7), more people can see that God is worthy of praise.

We receive the teaching and care of God's pastor-shepherds. Pastors are gifts from the ascended Christ to equip us for ministry (Ephesians 4:11–12). They have the responsibility to lead, guide, guard, and feed God's people (1 Peter 5:2; Acts 20:28), which they especially do in the context of the gathered church. One day they'll give an account to God for those he has placed in their care (Hebrews 13:17).

God intends for humble, servant-minded shepherds to care for those his Son has redeemed (Jeremiah 23:4). Rather than level the playing field by dismantling all authority structures, Jesus defined leaders in a new way—faithful servants who lead for God's glory rather than their own (Luke 22:25–27). Paul made sure leaders were appointed in the early churches, and he commended their authority (see 1 Thessalonians 5; Titus 1; 1 Timothy 3). Godly leaders in the church are a sign of God's blessing.

As worship leaders, we need mature pastors in our lives. We don't want to be on our own. Pastors ensure that we value biblical knowledge and godly character, not just musical chops. They remind us that worship is more than music. Most importantly, they lead us in caring for the church of God that "he obtained with his own blood" (Acts 20:28).

We're reminded that we've been drawn apart from the world and drawn together to God. Gathering together is a physical demonstration of our distinctness from the world and our unity in the gospel. Obviously, showing up at a church building is no guarantee we're unified. But meeting together reminds us of the gospel that has reconciled us to one another and makes us "eager to maintain the unity of the Spirit in the bond of peace" (Ephesians 4:3). It forces us to rub shoulders with those who are unlike us, maybe those we don't even like, and to recognize our need for mercy at the foot of the cross—together.

PUTTING EVENT AND EVERYDAY TOGETHER

Leading a fulfilling, faith-inspiring time of corporate worship is one of my primary tasks as a worship leader. How do I connect this worship with our everyday worship?

Often at the end of a time of singing I'll pray that the realities we've been declaring will be proclaimed in our daily lives. I might ask God to help us remember that he doesn't change when we're in the middle of trials. He's just as worthy of worship when our car breaks down as when we meet on

Sunday morning. I'll often pray that God will bring to mind the gospel truths we've been celebrating as we go through our week.

I might also lead songs that talk about living every day for God's glory, like the hymn "Take My Life and Let It Be" or "What Can I Do" by Paul Baloche and Graham Kendrick:

What can I do but thank you?
What can I do but give
My life to you?
Hallelujah, hallelujah!
What can I do but praise you?
Every day make everything I do
A hallelujah, a hallelujah.
Hallelujah![4]

We can also refer to nonmusical parts of the meeting as worship. "Let's continue our worship through our tithes and offerings." "Let's prepare our hearts to worship God as we hear his Word proclaimed." That helps people realize that everything we do for God's glory is worship.

In the end, worshiping God in all of life isn't just a matter of changing the way we use the word *worship* but of changing the way we think about Sunday morning's connection with the rest of the week. We all need help transferring the truth we sing about on Sunday into the daily details of our lives.

Sunday may be the high point of our week, but it's not the only point. During the week we live lives of worship when we love our families, resist temptation, courageously speak up for the oppressed, stand against evil, and proclaim the gospel. In all these things we are the worshiping church scattered.

But we grow weary in our battle against the world, our flesh, and the devil and need to be strengthened and encouraged by God's Word and the care of other saints. We want to fellowship with those to whom God has joined us through his Son's blood. So we meet to become the worshiping church gathered.

In both contexts—together and apart—we're aware that this is the reason we've been created: to magnify the greatness of God in Jesus Christ through the power of the Holy Spirit.

part four

RIGHT RELATIONSHIPS

chapter 28

ALWAYS PEOPLE

"Can we go home now?" I have no idea how many times I heard that question as my kids were growing up. If you have kids, you've probably heard it too. Then again, maybe you've heard it from your wife.

I'm usually asked that question after church on Sunday, as the final stragglers head to their cars. My kids learned early on that we were always the last ones to leave church on Sunday. Lunch and naps would have to wait.

Come to think of it, we're always the last ones to leave wherever we are. If it's someone else's house, we tend to be hanging around as the last guests are saying good night. We love being with people, whether we're having them over for dinner, catching up at a wedding, or vacationing together. We're relationship junkies.

A lot of the worship leaders I know are like that. But even if you aren't a people person, you'll always have them in your life, and learning how to relate to people for God's glory is part of what it means to be a worship leader.

In this last section I'll share thoughts on your most significant relationships, after your family. I'm talking about your church, your team, and your pastor. All three have been a significant means of grace to me over the years and have played a crucial role in my ministry. But before looking at these areas specifically, let's look at relationships in general.

TAKING STOCK OF YOUR RELATIONSHIPS

I've heard that the average length of employment for a paid music minister is two to three years. If that's accurate, and anecdotal evidence says it is, it's disappointing for at least two reasons.

First, it shows that guys are basing decisions about church involvement more on ministry opportunities than on what's best for them and their family. I know worship pastors who wouldn't be in their present church unless they were being paid. That's not good. Salary shouldn't be the primary means of determining where we serve. And you shouldn't work at a church you wouldn't attend.

Second, it suggests we're not working through the relational problems that inevitably confront leaders. We choose to avoid rather than solve them. Whether it's a pastor we can't get along with, a critical church, or a team that doesn't follow us (or doesn't exist), we find a reason to move on.

God has a better way. He intends to use our relational conflicts to make us more like his Son. And in the process we become more effective tools for serving the church and bringing him glory.

WHY WE CAN'T DO THIS ALONE

It's easy to forget what a privilege it is to serve our church, our team, and our pastor. We become more aware of what we don't like, what's going wrong, who isn't doing their job, who disagrees with us, and why people aren't responding.

Here are three things I've learned about why I need to work through obstacles in the relationships God has given me.

Sin Is Deceptive

I once counseled a friend who had a hard time receiving what I was saying to him about a particular sin. Finally I suggested, "I think this is a blind spot in your life."

"But I just don't see it!" he replied, slightly exasperated.

"Uh, that's why they call it a *blind* spot. Everyone sees it but you."

I can't tell you how often others have held up a mirror and showed me what I couldn't see. At one point some caring team members let me know I didn't seem very open to ideas from others. I thought I was running a semi-democracy, but it was more like "The Bob Show." Another time someone pulled me aside and said they noticed I tended to react sinfully to one of the band members when he shared his opinion. I wasn't as gracious as I thought. A pastor I worked with mentioned that I "bristled" whenever he questioned my plans, and his comment led me to see some deep-rooted pride in my heart.

I thank God for the people he has placed around me who help me see what I can't see myself.

We Need the Contributions of Others

I like to think I can do a great job leading worship with nothing but my own experience, resources, wisdom, and leadership gifting. But I can't. God never intended me to. I can certainly lead, but it won't be as effective or fruitful as when others are involved.

Why is the solo model of leadership so appealing? Because we're proud. If I'm the only one responsible for putting things together, I get all the credit. I lose sight of giving glory to God.

I've received song suggestions from pastors, team musicians, and church members. They're not all good, but hey, neither are all mine. People in the congregation have given me feedback about volume, the mix, and how songs are received. They've told me it's hard to learn the melody if I sing harmony half the time. Members of the team help come up with creative arranging ideas. Those are just a few of the ways I've benefited from the gifts, perspectives, and contributions of others.

My dependence on the contributions of others was on full display one Easter as I was writing this book. I couldn't be as involved as I would have liked. But I was asked to lead the corporate worship. So I did.

Anyone there that morning probably overestimated the part I played in putting it together. Here's what I *didn't* do: plan the meeting, choose the congregational songs, arrange the choir parts, rehearse the choir, audition the vocalists, choose the soloists, pick the Scriptures to be read, design the lighting, come up with creative vocal parts, schedule the musicians, find and arrange the special song, plan the song for the end of the meeting.

Here's what I *did* do:
1. Prayed.
2. Came to rehearsal.
3. Led.

(I wrote this as a list so it looks more impressive.)

I'm incredibly blessed to be in a large church where many gifted servants are eager to help out in whatever ways they can. In a different season I might have contributed more. And one day I won't be needed at all.

But the principle remains the same: Every week is another opportunity to benefit from the contributions and insights of others.

Relationships Are How We Worship God

If worship was just about leading songs, you and I might be home free. But God is just as interested in how we treat others as he is in our songs of praise. Actually, he's *more* interested.

Your congregation will never see some of your most significant acts of worship. They can take place while you're in a parking lot, sitting in front of your computer, on the phone, or in someone's home. They're the decisions you make to put selfishness to death so Christ might be more clearly seen in your life. It might be when you take fifteen minutes to find out how your bass player's new job is going. Or when you thank a guitarist before the meeting for his humility and tell him how easy it is to serve with him. It might be when you joyfully submit to your pastor's song choice (and later admit it was better than yours). Or when you respond quickly, humbly, and thoughtfully to an e-mail expressing a concern about the volume.

You don't hear bands playing at those moments, but if you're perceptive, you'll recognize that you're worshiping God. Jesus is receiving glory through your faithful obedience. God is being magnified.

WITH ONE VOICE

Relationships are messy. They don't always work out the way we'd like. Countless variables affect relationships, and sin comes in a million different packages. Nothing I say here will negate your need for constant dependence on the Holy Spirit. Your situation has nuances that will require you to search the Scriptures, pray for wisdom, and seek counsel.

But I know this: The church doesn't need leaders who love to lead people in worship but don't love the people they're serving. Working on musical transitions and flow is secondary in importance to bridging the relational gaps that may exist on our team. We can't praise God one moment, criticize our pastor the next, and think we're offering acceptable praise to God through Jesus Christ.

That's why I appreciate Paul's prayer in Romans 15:

May the God of endurance and encouragement grant you to live in such harmony with one another, in accord with Christ Jesus, that together you may with one voice glorify the God and Father of our Lord Jesus Christ. (vv. 5–6)

Living in harmony takes endurance and encouragement from God. It's not something we can accomplish on our own strength or in our own wisdom. We'll only make things worse.

So as you read this final section on honoring God in your relationships, I pray you'll recognize your need for his grace. I pray you will have fresh vision to serve others. And I pray that with one voice you, your pastor, your team, and your church will increasingly glorify the God and Father of our Lord Jesus Christ.

chapter 29

YOUR CHURCH

The feedback we get from the congregation isn't always glowing.

- Why in the world did you have Mary sing that solo? She's terrible.
- When are we going to sing more hymns?
- Why don't we do more songs by Chris Tomlin?
- You talk way too much. You sound like a frustrated wannabe preacher.
- Our last worship leader understood throne-room worship better than you apparently do.

I've had many communications like those. They help me remember that being a worship leader is more about leading people than leading songs. Caring for them and serving them is more important than pulling off a great meeting.

It takes a lot more time, thought, and energy.

It takes God.

THE PRIORITY OF PRAYER

The importance of prayer is something we need to hear over and over. If we don't pray for those in our church, we'll lack power, grace, and love as we lead them.

Pray for the church when you're planning songs. Pray for them during rehearsals. Pray for them as you're getting ready to lead. And pray for them also in your regular times with the Lord.

I've seen that *prayer helps me remember what I can't do*. Only the Spirit can actively open people's eyes to see the hope of the gospel, their glorious inheritance in the saints, and God's power at work in their lives (Ephesians 1:16–19).

Prayer opens my eyes to God's purpose. What I want from a meeting is often different from what God wants. I want everything to go smoothly, all the musicians to show up on time, the bass player and drummer to be in sync, that new song to blow everyone away, and people to tell me what a great job I did. God wants to remind a single mom that he hasn't deserted her even though her husband has. He wants to show a teenager that Jesus Christ is more dazzling, glorious, and fulfilling than the video game he's consumed with right now. He wants to free people from legalism and condemnation. He may want to heal someone or comfort a couple who just lost a child. And he wants to do it all by magnifying the greatness of the Savior in their eyes.

And *prayer cultivates care for others.* When I stand before my church, will I be more conscious of leading them or loving them? Will I think my role is to teach them or serve them? Leading and teaching are the activities; loving and serving are the motivation.

It's really not about me. At one time I didn't believe that. I thought that people were listening to me every moment, evaluating me, critiquing me, and appraising my ability as a keyboardist or worship leader. Of course, I was wrong. That's just how it seemed in my Bob-is-the-center-of-the-universe world.

Praying for the members of my church—*really* praying for them—helps me care more for God's people than for my sorry self.

ENCOURAGEMENT AND CORRECTION

Worship leaders, like all leaders, have the opportunity to relate both to people who love them and to those who don't.

Learning how to respond to both kinds takes wisdom and humility.

Receiving Compliments

awk-ward (ôk-wərd), adjective. How you feel when someone compliments you.

Why are compliments so difficult to receive?

Most of us, unless we're blatantly arrogant, feel embarrassed when someone encourages us. Maybe they're highlighting something we're not sure we should be encouraged about: "Hey, like, I loved those riffs, dude!" Or, "Thanks for not going as long as you usually do."

Or it could be their praise is a little unclear: "Great job today! I love it when you lead."

Maybe we're hearing what they *didn't* say: "I really liked the electric guitar today." (Could they even hear my piano?) "I loved that last song we sang." (Any of the others?) "Sam did a great job leading while you were gone." (How bad is it when I'm here?)

I've had all those thoughts at various times.

But even when it's a genuine compliment sincerely offered, we can feel uncomfortable. Usually we're battling the fact that we love being encouraged but don't want to be proud. We wish people wouldn't say anything, but another part of us is crying out, "More! *More!*" It's the dilemma of Romans 7:21: "when I want to do right, evil lies close at hand."

Here are some practices I've learned to help me receive encouragement (at least better than I used to):

Thank the person for taking the time to encourage you. I don't have to evaluate the accuracy of their encouragement. All I know is that they made a point to express gratefulness when they didn't have to say anything.

If the compliment is vague, ask for clarification. We're not fishing for more praise; it's just that it helps to know how God specifically worked in a person's heart. You might respond, "Thanks so much! So what is it about the meeting that encouraged you?" If someone isn't really sure what they liked, or if their second answer is just as vague ("It was just cool"), I usually say, "Great!" Not every interaction needs to be profound.

Express gratefulness for the opportunity to serve. My most common response to encouragement is, "It's a privilege and a joy." Because it is. God is giving me grace to follow the example of Paul who said, "For what we proclaim is not ourselves, but Jesus Christ as Lord, with ourselves as your servants for Jesus' sake" (2 Corinthians 4:5). More importantly, we're declaring our allegiance to the Savior who came not to be served but to serve (Mark 10:45).

Draw attention to the contributions of others. Most of the time when people encourage me, they're unaware of the parts others played. I can increase their awareness. "I'm just grateful to be on this team; these guys practice so hard." One of the best ways to turn awkwardness into gratefulness is to remember how God has used others in my life. And when I'm actively looking for evidences of grace in other people, I have less time to think about myself.

Internally and intentionally "transfer the glory to God." That's a phrase I first learned from C. J. Mahaney, who was quoting the Puritan pastor Thomas Watson. It means acknowledging that any benefit or fruit is because of his grace, and therefore all the glory is completely and rightfully his. It's not mine. So at some point after the meeting, possibly when you're driving home, it's wise to specifically give thanks to God and give him glory for all that you've received encouragement for.

None of this means we won't struggle later with pride. I may put someone's encouragement on constant replay in my mind, try to make others aware of how well I did, or exaggerate someone's comments in a later conversation. The best thing to do then is confess my pride to God and again transfer all the glory to him.

Receiving Criticism

Leaders, because of their public role, are always being evaluated. How do we prepare for the inevitable critique that comes with any leadership position?

By not being stupid. That's right, *stupid*.

Stupid is a word we didn't let our kids use when they were growing up. But God doesn't hesitate to use it to describe us at times. "Whoever loves discipline loves knowledge, but he who hates reproof is stupid" (Proverbs 12:1).

God tells me I'm stupid if I don't appreciate receiving correction. He wants me to *love* reproof and correction, not run from it. Why?

Because loving reproof makes me more aware of my need for God's grace in my life. It helps me fight self-exaltation. It's a sign I need others in the process of sanctification. And it's a way of acknowledging that *I don't know everything*.

In a word, loving reproof simply means being humble. It's receiving correction as a gift from God's loving, wise, and sovereign hand, sent to make us more like his precious Son.

So pray for correction. Ask God to bring people into your life who will point out where you're making mistakes, are sinning, or could do things better. Some of them (not all) are fearful of telling you what they really think. But you need to hear it.

Expect correction. When I'm surprised by critical feedback, it's usually because I'm looking for praise. Only perfect and proud people never anticipate doing something wrong. I know I'm not in the first category, and I don't want to be in the second.

Be proactive. Ask people you trust—family, pastor, friends, other leaders—for input. Ask for it when they have time enough to think about it and are convinced you really want to hear. And make sure they're honest with you.

Thank people who correct you. It's rarely easy for people to critique someone. So I want to thank them for caring enough to provide me with their observations, whether or not I agree with them.

Ask follow-up questions. Often my first tendency is to want to justify myself or shift blame—I want this conversation over as soon as possible. A better approach is to ask for further thoughts to fill out what they're saying. It will help you hear more clearly and respond more humbly. If the criticism you receive is serious or involves others, it may be wise to get a pastor involved. That will help you guard your own heart as well as the church.

Thank God for correction. Most criticisms are gifts from God. It's hard to see that when words are thoughtless, angry, sarcastic, or judgmental. But most feedback I receive isn't as strong as I need to hear and comes from hearts that want to serve. Even when given sinfully, reproofs remind us of our own self-deception and cast us upon the mercy of the Savior who covers all our sins.

And that's probably the main reason I resent criticism. I don't believe what God has said about me in the cross. I think there must be *some* aspect of my life, however small or pitiful, that's praiseworthy, meritorious, and beyond inspection.

Alfred Poirier provides this life-changing perspective:

> In light of God's judgment and justification of the sinner in the cross of Christ, we can begin to discover how to deal with any and all criticism. By agreeing with God's criticism of me in Christ's cross, I can face any criticism man may lay against me. In other words, no one can criticize me more than the cross has.[1]

What a thought. The cross is a loud statement of our sin, unworthiness, and need. And in light of the cross, we can receive criticism graciously because God, who knows our wickedness better than anyone else, has fully forgiven and justified us. We will never be brought into condemnation (Romans 8:1)! So we can confidently pray with David, "Let a righteous man strike me—it is a kindness; let him rebuke me—it is oil for my head; let my head not refuse it" (Psalm 141:5).

At the end of our lives, we'll probably look back and realize how the correction we received did more to make us like Christ than just about anything else. So why not thank God for it now?

OTHER LEADERSHIP CHALLENGES

Handling Song Suggestions

You know what it's like: People approach you and exude extravagant praise for a song they heard at a conference, on the radio, or at another church, and you brace yourself for the inevitable: "Why don't we sing this song at our church?"

How should you respond? Here's what I typically try to do.

First, I check my heart. I know this can sound redundant, but I have too much indwelling sin still hanging around to bypass this step. I've often assumed that someone suggesting a song means they're unsatisfied with the songs we've been doing. That's sinful judgment. Whatever my response, I want to speak graciously, humbly, and clearly.

After my heart-check, I thank them for their suggestion. It's great when people in the congregation actually care enough to offer an opinion. They've apparently encountered God in some way while singing that song, and they want others to have the same opportunity.

Third, I ask what they liked about the song. Maybe a particular line addressed a specific situation they're going through. Or maybe they just enjoyed the sound of the band or the catchiness of the melody. I don't know unless I ask.

Once I've listened to the song closely (and maybe obtained a few other opinions), I may decide it's not right for us, and I'll need to explain why. I don't want to dismiss a song just because "I don't like it." God has used many songs I didn't like to minister to people. However, just because a song is popular doesn't mean it's good or the best song for us to use.

Let me give you an example, using the popular song "Above All." There are many things I can commend about the song, but when asked to do it, my response might run something like this:

> "There are a number of things about this song I really like. The melody is beautiful and easy to remember. The lyrics wonderfully contrast God's greatness and Christ's humility at the cross. Both the poetic images and harmonic progressions are creative. But two parts concern me. The first is the line 'you took the fall.' It seems like an understated, almost colloquial way of describing what Jesus did. Plus, it's confusing.
>
> "The greater problem for me is the line 'and thought of me above all.'

I have no question that Jesus 'loved me and gave himself for me' (Galatians 2:20). But he didn't think of me 'above all.' Jesus went to the cross to satisfy God's righteous judgment against a sinful humanity. He thought above all of his Father's holiness, justice, and glory.

"This is no theological nuance. It's the difference between our faith being man-centered and God-centered. I don't think that's what the writers intended, but it might cause some confusion in people's minds. Other songs are clearer about the relationship between Jesus' loving me and wanting to glorify his Father."

After sharing my thoughts, I'd thank the person for suggesting a song and ask him or her to continue to do so.

My point here isn't to say no one should sing "Above All" but to give you an idea of how I'd respond. Actually, Paul Baloche, who co-wrote this song, is a good friend and has written many excellent songs for congregational worship. We've talked about those lines in "Above All," and I can assure you that neither he nor Lenny LeBlanc, the other writer, intended the song to magnify us rather than God. But that just shows that what we're meaning to say isn't always what people hear.

Other elements in a song that might cause me to shy away from using it include choruses that don't say much but are sung repeatedly, lack of clarity, lack of originality in music or lyrics, or scattered content that covers too many themes. At times I've changed my mind on using a particular song after thinking more about it or because it seemed to work in a specific context.

I'm sure we'll make some wrong decisions in choosing not to sing certain songs. But if our goal is always to sing songs that exalt God's glory in Christ in people's hearts and minds in the clearest and best ways, we won't have any regrets.

Introducing and Leading Through Changes

Another challenge worship leaders can face is helping people understand why things have changed. Most people enjoy the familiar. We get comfortable knowing what's coming. When things aren't the way they used to be, people usually want to know why (or they make up their own reasons). Small changes don't require any explanation as people adjust fairly quickly. But what seems small to us may not seem small to someone in our church.

Most worship leaders will have to introduce changes to the church at some point. If you've led your church well, these changes can be good. If you haven't, change usually creates problems. Or rather, exposes them.

Here are some ways of leading your church through change that will ensure problems:

- Make significant changes without telling anyone in advance.
- Give superficial reasons for changes.
- Emphasize wanting to make everybody happy.
- Disparage the past as you press toward the future.
- Pursue experience at the expense of doctrine.
- Adopt external changes without emphasizing the internal work of the Holy Spirit.
- Assume everyone in your church understands what worship is about.

Each church has unique challenges when it comes to change. Whatever your situation, the following principles can help change go a little easier.

Make sure your leaders are in agreement. Sometimes you read a book or attend a worship conference and come home bursting with innovative ideas and creative plans you can't *wait* to introduce to your church. Here's a suggestion. Wait. Leading a church through changes is ultimately the pastor's responsibility. Make sure he's fully behind any changes you want to make. Maybe you've built a significant degree of trust with him. That's great. But even if he trusts you, remember that you're serving him.

Regularly teach the church what biblical worship is. Your church will be more receptive to change when they understand what true worship is. But it doesn't matter how mature a church is, they'll need to be reminded how to worship biblically. Each week they're tempted by idols and deceived by indwelling sin. Also, we have guests and new Christians attending who come with various misconceptions about what we're doing. Finally, and perhaps most important, we all at times forget what we already know. What was once a faith-filled encounter with the living God becomes a dull, same-as-every-week experience that leaves us cold. We need to be reminded what a life-altering, awe-inspiring event worshiping God really is.

We can teach the church about worship in different ways. At least once a year we preach a message on the topic of worship. I regularly share a brief comment while I'm leading on some aspect of why we worship. You can also spell out your philosophy of worship on your web site.

Lead theologically. If you're introducing a new style of music, use this as an opportunity to teach that God's glory isn't expressed in only one music style. If you want to start repeating parts of songs, let the church know of your desire to be more responsive to the Spirit's leadings. Every time we make a change, it's an opportunity to ground people in biblical principles that will serve them in other contexts as well.

Lead humbly but confidently. Once you've prayed, done your homework, and prepared, don't second-guess your decision if you receive negative feedback. Humble confidence means we're open to questions but won't change course just because someone disagrees with us.

Teaching New Songs

Another aspect of leadership that has a significant impact on our relationship with the church is how and when we introduce new songs. This past year we taught the church fifteen new songs. We'll probably continue doing ten of them. (I used to try an average of two new songs a month, but people can only remember so much.)

We've taught new songs in a variety of ways over the years. We sometimes look for a place in the meeting, such as Communion, to present the song as a meditation that the congregation first listens to, then joins in. Some churches use the prelude or offering as an opportunity to present a new song that they sing congregationally the following week.

If the song is more up-tempo, I'll typically say something beforehand to help people understand some aspect of the song. I could say, "We'd like to introduce a new song this morning to help us celebrate God's lavish mercy displayed at the cross." Or "We're going to sing a new song this morning that helps us remember the ways God has been faithful to us." Teaching a new song is an opportunity to draw attention to the truth the song contains rather than allowing people's focus and emotions to center on the music. (It's not a good idea to introduce a new song with, "And now we're going to sing a really *kickin'* song!")

I usually tell the congregation to listen as we sing the verse and chorus, then invite them to join in. I may have them start singing on the chorus (if the song has one) rather than the verse because it's often easier to pick up. On other occasions, I'll teach the song line by line, having the congregation repeat each line after I sing it. That method can help people learn the melody more accurately.

I try to avoid starting the meeting with a song no one knows or doing more than one new song in a meeting. There have also been times when we just introduce a new song without saying anything because the song is easy to learn.

PRECIOUS IN THE EYES OF GOD

Leading in the church can be exhilarating one moment and exasperating the next. But God wants to ask you a question: *Do you love your church?*

God does. He never loses hope or gets discouraged. He never gets tired of hearing believers' almost-in-tune, somewhat together, faith-filled offerings of worship. He never gives up on his plan to reveal his glorious wisdom through the church (Ephesians 3:10).

We often look out on our congregation and see normal people, nothing special. But God sees his treasured possession. These are the people he purchased with the blood of his own Son (Acts 20:28). They're precious in his sight.

May they be precious in ours.

chapter 30

YOUR TEAM

No two worship teams are exactly alike. You may use the same instruments as another church, but musicians are a varied lot. They come from different backgrounds and experiences and have unique strengths and weaknesses.

For that reason, I can't go into the kind of detail that I'd like to in this chapter on relating to your team. Nor can I address every practical issue you'll face. That would take an entire book itself.

But what I can do is give you five categories to consider. Five ways to think about your team that will help you ask the right questions and pursue the right solutions. These aren't one-time decisions or actions but processes that, when faithfully practiced, create a way of relating—a culture—that honors God.

ESTABLISHING YOUR TEAM

Scripture doesn't define what our music team should look like. It depends on your church's size, your pastor's vision, your gifts, how much time you have, your church's schedule, and who's available.

There's no verse that says worship team musicians have to be a close-knit group, nor is there one that says they shouldn't be. It's okay to be flexible here and choose the structure that best fits your present goals and resources.

You might also consider including sound and tech personnel on your team. At the very least, make sure there's clear communication with and deep appreciation for those who take care of the technical details.

Different Roles

I unpacked a functional definition of a worship leader in Part Two of this book. What I didn't do there was insist that one person had to do all these things or should even attempt to do them. Likewise, a worship team is made up of people with different responsibilities.

As a leader, you provide oversight for the team not only musically but spiritually. The degree of spiritual oversight will vary depending on your spiritual gifts and the level of responsibility that your pastor has given you. You might even be a pastor at your church. But you don't have to be on staff to care for people's souls. It just means your concerns extend beyond making good music. When it comes to your team members, you're just as sensitive to the state of their hearts as you are to the precision of the notes they're playing.

Another role is the music director or "chief musician," as we used to call it in the eighties. This person's primary responsibility is to make sure the music is arranged, rehearsed, and performed well. A worship leader might fulfill this role, but not always. Sometimes I've divided the duties between an instrumental leader and a vocal leader. It helps during rehearsals to have someone else working with the vocalists while I work with the band.

Teams can also use a coordinator or facilitator. This is the person who makes sure songs are copied, people know the schedule and receive the songs, and all the pieces fit together. And it doesn't have to be you. If you don't have an administrative assistant, ask around. You might be surprised how willing people are to help out when they know a specific need exists.

Team Standards

In the New Testament, those who lead are held to a stricter standard for character (1 Timothy 3:2–12; Titus 1:5–9; James 3:1). Even though musicians aren't necessarily "elders" or "teachers," their presence in front of the congregation week after week implies that their life is worthy of emulation— not flawless, but demonstrating the fruit of the gospel. When that's not true, the church gets the message that worship is more about music than the way we live. Likewise, when non-Christian musicians are used, we're implying that the *art* of worship is more important than the *heart*.

That's why it's wise to have standards for our musicians that spell out responsibilities and expectations. Worship isn't a gig. It's the overflow of a life devoted to the glory of Jesus Christ. If standards aren't written down, they should be clearly communicated before someone joins the team.

When I first came to my current church, I took time to set clear standards for participation. We revisit that with everyone who joins the team and review it every few years together. It's better to remind someone of what you've already told them than to expect them to follow unspoken expectations.

At our church we require that each member of the worship team be:

1. A member of Covenant Life Church and actively involved in a small group.

2. In agreement with the doctrines and practices of Covenant Life Church.

3. Growing in their knowledge of and love for God through prayer and Bible study.

4. Able to genuinely and visibly engage with God as they lead others in corporate worship.

5. Committed to pursuing humility and servanthood.

6. Faithful and punctual in attending required meetings and rehearsals.

7. Committed to growing in their musical skill.

8. Faithful to communicate to the appropriate pastor any circumstances that might affect the integrity of their participation on the team.

At our church we interact closely with the pastors about who is on the music team. Before anyone is added, we make sure they have the full support of their pastor and small group leader. It's always easier to be careful about adding someone to the team than to ask them to leave later.

As your church grows, the spiritual standards shouldn't change. In a large church the impact of a godly team member will be greater, and so will the negative consequences if a member is involved in a pattern of unrepentant sin. As we grow in size, we'll be tempted to minimize spiritual maturity for the sake of musical excellence. That's a dangerous trade-off.

Level of Commitment

Many teams serve on a weekly basis, with the same musicians participating every Sunday. That schedule requires more from the leader in terms of preparation, care, and follow-up. If you have enough musicians, I'd try to schedule people one to three times a month. That enables them to serve in other ministries as well and provides variety for the church.

Some churches ask for a year-long commitment or even a signed one-year contract. A contract can communicate the significance of what you're asking people to do and also assures them they can reconsider their involvement in twelve months.

I used to expect the same degree of commitment from everyone on the team. I didn't want anyone to be perceived as a prima donna. Now I think there are good reasons for differing levels of commitment. (Selfishness isn't one of them.) Moms with young kids, students, and people who travel for their jobs can all have the opportunity to serve if we're flexible on how often they need to participate. Sometimes I've even let someone miss a rehearsal for the coming Sunday if it's justified and they have the musical skills to pull it off.

We need to evaluate our own level of commitment as well. Many worship leaders confess they never have enough time to do it all—arranging the songs, researching new ones, making the charts, calling people, sending out the schedule, practicing, and leading the weekly rehearsals.

Hudson Taylor said, "God's work done in God's way will never lack God's supply." That's why we shouldn't be doing *our* work in *our* way.

So maybe *all* should be redefined. Maybe all that stuff doesn't have to be done. (Or at least *you* don't have to do it.) One worship leader I talked to spent hours slaving over arrangements while his wife struggled with a severe illness. My counsel? Forget about the arrangements and care for your wife. The church will be able to worship God just fine without your horn charts.

I don't want to minimize the amount of work that faithfulness involves. But thinking about what serves the church most and what truly lasts reorients my priorities.

Another problem might be that you're wasting time in other ways, which prevents you from giving time to what you're supposed to be doing. Don't let wrong priorities rob you of the joy that comes from being faithful to God's agenda.

ENCOURAGING YOUR TEAM

I love our annual worship team Christmas party. During an evening of delicious food, rich fellowship, and much laughter, we typically honor two members of the team for their faithfulness and godly example and present each of them with a gift card to a local mall. But the highlight is sharing why they're being honored and then asking other members of the group to join in. Hearing specific words of encouragement for other members of the team is one of the most memorable moments of our year.

Our Christmas party is one of the many ways we try to cultivate a *culture of gratefulness*. That's an environment where people intentionally encourage evidences of grace they see in others rather than self-righteously criticizing their weaknesses.

Shelley is a vocalist on our team who has often inspired me in the area of encouragement. It's impossible to walk away from a conversation with her and not be more aware of God's grace. She never misses an opportunity to encourage others. Her words, her smile, and her enthusiasm all communicate that God is at work and that he's doing something very good.

That's how I want to be. That's how we all want to be.

When you think of the members of your team, what comes to mind? Problems or joys? Pain or pleasure? Whatever's in your heart will be revealed in your words and actions.

Every time you're with your team, make it a goal to identify and encourage evidences of grace in them. Who arrived early for rehearsal? Who stayed late to help tear down? Has anyone been spending time practicing at home? Who organized the music team cookout? Who has been serving faithfully in the midst of personal trials?

Expressing gratefulness can have a dramatic effect on a team that's not used to it. Sending notes or e-mails after a Sunday meeting or rehearsal thanking them for a particular way God used them is another way you can keep the conversation consistent.

God tells us we're to "outdo one another in showing honor" (Romans 12:10). When the team is together, we have an opportunity to highlight qualities and characteristics we'd like everyone on the team to emulate—humility, long-term faithfulness, servanthood, godliness, joy. It's not wrong to honor people for musical excellence, especially when it's the fruit of hard work. But everyone will know what's most important by what we bring to their attention most often.

If it's possible, include gifts for your team in your ministry budget. Gifts are a tangible expression of gratefulness and honor. At various times we've given out CDs, books, coffee shop gift cards, and gift certificates. You might also consider equipment for the instrumentalists, like drumsticks, strings, or a tuner. Gifts don't have to be expensive to make an impact.

At every rehearsal, it's easy to be most aware of what I need to get done and how little time I have. When that happens, my focus ends up being on an activity rather than on people. So I'm learning to ask questions before, after, and sometimes during a rehearsal. Learning what people are going through helps me remember that there's more to our relationships than making music together. I may find out about a significant transition like a move or a job change. When someone tells me about an illness or a potential financial challenge, I have an opportunity to pray right then for the situation. (If it's a serious issue, I make sure a pastor is involved.) Asking questions doesn't take much time, but it's one more way of encouraging your team.

EQUIPPING YOUR TEAM

We also serve our team by making sure they're equipped in the skills they need. The goal is to create a *culture of growth*.

You don't have to be the one doing the actual training. You just have to make sure people are motivated to grow in their skills and have the resources to do it.

Theological Growth

The primary source of growth for your team will come from the preached Word every week. But we have a unique opportunity to equip them in a knowledge of God and in an understanding of worship.

Resources abound in this area, but here are a few books I'd highly recommend: *Desiring God* and *When I Don't Desire God* by John Piper, *The Joy of Fearing God* by Jerry Bridges, *Living the Cross Centered Life* and *Humility: True Greatness* by C. J. Mahaney, *Knowing God* by J. I. Packer, *The Holiness of God* by R. C. Sproul, and *The Knowledge of the Holy* by A. W. Tozer.

We've had our group read a chapter from a book and come ready to share what they learned and how they were affected. You can also listen to a message,[1] read an article, or download materials from the Web. Another excellent resource is the chapter on worship in *Systematic Theology* by Wayne Grudem.

Musical Growth

An increasing number of worship team instrumentalists read from guitar charts. In that context I've identified eight crucial areas to work on:

- *time:* being able to play a consistent tempo
- *groove:* playing "in the pocket," being aware of a song's feel, usually provided by the bass and kick drum
- *space:* allowing room for other instruments to play
- *rhythm:* understanding and being able to play rhythmic patterns and hits
- *melody:* being able to create melodies that complement the congregational melody

- *ensemble:* playing together
- *dynamics:* using volume effectively
- *sensitivity:* playing what's appropriate and being able to respond to the leader's direction

Your church might have a combination of note-readers (usually pianists and solo instrumentalists) and chart readers. There are advantages to both, although in contemporary music, guitar charts definitely dominate.

Among other advantages, using sheet music means musicians can play songs without hearing them, rhythms can be written out precisely, and vocalists can learn the melody and harmony immediately. Musicians who play by ear learn by feel, repetition, and imitation, which has its own advantages. This allows for more freedom and creativity and sounds more current. Also, charts are generally shorter and easier to prepare.

When note-readers and chart-readers (or trained and untrained musicians) work together, tensions often develop. Both sides tend to think the other doesn't appreciate "real" music. In those cases, it's important that everyone is committed to growing in their weak areas.

It's also important to develop a common language of music. Trained musicians have a responsibility to speak in terms that untrained musicians can comprehend. It doesn't help when I tell the guitarist for the third time, "That chord comes on 4 *and*, not 3 *and*" when he doesn't know where 3 *or* 4 comes. I need to show him.

Working from a simple lead sheet with lyrics, chords, and basic rhythmic cues is often a good compromise.[2]

Vocalists are usually eager to grow in their gifts. Some of the important areas to focus on are caring for your voice, intonation, blending with others, solo styles, harmonizing, and following the leader.

Problems can also arise between vocalists who can read music and those who can't, but they're not insurmountable. Typically at least one individual can work out parts and teach them to the other vocalists, along with helping them develop their gifts. If you or a person on your team can't fill that role, suggest private lessons, community college courses, or the increasing number of training materials that are readily available.[3]

Our goal is to see everyone growing in their skills, so our team will have more tools and opportunities to serve God's people.

Rehearsals

I was talking to a worship leader once about his team's rehearsal schedule. "How often do you practice?" I asked. He told me three to four times a week. I was shocked. "Why?" I asked. He said practicing together made them a tighter band.

Tighter . . . and exhausted. I don't know anyone who has that kind of time. I certainly don't.

Besides, while practicing often *can* make you a better team, practicing *smart* is a better solution. That means coming prepared and spending time purposefully rather than simply playing through songs or jamming.

Rehearsals don't have to be the same every time. In fact, I'd encourage you to vary what you do. Possible activities include learning new songs, reviewing old ones, working on fresh arrangements, praying together, studying worship, working with the vocalists, working with the rhythm section, and having meals together.

While many teams rehearse every week, there's no rule requiring it. The frequency of rehearsals depends on your strengths and availability, the strengths and schedules of your team, and the vision of your pastor. It's a good idea to assess how often you rehearse at least once a year.

What if members of your team aren't motivated to practice outside rehearsals? How can we inspire them to take their playing to the next level? Here are some suggestions:

- Listen to and critique CDs together.
- Attend a concert as a team.
- Stimulate them by your own example of faithful practice.
- Ask people to share times when God used someone's musical skill to affect them.
- Ask more skilled members of the band to train less skilled ones.
- Watch a training video together.[4]
- Make a big deal when someone works extra hard to learn their songs well.
- Frequently mention the importance and benefits of outside practice.

EVALUATING YOUR TEAM

One of the best ways to motivate your team to continued growth is to offer consistent and thoughtful evaluation. Assessing your group's progress in different areas will also help develop a *culture of humility*.

If we want the members of our team to desire growth, we have to desire it ourselves. So we should lead the way in asking others for input and observations. *How did I do leading this morning? Was I clear? Are there any ways we could run rehearsals more effectively? Am I still overplaying?* If I'm regularly asking my team those kinds of questions, they'll realize it's okay to acknowledge their weaknesses in front of others. And it will make them more receptive to my observations in the areas of their musicianship, character, and gifts.

Musical Presentation

Not long after I arrived at Covenant Life, we started getting together for an evaluation meeting right after each service. Years later it remains one of the most fruitful practices we've established. The musicians and sound folks gather on stage, and the first thing I do is highlight how God was faithful to use us in spite of our flaws and mess-ups.

Then I run through the songs, pointing out specific things that were encouraging: "Jared, you did a great job catching my eye at the end of the second chorus on 'Blessed Be Your Name.' Thanks for paying attention. Ben, that was a strong beginning on acoustic for the third song. Roger, the synth voicings you used during the fourth song left plenty of room for the vocals. Speaking of vocals, thanks for remembering to sing unison the first time through the new song." I'll also typically take that opportunity to commend the sound team for the way they tirelessly and joyfully serve us.

Then I'll point out things that could have been better: "Don, remember that chord change in the turnaround for 'The Glories of Calvary.' Don't forget to write things down. Oh, you did? Well, then don't forget to read what you wrote. And what happened before the tag of 'Holy Is the Lord'? My signal was unclear? Oh, sorry about that. I'll try to give those earlier." We also discuss any monitor problems that came up.

I'll close by asking the group for their encouragement and critiques. Normally one of the other worship leaders or musicians who was in the congregation that morning offers his thoughts as well.

I don't want to give you the impression that these are heavy meetings. They usually take less than ten minutes. We laugh, poke fun at each other, and always express gratefulness once again that we get to serve the church with our musical gifts.

Consistent evaluation, given graciously and clearly, pops the bubble of self-exaltation and self-pity. You did well? That was God's grace! You messed up? Welcome to the club. And thank God for the blood of Jesus that perfects all our sin-stained offerings.

One small point: For evaluation to be effective, I have to be listening to others besides myself while we sing. A good monitor mix is a must. For years my monitor mix consisted of my piano, my vocal, and everyone else far in the background. No wonder I felt like the bottom dropped out when

I stopped playing! Make sure you can hear everyone so you can give them accurate thoughts about what they did.

Rehearsals provide another opportunity for evaluating your musical presentation. The best practice is to listen to a recording or watch a video of your previous meeting. Those don't lie. That can be a painful process, but there's nothing like a recording to open up blind eyes and deaf ears.

Character

Dave Campbell has been playing on our worship team for over twenty-five years. He's skilled, he's faithful, and he's humble. When I invite him to play for some special event he regularly asks, "Are you sure you don't want to give one of the younger guys an opportunity?"

Almost weekly he tells me how grateful he is to be serving in the church, what Charles Spurgeon referred to as "the dearest place on earth." He also is consistently on time, making sure his gear is set up before the rehearsal starts.

People like Dave—and we have many of them on our team—set the standard for what God is looking for in a musician.

Unfortunately, we can get used to hearing common refrains like these from church musicians: *Why does she get all the solos? I thought rehearsals were for people who aren't as gifted. Why am I playing only twice this quarter? My idea for the ending was much better than yours. I'm tired of the singers always getting special treatment. Are we singing that stupid song again?* We're prone to excuse such pride, self-serving, backbiting, and criticism because—well, we're musicians. What do you expect?

Being an artist is no justification for sin. If I care about my team, I'll hold them accountable to pursue godly character and will help them grow.[5] I'll take the time to follow up on questions or concerns I have about someone's behavior. If it turns out they're unwilling to change, I'll get a pastor involved and will possibly ask them to take a sabbatical. Their godly attitude is more important to me than their great musicianship.

Gifting

I should have a good idea of a person's gifting when he or she joins the team. But over time I want to be on the lookout for three things.

First, are they growing in their skills? Being part of the team doesn't mean you've arrived. It means now there's even greater motivation to improve.

Second, has the church outgrown an individual's gifting? A guitar player who can serve a church of seventy-five may not be your best choice once the church has grown to five hundred.

Third, have others come into the church who are as godly but more gifted than people on the team? We try to prepare our team for the inevitability of being replaced by regularly mentioning that possibility.

If you realize someone lacks the gifting to be part of the team, talk to him or her. I've found that when the bar of excellence is raised or when more gifted musicians show up, people often realize they shouldn't be on the team. If they don't figure it out, we have to tell them. We need to fear God more than their disapproval.

In thirty years I've taken members off the team only a handful of times. When I do, it's never easy. But I remind them that God has a unique place for them to serve. They'll enjoy serving with the gifts God has given them much more than trying to prove they can serve where he hasn't gifted them.

ENJOYING YOUR TEAM

Not long ago we rehearsed for three hours in preparation for a special Sunday morning. A three-hour rehearsal may seem normal to you, but it was way out of my comfort zone. Still, I was rejuvenated by our practice. I remember thinking how much I loved being with these people, working hard together, challenging each other, serving the church with our gifts. These weren't just church musicians and tech personnel; these were dear friends. We were bound together through the Savior and were committed to serving his church. I was experiencing the fruit of a *culture of joy*. It's the fruit of experiencing God's grace together and watching him work through us to glorify the Savior.

Of course, leading a team isn't always joyful. Rehearsals can get tense or boring. We can lose our best people to church plants, season-of-life changes, job transfers, or sin. Leading can bring challenges, frustrations, and disappointments. But failing to lead brings even worse fruit with none of the benefits.

Leading your team, whether it's made up of two, twenty, or two hundred, provides an opportunity for you to watch God work as you encourage, equip, evaluate, and enjoy those he has placed under your care.

God doesn't guarantee we'll have the biggest, most musically gifted, most enthusiastic, stable worship team in history. Or even in our city. We aren't guaranteed we'll have a team at all. But we can trust God's promise: "And let us not grow weary of doing good, for in due season we will reap, if we do not give up" (Galatians 6:9).

What kind of harvest can we expect to reap if we faithfully and humbly lead our team in the ways I've described? Musicians growing in their love for the gospel, for each other, and for serving in God's Kingdom. A church magnifying and encountering the glorious Savior on Sundays and every day. And the knowledge that God has glorified his Son through your life as you've led and served your team, by his grace.

And that's a rich harvest indeed.

chapter 31

YOUR PASTOR

In the years I've been leading corporate worship, I've had the privilege of serving with five different pastors. Each had his own style, ranging from uninvolved to very involved. One planned weeks in advance, another reviewed the songs with me Sunday morning, and another just wanted them in an e-mail.

None of them claimed to be musicians. I take that back. C. J. has told me repeatedly about his untapped innate musical talent. Definitely untapped.

Pastors come in all shapes and sizes. Some are carefree, happy that you're managing the music so they can take care of the preaching. Others are more involved, spelling out all the details in advance and not wanting you to swerve from them. Some are critical. You hear from them only when you've done something wrong.

The easiest pastors to work with are those who want to work as a team, but take full responsibility for the final outcome.

Whatever kind of pastor you serve with, God says he's a gift to you. In Ephesians 4:11–12 pastors and teachers are mentioned as gifts from the ascended Christ to equip the church for ministry. Worship leaders don't even receive a nod. That doesn't mean we have no place in God's plan. It just means that it's our responsibility to support our pastor and not set our own agenda.

SERVE YOUR PASTOR

Hebrews 13:17 tells us:

Obey your leaders and submit to them, for they are keeping watch over your souls, as those who will have to give an account. Let them do this with joy and not with groaning, for that would be of no advantage to you.

Did you get that? If I don't make it a joy for my pastor to lead me, it's of no advantage to *me*.

I don't think that way. I think it's to my advantage when I get *my* way with song choices, meeting flow, and other decisions on which the pastor and I disagree. God thinks differently.

God has given the pastor, not the worship leader, the ultimate responsibility for the direction of the church. That includes the musical portions of the meeting. When we're at odds, Scripture is clear: I'm the one who needs to submit.

Submitting to my pastor means serving him joyfully and humbly. I can do that better by knowing his priorities. What really matters to him? How much time does he want to give to singing the Word versus preaching the Word? To what does he think I should be giving my time? If I've listened well, this will be easier to do. Sometimes I've made important decisions about my work without even thinking to ask the guy I work for.

I've also gotten deep into planning and discovered I was headed in the wrong direction. One of my early goals at Covenant Life was to involve more people on the team. I wanted to have other people leading and to give different folks opportunities to sing solos. But C. J. wanted me to set a consistent model of leadership and keep the standard for soloists high. I had to readjust.

Asking for direction and clarity isn't a statement that you don't know what you're doing. It's a sign you want to serve someone else's plans, not your own.

That's especially true when it comes to planning the Sunday meeting. Do I present my songs as suggestions or the final list? Do I view the singing time as *my* time and resent any changes? I'm familiar with the sting in my heart when my pastor informs me I have to cut something. It's even worse when I'm told right before the meeting. My heart cries out, *But what about my plans, my arrangements, my transitions!*

What about your pride? God asks.

Worship leaders serve as those under authority. Our pastors should feel completely free to interrupt or adjust what we're doing because we're doing it to serve their priorities, not ours. Our meetings aren't made up of "my" time and "his" time. It's all God's time, and the pastor and I are on the same team. But my pastor has the final say about how that time gets used. I never want him to hesitate to ask me to cut a song, shorten the time we sing, or change something around when he thinks it's best. And I want to make it a joy for him to do so.

I also want to serve my pastor's preferences. That includes things like how (and how often) we communicate. Does he prefer e-mail, a phone call, or face-to-face conversation? Does he prefer talking about the next Sunday's songs on Tuesday or on Friday? I served one pastor who preferred doing it on Sunday morning. (Maybe because that's when I finally had the list ready.) It was a little tricky when he asked for changes, but we managed.

I want to factor in my pastor's musical preferences as well. If he doesn't like a certain song or soloist, and he's not quite sure why, I don't need to have a signed affidavit stating the reasons. Just knowing he doesn't prefer it should be enough.

I want to make his job a *joy*. That doesn't mean I can't humbly ask questions and dialogue with him. But I want to be sure I'm asking a question, not making an accusation.

There's probably no more effective way I can serve my pastor than simply by praying for him. He carries the weight of the church on his shoulders. He's the one God will hold accountable. At times I've noticed that I'm praying for the musical portion of the meeting and not even thinking about the preaching. Not much prayer support going on there. I also need to pray for my pastor's family, heart, health, schedule, decisions, and success. If he's not doing well, I won't be either.

LISTEN TO YOUR PASTOR

> *A fool takes no pleasure in understanding, but only in expressing his opinion. (Proverbs 18:2)*

Occasionally I'll be looking for a gift for Julie and wander into one of those soap-and-shampoo stores in the mall. Suddenly I'm accosted by a slightly-too-anxious salesperson. "May I help you?" she asks, all smiles. Obviously working for commission.

"Uh, sure." Without really asking me what I'm there to buy or who for, the salesperson shows me all the wonderful scents they're offering, what's on sale, the combo packages, the new arrivals. After a few minutes I drift away and out of the store.

The salesperson might have chalked up a sale if she'd simply asked me what my wife was like and what she enjoyed. But she was more concerned with selling a product than with learning what I wanted.

We can be like that when we're working with our pastor. We try to sell our ideas, our song choices, our style of ministry, our way of relating and can't figure out why he's not receptive. It's because we haven't taken the time to ask him questions and listen to his answers. Or maybe we think we've already heard what he has to say and just need to defend our viewpoint.

Listening takes time and self-control. We need to listen for a pastor's theology, his heart, his understanding of our role, the way he relates to his wife and children, the way he relates to his staff, and a dozen other details. I've known more than a few worship leaders who got into a bad situation by not listening with a discerning ear before they took a job at a church.

Pastors and worship leaders don't always speak the same language, especially when it comes to music. What he calls "simple" I call "dull." His "frantic" is my "jubilant." "Wordy" to him means "thoughtful" to me.

We need to define our terms, not argue about them. Maybe he wants more "upbeat" songs to get the people "going." You think that means he doesn't care enough about truth and wants you to musically manipulate the congregation. But maybe you pick slow songs too often, and people are nodding off.

Maybe he says you should be less preoccupied about theology in making song choices. It could be you tend to choose only weighty songs that don't take new believers into account. That's been my tendency, and I've benefited from input in that area.

Maybe he's told you, "I want more songs people can sing that tell God how much we love him!" Your song choices might be too complicated and void of affection for God.

Or he asks you to stop talking and just play the songs, so you don't interrupt the "flow." What he might mean is that you wander aimlessly when you speak.

Don't get defensive when your pastor asks you to do something different. Find out exactly what he's saying.

Your pastor might be the quiet type. But you can still listen to him. Listen to what he preaches on and what he emphasizes. Listen to what he gets excited about. Listen to what he *doesn't* say when he talks about the church. Most of all, listen carefully when he tells you what you're doing well and what you're not. Those are your cues for how to support him.

INITIATE

Do not withhold good from those to whom it is due, when it is in your power to do it. (Proverbs 3:27)

Serving your pastor doesn't rule out taking initiative or being creative. It just gives purpose and definition to your creativity.

Some pastors prefer a music minister who simply does what he's told. If that's your situation, then your opportunities to initiate are limited. But they still exist.

We can listen to songs and research what's being produced as well as what's being neglected. We can talk to other worship leaders about what they're doing in their churches. We can get ideas from *Worship Leader* magazine or web sites devoted to worship.[1] You won't agree with everything out there, but there's still plenty to learn.

Let your pastor know what you're doing and thinking about in this area. Don't surprise him. Initiate ideas in the planning stage. You'll have the advantage of getting feedback before you even try out something new.

Initiate encouragement as well. God wants us to notice how he's working in and through our pastors. Make a list of the things you appreciate about your pastor, then tell him. Be specific. The goal is to prime your encouragement pump so those kinds of expressions become a normal part of your relationship. Sometimes we think that too much encouragement will tempt someone to be proud or to take advantage of us. Maybe. But our trust is in God's Word, not in the percentages. God tells us to "encourage one another and build one another up" (1 Thessalonians 5:11). He knew how much we'd need it.

Another area to initiate is evaluation (of *us*, not the pastor). We've developed the practice of sending out an e-mail to our pastoral staff after an event, asking for their input and evaluation.

If you've never asked for the pastor's input, you might want to start by asking something like, "Any thoughts on how I could have done a better job last Sunday?" It may take a few tries before you get the answers you're looking for—honest ones. It's much easier for others to share their thoughts when we ask for them. It requires humility on our part, but isn't that what the Savior came to produce in us? Don't we want to be more like him? And won't it bring us joy to know we're serving God's people more effectively?

One of the most meaningful expressions of support to your pastor (and perhaps the most difficult to initiate) is communicating a willingness to step back or step down if he thinks someone else could do a more effective job of leading. That thought might be completely foreign to you. It shouldn't be. One day every one of us will be replaced.

GROW

If you're a leader in the church, everyone benefits when you grow. And everyone suffers when you don't. Particularly your pastor.

When you grow spiritually, he's confident that leading others in exalting Christ isn't simply a job to you. It's your life. As you grow in humility, he'll enjoy working with you more. As you grow in your love for God's Word, you'll be able to proclaim the Word more effectively with the songs you lead. As you grow in caring for your wife and children, the pastor is freed from concerns that you are dishonoring the Savior and the church by neglecting your home.

When you grow theologically, you'll be able to research topics that your pastor may not have studied. Why is singing so important to God? Does God care about what we do with our hands and feet in corporate worship? What is worship anyway? How do we help people focus on exalting God? How does worship in a meeting relate to worship in all of life? Our leading will also become more substantive and helpful for the church. We'll become more discerning about what songs are saying and how they can serve people.

When you grow musically, you'll have more tools available to serve your pastor. Are you at the place where you can lead any song your pastor asks for? If not, what do you need to learn to get there? Is your knowledge of music theory and your instrument just enough to get by, or are you anticipating future needs? Most pastors aren't knowledgeable in these areas, so it's even more important that we take the initiative to make progress musically.

Administratively, we can grow in serving our pastor by figuring out ways to communicate more quickly, more clearly, more effectively. Aesthetically we can think about how attractive or appealing the musicians and stage look on a Sunday morning.

We can grow technologically, too. I'm not an equipment geek, but many times my basic knowledge of sound systems and equipment has enabled me to say whether we could accomplish a specific agenda for a meeting or improve the way we were doing things.

WHEN YOU DISAGREE

How do you serve and support your pastor when you don't think his approach is biblical? What do you do if your pastor asks you to do things you don't think will serve the church in the long run? What if you have a hard time trusting your pastor?

First, make sure you've rightly identified the issues. Conflicts arise for different reasons. Some are theological. You may disagree about the worship leader's role, the goals of corporate worship, or how the Holy Spirit reveals his active presence during the meeting. Some differences are methodological. You don't see eye to eye on the way things are done or the systems you're using. Some conflicts spring from different cultural or generational assumptions. "Of course everyone will like this song!" reveals how narrow-minded our thinking can be.

But the root issues are almost always tied to sin. Selfish ambition leads to comparison, envy, offense, and slander. Uncharitable judgments become the norm. *He's cutting a song again because he doesn't care about worship.* We think we're being discerning. Actually, we're being judgmental. If that describes your present relationship with your pastor, there's no other way out but confession and repentance.

Second, exhaust every avenue of resolution. If your relationship with your pastor isn't already a matter of prayer, start there. Then humbly ask him questions to better understand his thinking. If you discover you really disagree over theological issues, talk through them. Suggest that he read an article or a chapter of a book or listen to a message that clearly defines what you think he's missing. Ask him to make similar recommendations for you. Then discuss them together. (Vaughan Roberts's *True Worship* might be a great place to start, or the first chapter of *Worship by the Book*, edited by D. A. Carson.) Make sure you understand how he perceives your role.

If you see that you've sinned, confess it clearly and fully. Ask him for observations about your heart, your words, and your life. If necessary, determine together if you should involve anyone else.

And be patient. Allow God to work over time. A few weeks or months often brings a clearer perspective. Things you thought were *very* important turn out to be not so important after all.

Third, stay or move on in faith. I served in one church where I thought the challenges I experienced with my pastor were primarily his problem. By God's grace, my perspective changed. A discerning friend pointed out that my lack of support for my pastor was rooted in pride, a most serious sin in God's eyes. I'd wanted him not only to conform to my ideas but to applaud them. After I stopped sinfully judging his motives, things changed dramatically. I had renewed faith to support him because—well, by the grace of God, I changed.

There are times, though, when disagreement about theological issues, your role and responsibilities, or your assessment of his character makes it difficult to remain at that church. The differences are too significant to ignore. In those instances, after sufficient prayer and counsel, it might be wise to move on. One thing is certain: you need to be in a church where you can fully support your pastor. And if you do leave, do everything you can to leave with his blessing.

YOU, TOO, NEED SUPPORT

If a church is going to be served well, it's not only the pastor who needs support—the worship leader does too.

That's why this book's final chapter is addressed to pastors. If you're a worship leader, you might suggest that your pastor read it. You can tell him I asked you to pass it on. It's meant to equip and encourage him in his role of overseeing the corporate worship of his church.

And if you're a pastor, thank you for reading this book and demonstrating your desire to grow in your knowledge of worship. The last chapter's just for you.

chapter 32

SOME THOUGHTS FOR PASTORS

I'd been at my new church for only a few months when C. J., my senior pastor, came into my office with a stack of books.

"My friend, I think you would be well served by reading these."

Little did I realize what a difference his simple act of generosity was going to make in my life.

Included in the stack was *Engaging with God* by David Peterson. As I read it, I was stunned. Here was a scholar who took the Bible and worshiping God seriously. And he was able to connect them! I began to see how little I actually understood biblical worship.

I learned that the Bible uses the word *worship* in a much broader way than I was using it. I thought worship was primarily about singing. That's why I called myself a worship leader. But I came to see that worship involves my whole life—my words, my thoughts, my actions. Music was a part of that, but certainly not the whole picture.

C. J.'s initiative and generosity had a profound influence on my understanding and practice of worship. But he did more than give me books. Over the following months and years C. J. taught me more about leading worship than anyone I know. I've come to understand the centrality of the gospel in our worship, the importance of God's Word, and our need for the Spirit's empowering presence. C. J.'s constant encouragement has made my ministry as a worship leader easier, more effective, and more fruitful. And he doesn't even play an instrument.

Why am I telling you about C. J.? I hope you will serve your worship leader like C. J. has served me for so many years. I hope more pastors become like him. That's why I've written this chapter. Worship leaders need pastors who are more passionate about glorifying Jesus Christ than they are. They need pastors who are willing to lead them, care for them, and speak the truth to them.

The church music landscape has changed dramatically over recent decades. In many churches, singing now occupies up to half the meeting, led by a musician who may or may not have theological training or pastoral gifts. People often choose churches more for the music than for the preaching or doctrine. It's been suggested that music is a new sacrament that mediates God's presence to us. Obviously, there are reasons for great concern.

For twenty years I've functioned both as a corporate worship leader and as a pastor. I know pastors have plenty to do, but one of the most important things they can do is make sure their churches understand and practice biblical worship. Maybe you already have that conviction, and what you read here will be fresh encouragement. Or maybe you've turned over the responsibility for worship in your church to someone else. Or maybe you're not sure what to think.

Whatever your situation, here are five suggestions for how you can serve your worship leader more effectively. I hope you find them helpful.

RECOGNIZE YOUR OWN ROLE IN LEADING WORSHIP

On most Wednesday mornings from September to May, I have the privilege of teaching the students in our Pastors College about worship. The PC is a ten-month school of intensive training for men who will serve as pastors or church planters. Every Wednesday one of the students leads us in corporate worship for thirty minutes. For the next fifteen minutes I encourage the leader and then suggest things he could have done differently.

Only a few of the students can play an instrument, and not everyone can sing. In fact, one year we were led by a student who was completely tone-deaf. He actually did a pretty good job. Why do I ask these pastors and future pastors to lead us in worship despite their lack of musical gifting? Because leading worship is a pastoral role before it's a musical one. Music certainly plays a part, but without a pastor's involvement, the songs we sing may do more harm than good.

You may not own an instrument or know how to play one. But your congregation looks to you to know what it means to be a worshiper. You are the primary worship leader in your church.

A church's response to God's greatness and grace rarely rises above the example of its pastor. Your congregation is watching and listening to you on Sunday, and not just when you preach. What are they learning? What kind of example do you provide for them?

If you fiddle with your sermon notes while everyone else is praising God, they may infer that singing is optional. If you look around anxiously to make sure the technical details are being taken care of, they might conclude that the priority of Sunday morning is the performance, not their participation. If you sing halfheartedly, they may assume that passion for God isn't that important. But know this: your church is watching you.

God has called pastors to feed, lead, care for, and protect the members of the church. We tend to think preaching and personal pastoral care are the only ways we can fulfill those ministry responsibilities. But let's not overlook how corporate worship—thoughtfully, passionately, and skillfully led—can be a means of fulfilling those goals.

As a pastor, you can feed the church by making sure your worship leader chooses songs for their theologically balanced lyrics, not for their popularity. You can lead the church by directing their attention to what's important and by explaining the role of music in worship. You exercise care when you highlight songs that remind the church of God's promises and faithfulness in the midst of their trials, especially as he has revealed them to us in the gospel. You protect your church from the world by finding songs that remind them of God's holiness and the infinitely superior joy that Christ offers us.

Being the primary worship leader also means helping people understand what biblical worship entails. Because worship has become such a buzzword in recent years, we think we understand it better than ever. I think the opposite might be true. We think of worship as a feeling, a mood, or (most often) a style of music. We buy worship CDs, sing worship songs, go to worship conferences, tune into worship radio stations, and support worship artists. You'd almost think we're the first generation to think about worship or to worship God authentically. Hardly. The church has been wrestling through worship questions for centuries and has often come up with more compelling answers than we have. And the biblical picture of worship is far richer, more complex, deeper, more fulfilling, and more comprehensive than our present "worship" culture suggests.

That's why pastors need to study the theology of worship. As helpful as the Christian worship industry can be, we can't allow it to dictate and define what biblical worship is. There are an increasing number of books that ground our understanding of worship in Scripture and not in passing trends. If we want to serve our church, serve our worship leader, and please God, we'll find the time to read them and to teach our church what we learn on this most important topic.[1]

KNOW WHAT TO LOOK FOR IN A WORSHIP LEADER

Most of us think a typical worship leader is someone who can play the guitar, lead vocally, write original songs, lead a band, and plan half of your Sunday meeting. Maybe he'll even record a CD someday.

Those kinds of leaders are rare. And those certainly aren't the standards God sets.

Let me propose another list of qualifications.

Humility

A pastor called me once for counsel. His worship leader was resisting his request to submit his list of Sunday songs in advance. He thought that music was his domain and preaching was the pastor's responsibility. My friend was unsure if it was right for him to insist that the worship leader comply. He thought that might be too forward or demanding.

Actually, it would be wrong for this pastor *not* to graciously but firmly insist. Every pastor will have to give an account to God for the members of his church (Hebrews 13:17). If your worship leader isn't willing to run his plans by you for your evaluation and approval, he won't be serving you or the church effectively. And the risk is greater that he'll do things that harm rather than help the church.

Along with being willing to submit his plans to you, here are other evidences that a worship leader is pursuing humility:

• He doesn't compete with you for your congregation's allegiance.
• He welcomes and even requests evaluation about how he's doing.
• He wants to serve your vision for the church rather than his own.
• He's happy to change his plans when you ask him to.
• He doesn't view serving in the church as a mere stepping-stone to another position or a way to advance his personal musical career.

Your worship leader won't be completely humble. Neither will you. That's why God sent his Son to be our Savior and why meditating on the gospel is a crucial aspect of pursuing humility. It's impossible to boast as we remember what took place at the cross.

If this is an area where you're deficient, I can't think of a better resource to recommend than C. J.'s book *Humility: True Greatness*. I'd strongly suggest you read it together.

The important thing to remember is that if someone wants to lead worship in your church because he loves the spotlight and attention, he's the wrong person for the job, no matter how gifted he is.

Godly Character

I'd like to think this goes without saying, but it doesn't. At a recent conference a man came up to me and said he was aware of another worship leader in his town who was involved in sexual immorality. He wasn't sure the pastor was aware of the situation but knew that the worship leader hadn't been asked to step down. I encouraged the man talking to me to tell his unrepentant friend that if he didn't talk to his pastor in two weeks, he would do it for him. There was a good chance he'd lose a friend in the process.

That counsel might sound harsh to you. I hope not. Those who lead public worship in the church aren't just holding down a job. They're representing the Savior, Jesus Christ. When leaders engage in ongoing sin, it brings disgrace to his name, his church, and his mission.

If we truly care about God's people, we can't value musical skill over godliness. It's best to have both, but if we have to choose, Christlikeness wins hands down.

Godly character includes the qualities for leadership listed in 1 Timothy 3 and Titus 1—qualities such as self-control, respectability, sober-mindedness, and humility. Raising up leaders from within your church gives you the advantage of knowing someone's character well. If you hire from outside the church, take sufficient time, ask enough probing questions, and pursue credible references to make sure the person you're interviewing is truly qualified.

Love for Good Theology

Your worship leader doesn't need a Master of Divinity degree from a seminary to serve your church effectively. But he should have an appetite and aptitude for sound doctrine. He should be more concerned about the lyrics the church sings than the groove they're sung to. He should make sure that "the word of Christ" is dwelling in us richly as we sing (Colossians 3:16).

Music is a powerful tool. It can move people to joy or tears, celebration or reflection. But music is a carrier of God's truth, not the truth itself. Jesus said the truth, not emotional highs, will set us free.

A love for good theology shows itself by seeking to affect people with the gospel and God's Word rather than with a musical progression or a new arrangement. Creativity and fresh musical treatments can bring new life to overly familiar lyrics. But that's different from choosing a song simply because it's upbeat and has a great melodic hook in the chorus. Younger worship leaders who might be prone to miss that distinction need to be patiently and carefully mentored in this area.

In a musically infatuated culture the church should stand out as a place where making music is an *act* of worship, not an *idol* of worship.

Leadership Gifting

Leading worship involves just that—leading. And we can't assume that a competent musician is also a competent leader. Congregations aren't served and Christ isn't honored when the individual in front doesn't give clear signals, is unsure where he's headed, or doesn't make sense when he speaks. You don't want people in the church spending time trying to figure out what the worship leader is going to do next or what he just said. They should be focusing on God's grace in Christ. That requires good leadership.

Leadership gifts are also needed for working with a team of musicians. What will he do when people consistently don't show up on time? How will he resolve a conflict between two members of the team? What will he do to help those he's serving grow spiritually? Do people on the team respect him? Answering those questions will give you an idea of your worship leader's leadership gifting. If he's not able to handle those situations well, you'll need to find someone to help him lead. And if you're in a smaller church, that someone is most likely you.

Musical Skill

Finally, it's helpful when your worship leader knows music well enough to be able to fulfill your requests. That standard varies widely from church to church. You may want a fully arranged horn section each Sunday, with full choir and band. You might be satisfied with choosing from a small repertoire of songs that are easier to play.

Keep in mind that your worship leader may be someone with less musical skill but strong leadership gifts. In that case you need a strong lead musician who can both direct the other musicians and follow the worship leader. Also, if you have a worship leader who is weak in theological foundations, don't ask him to do what he's not equipped to do. Have others make comments about songs. In the meantime you can benefit from his musical gifts and help him grow in his understanding of Scripture.

EQUIP AND ENCOURAGE YOUR WORSHIP LEADER

One of the best ways to show you care for your worship leader is to supply him with materials to help him grow.

You can start with a book allowance. Even if it's small, this sends the message that you expect him to grow in his knowledge of worshiping God.

I've been in more than one bookstore with C. J. when he's pointed out books I might be interested in or bought them for me himself. He's sent me articles and brought home books and messages on worship from conferences that he's attended. He'll often follow up on what I've read or listened to. I can almost feel that whenever he's buying something for himself, he's also asking, "What about Bob?" (What a great name for a movie.)

Sending your worship leader to a conference is another way to equip him, and it doesn't have to be a worship conference. I've benefited immensely from attending conferences that helped me grow in my knowledge of Scripture and biblical leadership. If you really want to invest in his life and build your team, go together. God has often brought surprising guidance and help during casual conversations with C. J. while I was with him on a long trip.

Encouragement will enable your worship leader to function at his best. Hebrews 3:13 tells us that exhorting or encouraging others will keep them from being "hardened by the deceitfulness of sin." If you don't want a worship leader struggling with comparison, bitterness, discouragement, or envy, try encouraging him. You'll be amazed at the results.

You might be thinking, "But you don't know *my* worship leader." That's true. But I do know that the apostle Paul, when writing a primarily corrective letter to the Corinthian church, started out by telling them, "I give thanks to my God always for you because of the grace of God that was given you in Christ Jesus" (1 Corinthians 1:4). If Paul could encourage the Corinthians, you can encourage your worship leader.

Look for areas in his life where you see God at work. Maybe it's in his growing understanding and application of Scripture. Perhaps it was a creative musical idea. Every time I'm encouraged for stretching out musically, it increases my desire to find new ways to express God's glory.

If your worship leader tends to be tied to his plan every week, pour on the accolades when he does something spontaneous. On the other hand, if he unexpectedly stays within the allotted time one Sunday, let him know how appreciative you are. If he usually talks too long but keeps it brief one

Sunday, let him know. But make sure it's real encouragement, not something like, "Hey, Jeff, thanks for not going on and on like you usually do. What happened, did you blank out?"

Encouragement has the greatest impact when it's a way of life. Look for every opportunity to point out what your worship leader is doing right.

Express your encouragement publicly as well as privately. Tell the church how grateful you are for your worship leader's preparation, diligence, and example. Mention gifting, but don't major on it. You want people to respect your worship leader because of his godly character, not simply because he has musical ability or can sing well.

A generous budget for CDs, tapes, and equipment is also a great way to encourage and equip a worship leader. It makes a loud statement about your support. A worship leader shouldn't feel he has to fight you for purchases. Have him clarify what the needs of the church are and present a proposal. Then get back to him in a reasonable amount of time. If the budget has to be approved by others, go to bat for him. Better sound equipment can improve not only the music but the speaking. Since most of what we do as pastors depends on effective communication, you'll rarely regret investing money in purchases for sound equipment.[2]

BE FAITHFUL TO PLAN AND EVALUATE

Faithful encouragement will open the door for constructive evaluation. Your worship leader needs your observations and discernment.

It begins when you plan songs. Take responsibility for helping your worship leader choose songs that will most benefit the congregation. Whether you come up with a list of songs or you review a list put together by your worship leader depends on the maturity of your worship leader and how much you trust him.

Weekly song planning is also a good time to equip your worship leader as to why certain songs are better than others, what the lyrics mean, and what he might say in introductions and transitions. C. J. once told me, "I can tell the difference between when you prepare what you're going to say and when you don't." Message received. That's all he needed to say.

After a meeting, it's wise to share your thoughts as soon as possible. If you can't do it right after the meeting, it might be an e-mail later that week, a phone call, or a personal meeting. Do what fits your schedule. Even if a certain situation might never arise again, communication about what took place can help establish trust and teach discernment.

During my first few years at Covenant Life Church, C. J. would find me after almost every meeting to provide me with his encouragement and critique. He always started with encouragement. He took note of everything from my leadership to the songs to the arrangements to the sound. Then he'd share thoughts on what I could do differently. He always began with, "Now these are very small things, and they didn't in any way affect our ability to worship God this morning." His consistent feedback over a period of time has helped me grow in many ways.

One Sunday I shared briefly from Romans 8:32: "He who did not spare his own Son but gave him up for us all, how will he not also with him graciously give us all things?" I encouraged those who doubted God's provision to trust God's promise here—he would graciously give them all things. Afterward C. J. made the simple point that I didn't mention the logic of this verse: If God would give up his own Son as an atoning sacrifice for our sins, surely he would give us anything else that's good for us. His counsel was: Never mention the cross without some reference to what God accomplished there. I've never forgotten it.

Specific observations are the most helpful. Simply telling your worship leader, "It didn't feel like the Holy Spirit" is so vague it's completely useless. "The second song could have been faster" is more helpful than "Worship really didn't get off the ground this morning." It's better to say, "I thought you shouldn't have said anything after the third song" than "You talk way too much." Also, pointing out patterns is better than criticizing every single mistake you noticed.

Remember how you'd want others to treat you. That thought alone should help you balance your evaluation with large doses of encouragement.

RESOLVE CONFLICT BIBLICALLY

One of the best ways you can resolve conflict is by seeking to be humble before it starts. It's a good idea to regularly ask your worship leader how you could serve him more effectively. You might be surprised at the simple things that could improve your relationship and communication.

If you're having difficulties working with your worship leader, don't automatically assume he's at fault. He may not seem supportive of your leadership, but maybe you're always asking him to change things at the last minute. He might seem unorganized, but your concern may be more about how it affects your reputation. God will often use the sins of others to expose weaknesses in our own lives.

When there have been misunderstandings or disagreements, take time to talk through the reasons. It's not uncommon for worship leaders to feel like their pastors don't talk with them often enough. Sooner or later that lack of communication will create problems, or rather reveal them. It might be helpful to review this book's Part Three, "Healthy Tensions," to determine where you have different but complementary perspectives.

There are many reasons why pastors and worship leaders don't get along. Some are theological, some are methodological, some are the temptations common to man. Things like sinful judgment, comparison, pride, and impatience. It is often a combination of factors. Sin is deceptive, and the enemy works overtime to bring discontent and division. In some cases it's helpful to ask someone else you trust to help you work through the issues. In every case it's helpful to make your relationship a matter of regular prayer.

If you've sinned against your worship leader, specific confession and repentance are vital to working together. Acknowledge where you've sought your own way or your own recognition. And don't make confession a one-time occurrence. Keep a short account.

God intends your relationship with your worship leader to be one of joy, mutual respect, and fruitfulness. And with confidence in his Word, dependence on his Spirit, and reliance on the gospel, that's exactly what it will be.

A FINAL WORD

One of my desires in writing this book, and specifically this chapter, was to speak to pastors about the role they play in leading worship in their church. It's not secondary, and it's not optional. It's crucial. Many churches today are weaker and worldlier because pastors have abdicated that role. Thousands of pastors have looked to the culture rather than to the Bible to determine how their church will worship God.

I thank God that C. J. wasn't one of those pastors. He has taken seriously his responsibility to train the church in biblical worship. He's taken even more seriously his responsibility to model what it means to be a worshiper.

It's hard to say where I'd be and what I'd be doing apart from his influence, discernment, care, and guidance. I know I'd be far less effective as a worship leader. More importantly, I don't think I'd love my Savior as much.

That's because what has affected me most about C. J. hasn't been his evaluation, instruction, or direction, although those have been significant means of grace to me. What has affected me most about him has been his life. I've simply never met someone who more passionately, consistently, or joyfully communicates a genuine desire to see Jesus Christ glorified. No one has directed my eyes more faithfully to the gospel of grace and the beauty of the cross. And I know I'm not the only one who could say that.

What would your church and worship leader say about you? How seriously would they say you take your responsibility to teach your church what it means to worship God? What would they say about your example? What would your family say?

What would God say?

In the end, his is the only evaluation that counts.

Now to him who is able to keep you from stumbling and to present you blameless before the presence of his glory with great joy, to the only God, our Savior, through Jesus Christ our Lord, be glory, majesty, dominion, and authority, before all time and now and forever. Amen. (Jude 24–25)

A BRIEF ANNOTATED
BIBLIOGRAPHY

These are a few of the books I've benefited from over the years. The titles preceded by an asterisk are the ones I recommend most highly.

WORSHIP

Allen, Ronald, and Gordon Borror. *Worship: Rediscovering the Missing Jewel*. Portland: Multnomah, 1982.

    Written by a church musician and an Old Testament professor, this book is theological, devotional, and practical. Currently out of print but worth tracking down.

Best, Harold. *Unceasing Worship: Biblical Perspectives on Worship and the Arts*. Downers Grove, IL: InterVarsity Press, 2003.

    An insightful look at what it means to be a continuous worshiper. Harold's thoughts on how we idolize music and art, and how we can use them in a way that glorifies the Savior, are outstanding.

Carson, D. A., editor. *Worship: Adoration and Action*, Grand Rapids, MI: Baker, 1993.

    Theological, historical, and confessional studies produced by the Faith and Church Study Unit of the Theological Commission of the World Evangelical Fellowship. Some excellent and thorough treatments.

*Carson, D. A. *Worship by the Book*. Grand Rapids, MI: Zondervan, 2002.

    Four perspectives on how corporate worship should be shaped and governed by Scripture. The first chapter by Carson is worth the price of the book.

Due, Noel. *Created for Worship*. Geanies House, Fearn, Ross-shire, Scotland: Christian Focus, 2005.

    A thick read but contains a number of gems. Due weaves various biblical, theological themes into the study of worship. His application is sparse but meaningfully applied.

Frame, John M. *Contemporary Worship Music: A Biblical Defense*. Phillipsburg, NJ: P&R, 1997.

_____. *Worship in Spirit and Truth*. Phillipsburg, NJ: P&R, 1996.

    Both of Frame's books are biblical, practical, and easy to read. While written from a Presbyterian perspective, any church will benefit from his insights.

*Peterson, David. *Engaging with God: A Biblical Theology of Worship*. Grand Rapids, MI: Eerdmans, 1992.

A thorough and reverent exposition of biblical worship. Peterson is a New Testament scholar, and his treatment of worship is eminently Christ-exalting and gospel-centered. He highlights the connection between worship and edification.

Rayburn, Robert. *O Come, Let Us Worship*. Grand Rapids, MI: Baker, 1980.

A readable, informative volume with many good points concerning the theology and application of biblical worship in the church. A proponent of a more formal, planned liturgy. Out of print.

Roberts, Vaughan. *True Worship*. Cox and Wymjan, Reading, Berkshire, UK: Authentic Lifestyle, 2002.

A short but clear and biblical book on the nature of worship that honors God. Emphasizes worship as edification.

*Ross, Allen P. *Recalling the Hope of Glory: Biblical Worship from the Garden to the New Creation*. Grand Rapids, MI: Kregel, 2006.

Dr. Ross is an Old Testament professor who does a brilliant job of helping us see how worship in the Old Testament applies to us today. While acknowledging that worship is lived out in the entirety of life, he focuses primarily on worship as a corporate event.

GOD

Frame, John. *The Doctrine of God: A Theology of Lordship*. Phillipsburg, NJ: P&R, 2002.

A comprehensive and passionate exploration of God's attributes and acts. For the serious student of God. But shouldn't that describe all of us?

*Packer, J.I. *Knowing God*. Downers Grove, IL: InterVarsity Press, 1993.

Over one million copies sold, and for good reason. Packer writes in a way that is eminently readable, biblical, and devotional. You'll know God better after studying this book.

Piper, John. *The Pleasures of God*. Sisters, OR: Multnomah, 1992.

A must read for every Christian who wants his or her joy in God to be rooted in God's joy in himself.

Tozer, A. W. *The Knowledge of the Holy*. New York: Harper San Francisco, 1978.

A brief but insightful introduction to the attributes of God and their meaning for our lives.

Ware, Bruce. *Father, Son, and Holy Spirit: Relationships, Roles, and Relevance*. Wheaton, IL: Crossway Books, 2005.

A clear introduction to the doctrine of the Trinity and its significance for us.

THE PERSON AND WORK OF CHRIST

Bridges, Jerry. *The Gospel for Real Life*. Colorado Springs: NavPress, 2002.

An excellent introduction to understanding how the gospel makes a difference in our lives.

*Carson, D. A. *The Cross and Christian Ministry*. Grand Rapids, MI: Baker, 1993.

Using different passages in 1 Corinthians, Carson shows how "the cross stands as the test and the standard of all vital Christian ministry." He explains how the cross shapes our understanding and practice of preaching, the Holy Spirit, factionalism, leadership, and being a world Christian.

Morris, Leon. *The Atonement: Its Meaning and Significance*: Downers Grove, IL: InterVarsity Press, 1983.

A readable but profound treatment of various aspects of the atoning work of Christ.

*Stott, John. *The Cross of Christ*: Downers Grove, IL: InterVarsity Press, 1986.

One of the definitive works on the meaning and glory of the cross. Worth reading and re-reading.

THE HOLY SPIRIT

*Carson, D. A. *Showing the Spirit: A Theological Exposition of 1 Corinthians 12–14.* Grand Rapids, MI: Baker, 1996.

An insightful, pastoral, and biblical study of the validity and function of the gifts of the Spirit.

Fee, Gordon. *God's Empowering Presence*. Peabody, MA: Hendrickson, 1994.

A thorough and comprehensive study of the Holy Spirit in the letters of Paul. Dr. Fee has also written a shorter version entitled *Paul, the Spirit, and the People of God.*

Grudem, Wayne. *The Gift of Prophecy in the New Testament and Today.* Wheaton, IL: Crossway Books, 2000.

A careful, biblical, and practical treatment of the gift of prophecy and how it should function in the church.

THEOLOGY

Grudem, Wayne. *Systematic Theology.* Grand Rapids, MI: Zondervan, 1994.

A thorough explanation of what the Bible teaches on a multitude of topics. Grudem's style is biblical, insightful, practical, and devotional. My good friend Jeff Purswell edited this book down into a shorter volume called *Bible Doctrine.*

Packer, J. I. *Concise Theology.* Wheaton, IL: Tyndale House, 1993.

A brief introduction to essential doctrines of the Christian faith.

*Roberts, Vaughan. *God's Big Picture.* Downers Grove, IL: InterVarsity Press, 2003.

A brief and helpful introduction to biblical theology and understanding the unifying themes of the Bible.

GROWING IN HOLINESS

Bridges, Jerry. *The Discipline of Grace.* Colorado Springs: NavPress, 1994.

God used the truths in this book to help me understand that the changes God wants to bring about in me are all by his grace and for his glory.

Lundgaard, Kris. *The Enemy Within.* Phillipsburg, NJ: P&R, 1998.

A reader-friendly introduction to the doctrine of indwelling sin—how it deceives, how it works, and how to overcome it through the gospel.

*Mahaney, C. J. *Humility: True Greatness.* Sisters, OR: Multnomah, 2005.

A biblical, insightful, and practical book for understanding what humility is and how to pursue it by the grace of God.

*_____. *Living the Cross Centered Life*. Sisters, OR: Multnomah, 2006.

Having watched C. J. live this way for decades, I can assure you this book will help you more fully enjoy the fruit of what Christ accomplished at the cross for us.

Owen, John. Edited by Justin Taylor and Kelly Kapic. *Overcoming Sin and Temptation*. Wheaton, IL: Crossway Books, 2006.

An edited version of John Owens's treatise on indwelling sin. If you want to know your heart better, fight sin more effectively, and love the Savior more, this book is invaluable.

*Piper, John. *When I Don't Desire God*. Wheaton, IL: Crossway Books, 2004.

One of the most practical and biblical books I've ever read to aid us in our fight for joy in God.

Storms, Sam. *Signs of the Spirit: An Interpretation of Jonathan Edwards's "Religious Affections."* Wheaton, IL: Crossway Books, 2007.

A refreshing rendition of the Puritan classic. If you're wondering how to think of emotions in your relationship with God, this book will help.

Welch, Ed. *When People Are Big & God Is Small*. Phillipsburg, NJ: P&R, 1997.

Biblical teaching on overcoming the fear of man and the craving for approval.

THE CHURCH

Dever, Mark. *What Is a Healthy Church?* Wheaton, IL: Crossway Books, 2007.

A clear statement of what kind of church communities we should be seeking and building.

Harris, Joshua. *Stop Dating the Church*. Sisters, OR: Multnomah, 2004.

A great book to develop conviction about the importance of being involved in a local church, written by my good friend and pastor.

White, James F. *Documents of Christian Worship: Descriptive and Interpretive Sources*. Louisville: Westminster/John Knox Press, 1992.

A valuable collection of primary sources on the history of worship in the Western church.

Whitney, Donald. *Spiritual Disciplines Within the Church*. Chicago: Moody Press, 1996.

A valuable, readable resource for understanding the biblical nature and importance of the church.

MUSIC

*Best, Harold M. *Music Through the Eyes of Faith*. San Francisco: Harper, 1993.

A balanced and thought-provoking book on the meaning and use of music for God's glory, written by a former Dean of Music at Wheaton College.

Kidd, Reggie M. *With One Voice: Discovering Christ's Song in Your Worship*. Grand Rapids, MI: Baker, 2005.

A compelling and engaging apologetic for the use of various musical styles in congregational song, all flowing from the song of the Savior in our midst.

Page, Nick. *And Now Let's Move into a Time of Nonsense.* Waynesboro, GA: Authentic Media, 2004.

A brief, insightful, humorous, and helpful book on what makes a great congregational song.

Roff, Lawrence C. *Let Us Sing.* Norcross, GA: Great Commission Publications, 1991.

A brief but informative history of Christian congregational song.

Thiessen, Donald. *Psalms, Hymns and Spiritual Songs: What the Bible Says about Music.* Chicago: Cornerstone Press, 1994.

A collection of all the references to music in the Bible.

DEVOTIONALS

*Bennett, Arthur, ed. *The Valley of Vision: A Collection of Puritan Prayers and Devotions.* Carlisle, PA: Banner of Truth Trust, 1983.

These collected one page prayers model a relationship with God that grieves over sin, loves the gospel, rejoices in God's attributes, and seeks to live for God's glory.

Carson, D. A. *For the Love of God, Vols. 1 & 2.* Wheaton, IL: Crossway Books, 1998, 1999.

Two of the most helpful devotional commentaries on the Bible you'll find. Carson provides historical background, helps you understand Scripture in its redemptive context, and makes gospel-centered application.

Piper, John. *Desiring God.* Sisters, OR: Multnomah, 1996.

An exposition of John Piper's saying, "God is most glorified in us when we are most satisfied in him." God used this book in my life to turn duty into delight.

Tozer, A. W. *The Pursuit of God.* Camp Hill, PA: Christian Publications, 1982.

A classic devotional that reminds us, "We pursue God because, and only because, He has first put an urge within us that spurs us to the pursuit."

SPECIAL THANKS

To Lane Dennis, for the privilege of writing a book for Crossway, one of my favorite publishers.

To Al Fisher, for your encouragement, graciousness, and patience in the unexpectedly long process of writing.

To Josh Dennis, Ted Griffin, and all the folks at Crossway who work so faithfully to provide the church with substantive, biblical, gospel-centered, God-glorifying books.

To Thomas Womack, for the thoughtful, careful, insightful, humble editing that you put into this book. Thank you for providing the outline and for helping me say things clearly and much more concisely.

To David Peterson, John Piper, and Harold Best. God used your books to help me understand the biblical theology of worship, the importance of passion in worship, and the role of music in worship, all for the glory of Jesus Christ.

To Ken Boer, Eric Hughes, Jon Payne, Pat Sczebel, Joseph Stigora, and Todd Twining, for helping me oversee music and worship in Sovereign Grace churches and for your encouragement, counsel, and friendship during and beyond the writing of this book.

To the staff of Sovereign Grace Ministries, whose unseen, faithful labors are being used by God to glorify the Savior and change lives throughout the world.

To the pastors and members of Covenant Life Church, for modeling Christ-exalting worship through humble servanthood, genuine encouragement, faithful prayer, and passionate gospel-centeredness. Living among you is a continual reminder of God's kindness to me.

To the members of my care group—Gary Ricucci, Jeff Purswell, Pat Ennis, and C. J. Mahaney. I can't imagine not having you as friends.

To Josh Harris, not only for the example you've set as a writer, but for your encouragement over the years. Both have been a means of grace to me.

To Jeff Purswell, the smartest friend I have. Knowing you has truly been one of the highlights of my life. Thank you for helping me treasure God's words more than my own. Thank you for the humility, grace, and patience you've shown in helping me think more biblically. And thanks for helping this book be better than it would have been.

To C. J. Mahaney. No one, other than my wife, has had more of an influence on me. I've told you in private, and I'll say it here—if I had a choice between hearing you preach and watching your life, I'd easily choose the second. Your preaching is amazing. But your life is even more so. Thank you for consistently teaching and modeling what it means to live for the glory of the Savior. Thank you for asking me to rewrite this book after seeing the first draft. Thanks for taking so much time to go over the contents. And thank you for asking me to come to Covenant Life ten years ago. My life has never been the same since.

To my children—Megan, Jordan, Devon, Chelsea, Brittany, and Mckenzie—for the patience you displayed and the encouragement you gave me while I wrote this book. More importantly, thank you for making it such a joy to be your dad. And, Chelsea, thanks for all the administrative work you did to get this book out.

To Julie, my precious wife, my best friend, my most enthusiastic encourager, and my greatest gift from God after salvation. You are indeed "far more precious than jewels." Thank you for being patient with me in so many ways, especially as I wrote this book.

Finally, to my Lord and Savior, Jesus Christ, who opened the way to the Father and filled me with his Spirit. May this book be used to bring glory to your matchless name.

NOTES

Chapter 2: My Heart: What Do I Love?

1. Isaac Watts, *Discourses on the Love of God*, printed by J. Catnach, 1798, 12.

Chapter 3: My Mind: What Do I Believe?

1. Charles Spurgeon, Sermon #542 on 2 Timothy 4:13, November 29, 1863. *Metropolitan Tabernacle Pulpit*, 9 (1863); www.spurgeon.org/sermons/0542.htm.

Chapter 4: My Hands: What Do I Practice?

1. From a message called "More Desirable Than Gifts," given at the Sovereign Grace Small Group Leaders Conference, 1998.
2. "What Unites Us in Worship at Bethlehem?"; http://www.desiringgod.org/ResourceLibrary/TasteAndSee/ByDate/2003/1241_What_Unites_Us_in_Worship_at_Bethlehem/.
3. Among the many online music theory courses available, I'd check out www.musictheory.ca. Also Sibelius sells a comprehensive theory course called Musition at www.sibelius.com/products/musition
4. Guitarists should check out the Learn & Master Guitar series at http://www.learnandmasterguitar.com.

Chapter 5: My Life: What Do I Model?

1. See 2 Corinthians 6:7; Ephesians 4:29; Colossians 4:6; Titus 2:8.
2. An excellent study on why we use the words we do is Paul Tripp's *War of Words* (Phillipsburg, NJ: P&R, 2000).
3. One of the best resources I've found in the fight against sexual temptation is *Sex Is Not the Problem (Lust Is)* by Joshua Harris (Sisters, OR: Multnomah, 2005).

Chapter 6: So What Does a Worship Leader Do?

1. Andrew Wilson-Dickson, *A Brief History of Christian Music* (Oxford, UK: Lion Hudson, 1997).
2. Gordon MacDonald, "To Find a Worship Leader," *Leadership Journal,* Spring 2002.
3. Tony Payne interview with D. A. Carson, *The Briefing,* Issue #232, Matthias Media, 2000.
4. Throughout this book I use masculine pronouns when I'm talking about an individual worship leader. There are a number of reasons for this. First, I believe Scripture teaches a complementarian view of manhood and womanhood. That is, men and women are both created in the image of God and are of equal worth before God, but he has assigned them different but equally valuable roles in the family and in the church. A helpful resource on this topic is *Fifty Crucial Questions* by John Piper and Wayne Grudem, published by the Council on Biblical Manhood and Womanhood and available online at http://www.cbmw.org/Store/Books/50-Crucial-Questions. Second,

in Sovereign Grace churches and in this book, the task of a worship leader includes teaching and leading the gathered church. In addition to leading music, they direct people's hearts, minds, and wills to the truths they're singing. We believe these teaching and leading roles are pastoral in nature and that Scripture reserves pastoral functions in the corporate meeting for males. For that reason, all our worship leaders are men. But women make a significant contribution to our corporate worship through singing, playing instruments, reading Scripture, writing and arranging songs, leading choirs, modeling expressive engagement, contributing through spiritual gifts, and more. Third, while there are occasions when women could lead worship (such as in a gathering of women), I thought switching back and forth between male and female pronouns would create confusion.

Chapter 7: A Faithful Worship Leader . . .

1. Harold Best, *Music Through the Eyes of Faith* (San Francisco: HarperOne, 1993), 116.

Chapter 8: . . . Magnifies the Greatness of God . . .

1. J. I. Packer, *Knowing God* (Downers Grove, IL: InterVarsity Press, 1993), 83.
2. John Owen, *The Glory of Christ* (Carlisle, PA: Banner of Truth Trust, 1994), 54.
3. John Stott, *Authentic Christianity* (Downers Grove, IL: InterVarsity Press, 1996), 250.
4. I've included more recommended books in the bibliography at the end of this book.
5. John Piper, *Desiring God* (Sisters, OR: Multnomah, 2003), 68.
6. More professions of faithfulness and desire are found in Psalm 52:9, 75:9, and 119:33.
7. Isaac Watts, *A Guide to Prayer* (Carlisle, PA: Banner of Truth, 2001), 28.

Chapter 9: . . . In Jesus Christ . . .

1. D. A. Carson, "Worship under the Word," in *Worship by the Book*, ed. D. A. Carson (Grand Rapids, MI: Zondervan, 2002), 37.
2. C. J. Mahaney, *Living the Cross Centered Life* (Sisters, OR: Multnomah, 2002), 61.
3. As quoted by John Stott in *The Cross of Christ* (Downers Grove, IL: InterVarsity Press, 1986), 43.
4. From "Across the Great Divide," by Mark Altrogge, copyright 2001 Sovereign Grace Praise.
5. Harold Best, *Music Through the Eyes of Faith* (New York: HarperOne, 1993), 155–156.
6. John Owen, *The Glory of Christ* (Carlisle, PA: Banner of Truth Trust, 1994), 25.
7. David Prior, *Message of 1 Corinthians: Life in the Local Church* (Downers Grove, IL: InterVarsity Press, 1985), 51.
8. Jim Elliff, *The Glory of Christ*, ed. John Armstrong (Wheaton, IL: Crossway Books, 2002), 78.
9. *The Collected Essays, Journalism and Letters of George Orwell: In Front of Your Nose, 1945–1950*, Sonia Orwell and Ian Angus, eds. (New York: Harcourt Brace Jovanovich, 1968), 125.
10. Frederick Leahy, *The Cross He Bore* (Carlisle, PA: Banner of Truth, 1996), 45.

Chapter 10: . . . Through the Power of the Holy Spirit . . .

1. Robert Rayburn, *O Come Let Us Worship* (Grand Rapids, MI: Baker, 1980), 22.

2. D. Martyn Lloyd-Jones, from the sermon "The Living God," June 1971; http://www.mlj.org.uk/emw_mag/article4.htm.

3. Gordon Fee, *Paul, The Spirit, and the People of God* (Peabody, MA: Hendrickson Publishers, 1996), 188.

Chapter 11: . . . Skillfully Combining God's Word . . .

1. John Stott, *The Contemporary Christian: Applying God's Word to Today's World* (Downers Grove, IL: InterVarsity Press, 1995), 174.

2. "The Gospel Song," words by Drew Jones, music by Bob Kauflin, copyright © 2002 by Sovereign Grace Worship (ASCAP); Sovereign Grace Praise (BMI), Sovereign Grace Music, a division of Sovereign Grace Ministries. Available at http://www.sovereign-gracestore.com/ProductInfo.aspx?productid=M4055-15-51?.

3. Nick Page, *And Now Let's Move into a Time of Nonsense: Why Worship Songs Are Failing the Church* (Waynesboro, GA: Authentic Media, 2004), 59.

4. In his book *Simplify Your Spiritual Life* (Colorado Springs: NavPress, 2003), Donald Whitney addresses this topic in a chapter entitled "Pray Scripture."

Chapter 12: . . . With Music . . . (Part One: What Kind?)

1. Taken from Martin Luther's foreword to Georg Rhau's *Symphoniae iucundae*, published in 1538, a collection of fifty-two chorale motets and Latin motets of old masters, likely intended for amateur singers.

2. As quoted by John Piper in *A God-Entranced Vision of All Things* (Wheaton, IL: Crossway Books, 2004), 242.

3. Michael S. Hamilton, "The Triumph of the Praise Songs," *Christianity Today,* July 12, 1999, 28.

Chapter 13: . . . With Music . . . (Part Two: Planning Sunday's Songs)

1. This list is adapted from one by Graham Kendrick that I came across on the Internet a few years ago. That web page is no longer available.

2. One of the most helpful discussions on modulations I've come across is in Greg Scheer's book *The Art of Worship* (Grand Rapids, MI: Baker, 2006), 112–120.

3. An example of a corporate Confession can be found at http://www.worshipmatters.com/2006/08/corporate-confession-at-the-worship-god-conference.

Chapter 14: . . . Thereby Motivating the Gathered Church . . .

1. D. A. Carson, "Worship under the Word," in *Worship by the Book*, ed. D. A. Carson (Grand Rapids, MI: Zondervan, 2002), 59.

2. David Peterson, *Engaging with God: A Biblical Theology of Worship* (Downers Grove, IL: InterVarsity Press, 2002), 21.

Chapter 15: . . . To Proclaim the Gospel . . .

1. From "Before the Throne of God Above," lyrics by Charitie Lees Bancroft, music by Vikki Cook. Copyright © 1997 by Sovereign Grace Worship (ASCAP), Sovereign Grace Music, a division of Sovereign Grace Ministries.

2. From "Before the Cross," by Jon Payne, copyright © 2003 by Sovereign Grace Worship (ASCAP), Sovereign Grace Music, a division of Sovereign Grace Ministries.

3. C. J. Mahaney, *Living the Cross Centered Life* (Sisters, OR: Multnomah, 2006), 112.

4. From "Grace Unmeasured," by Bob Kauflin, copyright © 2005 Sovereign Grace Praise, Sovereign Grace Music, a division of Sovereign Grace Ministries.

5. Along with Scripture, two books I've found helpful for proclaiming the gospel to myself are *A Gospel Primer for Christians* by Milton Vincent (Bemidji, MN: Focus Publishing, 2008) and *The Valley of Vision: A Collection of Puritan Prayers and Devotions*, ed. Arthur Bennett (Carlisle, PA: Banner of Truth Trust, 1975).

6. Mahaney, *Living the Cross Centered Life*, 132.

Chapter 16: . . . To Cherish God's Presence . . .

1. D. A. Carson, "Worship under the Word," in *Worship by the Book*, ed. D. A. Carson (Grand Rapids, MI: Zondervan, 2002), 50–51.

2. Harold Best, *Music Through the Eyes of Faith* (New York: HarperOne, 1993), 153.

3. Wayne Grudem, *Systematic Theology* (Grand Rapids, MI: Zondervan, 1994), 641.

4. Gordon Fee, *Paul, the Spirit, and the People of God* (Peabody, MA: Hendrickson, 1996), xiii.

5. I'm not seeking to persuade anyone that certain spiritual gifts are still in operation today. Others have done a much better job of this than I could. Some resources I've found especially helpful are *Showing the Spirit* by D. A. Carson (Grand Rapids, MI: Baker, 1996), *Paul, the Spirit, and the People of God* by Gordon Fee, and *Who's Afraid of the Holy Spirit?*, edited by Daniel Wallace and M. James Sawyer (Dallas: Biblical Studies Press, 2004). Also, Jeff Purswell has given two helpful messages, "Understanding and Experiencing the Holy Spirit" and "Non-Spectacular Gifts," which are available at http://www.sovereigngracestore.com/Productinfo.aspx?productid=A2240-05-51 and http://www.sovereigngracestore.com/Productinfo.aspx?productid=A1235-04-51. I think that much of the disagreement and at times animosity between charismatics and cessationists is a result of people using gifts from the Holy Spirit in a proud way. I think some well-known charismatics have received genuine gifts from God, but their usefulness is limited or negated due to blatant self-promotion, financial deception, or theological error. Works of power are no excuse for disobedience.

6. When I first started singing spontaneous songs, I wrestled with the biblical basis for the gift. I learned that prophesying in the Old Testament often had musical accompaniment (1 Chronicles 25:1; 1 Samuel 10:5; 2 Kings 3:14–16). Ephesians 5:18–19 connects being filled with the Spirit with singing. And the effects of prophecy listed in 1 Corinthians 14:3—building up, "encouragement," and "consolation"—were frequently the effect of this gift. So I told the Lord that if I felt I was to sing a song in a particular meeting, I would do it and let him take care of the results. I would focus on being prepared, humble, and faithful. Since that time I've seen God use spontaneous songs on countless occasions to encourage and speak to groups as well as individuals—including single mothers, those in the midst of suffering, young men, widows, and adopted children.

7. Grudem, *Systematic Theology*, 176.

8. Allen P. Ross, *Recalling the Hope of Glory: Biblical Worship from the Garden to the New Creation* (Grand Rapids, MI: Kregel, 2006), 474.

9. C. S. Lewis, *The Last Battle* (New York: Collier, 1956), 183.

Chapter 17: . . . And to Live for God's Glory

1. From "A Debtor to Mercy Alone," words by Augustus M. Toplady, music and alternate words by Bob Kauflin. Copyright © 1998 by Sovereign Grace Praise (BMI), Sovereign Grace Music, a division of Sovereign Grace Ministries.

2. From "God Moves," original words by William Cowper, music and additional words by Bob Kauflin. Copyright © 2005 by Sovereign Grace Praise (BMI), Sovereign Grace Music, a division of Sovereign Grace Ministries.

3. W. M. Clow, quoted in John Stott, *The Cross of Christ* (Downers Grove, IL: InterVarsity Press, 2006), 257–258.

4. From "Jesus, Thank You," by Pat Sczebel. Copyright © 2003 by Integrity's Hosanna! Music (ASCAP)/Sovereign Grace Worship (ASCAP), Sovereign Grace Music, a division of Sovereign Grace Ministries.

5. "In the Presence," by Mark Altrogge. Copyright © 1999, Sovereign Grace Praise (BMI)/Integrity's Hosanna! Music (ASCAP), Sovereign Grace Music, a division of Sovereign Grace Ministries.

6. From "High Above All Things," by Mark Altrogge. Copyright © 2001 by Sovereign Grace Praise (BMI), Sovereign Grace Music, a division of Sovereign Grace Ministries.

7. From "Let Your Kingdom Come," by Bob Kauflin. Copyright © 2006 Sovereign Grace Praise (BMI), Sovereign Grace Music, a division of Sovereign Grace Ministries.

8. Allen P. Ross, *Recalling the Hope of Glory: Biblical Worship from the Garden to the New Creation* (Grand Rapids, MI: Kregel, 2006), 60.

Chapter 18: Guiding Principles

1. You can find a helpful presentation and defense of the regulative principle in chapters 2–4 of *Give Praise to God: A Vision for Reforming Worship*, ed. Philip Ryken, Derek Thomas, and J. Ligon Duncan III (Phillipsburg, NJ: P&R, 2003).

2. Allen P. Ross, *Recalling the Hope of Glory: Biblical Worship from the Garden to the New Creation* (Grand Rapids, MI: Kregel, 2006), 470.

Chapter 19: Transcendent and Immanent

1. See John Frame's excellent discussion on God's transcendence in *The Doctrine of God* (Phillipsburg, NJ: P&R, 2002), Chapter 7.

2. D. A. Carson, *The Difficult Doctrine of the Love of God* (Wheaton, IL: Crossway Books, 2000), 41.

3. "O Sacred King," by Matt Redman. Copyright © 1999 by Kingsway's Thankyou Music.

4. Dr. Piper's sermon series "Gravity and Gladness on Sunday Morning" is available at http://www.desiringgod.org/ResourceLibrary/Seminars/1724 Gravity_and_Gladness_on_Sunday_Morning.

5. Charles H. Spurgeon, *The Power of the Cross of Christ*, ed. Lance Wubbels (Lynnwood, WA: Emerald Books, 1995), 66.

Chapter 20: Head and Heart

1. Jonathan Edwards, "Some Thoughts Concerning the Revival," in *The Works of Jonathan Edwards*, Vol. 4, *The Great Awakening*, ed. C. C. Goen (New Haven, CT: Yale University Press, 1972), 387.

2. Kelly Carpenter, "Draw Me Close to You." Copyright © 1994 by Mercy/Vineyard Publishing.

3. C. J. Mahaney, *Sex, Romance, and the Glory of God* (Wheaton, IL: Crossway Books, 2004), 12.

Chapter 21: Internal and External

1. These guidelines are adapted from Mark Alderton, a pastor of Sovereign Grace Fellowship in Bloomington, Minnesota.

2. From "In Christ Alone," by Stuart Townend and Keith Getty. Copyright © 2001 by Kingsway's Thankyou Music.

Chapter 22: Vertical and Horizontal

1. From the sermon "Why Expositional Preaching Is Particularly Glorifying to God" by John Piper; http://www.desiringgod.org/ResourceLibrary/ConferenceMessages/ByDate/1756_Why_Expositional_Preaching_is_Particularly_Glorifying_to_God/.
2. Donald Whitney, *Spiritual Disciplines for the Christian Life* (Colorado Springs: NavPress, 1977), 77.
3. David Peterson, *Engaging with God: A Biblical Theology of Worship* (Downers Grove, IL: InterVarsity Press, 2002), 215, 221. Chapter 7 of Peterson's book specifically expands upon the connection between the vertical and horizontal aspects of worship.

Chapter 23: Planned and Spontaneous

1. As quoted by Tony Sargent in *The Sacred Anointing* (Wheaton, IL: Crossway Books, 1994), 57.
2. From Sermon #878, "A Well-Ordered Life"; http://spurgeongems.org/vols13-15/chs878.pdf.

Chapter 24: Rooted and Relevant

1. Os Guinness, *Prophetic Untimeliness: A Challenge to the Idol of Relevance* (Grand Rapids, MI: Baker, 2005), 15.

Chapter 25: Skilled and Authentic

1. Reggie Kidd, *With One Voice: Discovering Christ's Song in Our Worship* (Grand Rapids, MI: Baker, 2005), 101–102.

Chapter 26: For the Church and for Unbelievers

1. Quoted in Mark Dever, "Baptized Pagans"; http://blog.togetherforthegospel.org/2006/03/baptized_pagans.html.
2. D. A. Carson, *The Cross and Christian Ministry* (Grand Rapids, MI: Baker, 2004), 80–81.

Chapter 27: Event and Everyday

1. David Peterson, *Engaging with God: A Biblical Theology of Worship* (Downers Grove, IL: InterVarsity Press, 2002), 175.
2. Harold Best, *Music Through the Eyes of Faith* (New York: HarperOne, 1993), 147.
3. Donald Whitney, *Spiritual Disciplines Within the Church: Participating Fully in the Body of Christ* (Chicago: Moody Publishing, 1996), 77.
4. "What Can I Do," by Paul Baloche and Graham Kendrick. Copyright © 2005 by Integrity's Hosanna! Music.

Chapter 29: Your Church

1. Alfred Poirier, "The Cross and Criticism," *The Journal of Biblical Counseling*, Vol. 17, Number 3, Spring 1999, 19.

Chapter 30: Your Team

1. Many messages on worship are available from the Sovereign Grace web site (www.sovereigngracestore.com/category.aspx?CategoryID=1732), as well as the Desiring God web site (www.desiringgod.org/ResourceLibrary/Sermons/ByTopic/60).

2. The two most popular notation software programs at the moment are Finale and Sibelius. Having worked with both, I prefer Sibelius (www.sibelius.com) for its ease of use and flexibility. Another helpful site for pre-written charts is www.praisecharts.com.

3. Greg Scheer gives great counsel for developing vocal harmonies on pages 130–138 of *The Art of Worship* (Grand Rapids, MI: Baker, 2006). Another valuable resource is vocalcoach.com.

4. Two resources for training videos are www.leadworship.com and www.musicacademy. co.uk. Make sure you preview any video you'd show to your team to assess its suitability.

5. C. J. Mahaney's book *Humility: True Greatness* effectively addresses issues with which every musician deals.

Chapter 31: Your Pastor

1. The number of blogs and web sites devoted to music and worship is growing weekly. Here are a few I recommend: www.worshipmatters.com (my blog); www.blog.worship. com (multiple contributors, multiple resources); www.sbts.edu/Adademics/Schools/ Church_Music_and_Worship/Institute_for_Christian_Worship.aspx (resources from classes at Southern Baptist Theological Seminary).

Chapter 32: Some Thoughts for Pastors

1. I've suggested a number of helpful books on the theology of worship in the bibliography.

2. If you're involved in a church plant, we've had great experiences with Portable Church Industries (www.portablechurch.com), a one-stop solution for churches that meet in rented facilities.

SCRIPTURE INDEX

105:2	64	*Lamentations*	
105:3	91	3:23	161
105:4	137		
106:36	21-22	*Zephaniah*	
108:1	170	3:17	99
111	64-65		
111:1–2	94	*Matthew*	
111:2	64	1:23	161
115:8	22	12:6	52
117	122, 186	12:36	45
117:1–2	64	15:3–9	91
119	63	15:8–9	169
119:97	92	18:15–17	202
119:172	63	18:20	138
121	186	22:37	25
134:2	171	25:21, 23	60
139:7–8	137	26:30	99
141:5	223		
145	96, 186	*Mark*	
145:3	61	1:36–38	59
145:7	209	10:45	221
145:8–9	63	12:30	154
148:5	64		
149	154	*Luke*	
149:3	154	22:25–27	209
150	98	24:27	91
150:3–4	171		
150:3–5	102	*John*	
		2:19	69
Proverbs		3:16	148
3:27	245	4:21–23	69-70
4:23	169	4:23–24	52
12:1	222	8:32	27
18:2	243	14:6	27
28:13	45	15:12	148
29:25	172	15:14–15	161
		15:26	125
Ecclesiastes		16:13	27
4:9	111	17:5	175
		17:17	27
Isaiah		17:21	204
1:15	171		
6	114	*Acts*	
6:5	160	2:42	91
7:14	161	17:28	160
45:16	21	20:28	209, 228
46:9	160	20:29–30	31
53	94		
53:4	132	*Romans*	
57:15	163	1:9	206
		1:16	204
Jeremiah		1:18	27
7:21–26	74	7:21	221
13:10	74	8:1	130, 223
23:4	209	8:18	132

2 Thessalonians
2:10 27

1 Timothy
2:1–2 155
2:4 27, 148
2:5 53, 70
2:8 172
3 209, 253
3:2–12 230
4:12 44-47
4:13 91, 94
4:16 138
6:16 160, 175

2 Timothy
3:2, 4 24
3:16 89
4:2 91, 155
4:3 58
4:13 29

Titus
1 209, 253
1:5–9 230
1:9 28
2:13–14 133
2:14 47-48

Hebrews
1:3 76
3:13 255
4:12 138
4:15 161
7:25 75
7:26 75
8:13 70
9:23–28 52
9:24 141
10:7 78
10:19–22 53, 65, 73
10:24–25 178
11:3 64
11:6 47, 169
12:23 190
12:28 154, 172
12:28–29 160
13:15 206
13:16 206
13:17 54, 241-242, 252

James
1:27 154
3:1 230
3:8–10 45

1 Peter
1:16 147
2:4–5 201
2:5 35, 74, 126, 202
2:9 53, 100, 129
2:11 83
2:24 72, 132
3:18 72
4:10 37
5:2 209
5:8 83

2 Peter
2:1 31
3:9 148

1 John
2:15–17 83
3:1 100
3:16 46
3:18 46
4:10 72
4:20 148
5:21 22

Jude
20 83
24–25 259

Revelation
1:17 160
5:5 77
5:9–10 77
5:12 77
15:3 98
21:3–4 142
21:22 141

GENERAL INDEX

For many years I've had the privilege of serving alongside other musicians and pastors in Sovereign Grace Ministries to produce gospel-centered resources for the local church. Here are a few that I think will encourage you. For more, visit www.SovereignGraceStore.com or www.SovereignGraceMusic.org.

— **Bob Kauflin**

Valley of Vision
Worship songs inspired by the classic book of Puritan prayers, *The Valley of Vision* (edited by Arthur Bennett). www.ValleyofVision.org

Worship God Live
Recorded live in 2005 at Covenant Life Church in Maryland, this project features 14 God-exalting songs from various songwriters. I was privileged to lead worship for the recording along with Pat Sczebel.

Upward: The Bob Kauflin Hymns Project
I selected, adapted, and arranged these songs because we believe that hymns still speak with power. Some are familiar, some new, and some newly revised, but all move us to look upward toward the Savior.

Living the Cross Centered Life
C.J. Mahaney
The gospel: God sent his Son to the cross to bear his wrath for sinners. This all-important message is the core of C.J. Mahaney's book *Living the Cross Centered Life,* subtitled *Keeping the Gospel the Main Thing.*

Humility: True Greatness
C.J. Mahaney
C.J. gives biblical, practical, and proven counsel for fighting the enemy of your soul — pride — and actively pursuing your best friend — humility.

Stop Dating the Church
Joshua Harris
Whether you are looking for a church or have been a member for twenty years, this book will inspire fresh passion for the significance and purpose of the local church.

SOVEREIGN GRACE®
MINISTRIES